For Leonard — my unforgettable
collaborator in so many good
things and my enduring friend.
With much affection and
respect,
Vick L—

August 3, 1988

Beyond Malice

Beyond Malice

The Media's Years of Reckoning

Richard M. Clurman

Transaction Books
New Brunswick (USA) and Oxford (UK)

Library of Congress Catalog Number: 88-12339
ISBN 0-88738-234-7
Printed in the United States of America

Library of Congress Cataloging-in-Publication Data

Clurman, Richard M.
  Beyond malice : the media's years of reckoning / Richard M.
Clurman..
    p.   cm.
  Includes index.
  ISBN 0-88738-234-7
  1. Press—United States—Influence. 2. Press—United States—His-
tory—20th century. 3. Journalism—Political aspects—United
States. 4. Journalism—United States—Objectivity. 5. Public opinion—
United States. 6. Journalistic ethics—United States. 7. Journalism—
Social aspects—United States. I. Title.
PN4888.I53C56   1988
302.2′34′0973—dc19   88-12339
                                                          CIP

To Teddy White

In whose memory—I wish I'd done better.

Contents

Forethoughts: Why "I"?

We editors stand for the free press. That was enough in Jefferson's day—and even in Hearst's. But, in my time, all journalists feel compelled to announce themselves as the free and responsible press. We would no more go around without our cloak of responsibility than a lady would be caught without her mink.

—Henry R. Luce, 1962

One of the first lessons I learned in professional journalism came from a plainspoken managing editor whose origins were in midwestern newspapering. "Journalists," he said, although he preferred the word *reporters,* "should be read but not seen." The perpendicular pronoun, "I," never survived his sharp copy pencil. He always wanted to know about "them" not about "us."

Because this is a book about the rising tension between *contemporary* journalists and the people and events they cover, there are very few copy pencils left. They have been replaced by the ballpoint and tape recorder (for notes), the video terminal (for writing and editing) and the television screen (for looking at the world). In this new era it seems important to me that journalists at times reveal background about themselves as they routinely do about others. How else can you know who's talking to you? How can you evaluate the information, opinions, selection of what goes in and what stays out, unless you know about the people who are giving it to you?

So I begin by using the first person more than my old editor would ever have tolerated. I view it as disclosure or orientation for readers—not an exercise in reminiscence or personal vanity. You will have to decide for yourself.

The eighth floor of the Time & Life Building, in Manhattan's Rockefeller Center, is equipped with a large suite, richly appointed, for meetings,

1

receptions, dinners and other ceremonials. On one such occasion, in the early 1960s when the building was new, two imposing men stood in a corner of the suite, away from the crush, locked in solitary conversation. Physically they bore some slight resemblance to each other. Born a year apart, both were tall, white-haired and visibly intense. Almost everything else about them was different.

They were friendly adversaries, agreeing on only one shared basic proposition. It sounds pretentious today—as it did then—to restate their premise but they often did so themselves without self-consciousness. They both were fond of saying, in one way or another, that they were in search of the "truth" and how to apply it to their own and other people's lives. They reveled in such lofty formulations.

They were democratic enough about it. Unlike some evangelists, or tyrants, they did not impose whatever truth they found on others. They just proclaimed it and hoped to convince. But even that basic starting point created no real bond between them. The common foundation they both built upon had little to do with the materials they used or the structures each erected.

One was Henry ("Harry") R. Luce, the son of a Presbyterian missionary to China. He was the founder of what became the largest magazine publishing company in the world. Luce was a brusque, question-asking journalistic genius who, when he was finished inquiring, knew the Truth and expressed it in print and pictures, or spoke it with stylish, albeit stammering, confidence. He passionately believed in individualism, God, the United States and Time Inc.—probably in reverse order. His Truth tended to be Republican in domestic politics, relentlessly American and capitalist in world affairs. It was religiously humanitarian, even egalitarian in social outlook. The rule of law was his second Bible. "There is no such thing as objectivity," was his working creed, "only fairness." His magazines never tried to be objective—and they were not always fair. Above all, he was proudly opinionated in his journalism.

Once, just before he was to appear before a large college audience, he summoned me to his dining room for a quick briefing on what I expected the students would ask him. I said I was sure they would press him on the one question that everybody always raised. Someone was certain to ask how *Time,* which he invented (along with *Life, Fortune* and *Sports Illustrated*), could call itself a "newsmagazine" yet be so full of opinions. "What's the answer?" he asked. I demurred, suggesting he knew better than I. He would have none of that and insisted I tell him how I responded when someone pressed me on that point. He seemed impressed with *my* standard, lengthy explanation of *his* philosophy, and flew off to meet his audience. Sure enough it was the first question thrown at him. Before answering, he paused a long few seconds, then ignoring my solemn approach, blurted out: "Well, I created the word newsmagazine. I guess I can define it any way I damn well please." I worked for Luce for twenty exhilarating years.

The other man in that crowded Time Inc. reception room was Robert Maynard Hutchins, as much an innovator in education as Luce was in journalism. At twenty-eight he was dean of the Yale Law School, at thirty president of the University of Chicago. For him truth—with a small "t"— lay in the wisdom of the ages, compacted into his and Mortimer Adler's *Great Books of the Western World.* Hutchins' god—with a small "g"— was reason, rooted in Aristotle and refined by Thomas Aquinas. I was his student and admirer. He even gave me my degree, which, typically, was of his own creation. It was a Ph.B. (bachelor of philosophy), which often turns up in print with a mistaken but more impressive "D."

Before I knew him, I had been a grammar school, high school and army newspaper editor. So it was at least not out of character when I suggested to him that the University of Chicago, then one of the most intense academic centers in the world, should have a daily newspaper equal in excellence to the university's other distinctions. He skeptically agreed and encouraged me to go ahead. The result, in keeping with the atmosphere he radiated, was not a daily but a quarterly journal, the *University Observer,* so highbrow that though I started it, I didn't understand half the articles we printed. (The *only* intellectual eminence who declined our invitation to write for the first issue was my celebrated uncle and friend, the theatrical director-critic Harold Clurman. He turned me down on the ground that he wrote only for magazines that paid.)

I never found out whatever Luce and Hutchins were discussing that day in the Time & Life building because I interrupted them, a habit I've never been able to shake when something I consider to be of high importance assails me. Quite deliberately, I walked over and said, "Excuse me, but this is a unique moment for me." They accepted my surprising intervention, silently waiting for me to justify it.

"I'm standing here," I said, "in the presence of the two living men who've had the most intellectual influence on me." Luce, arching his eyebrows at my cosmic declaration, as he always did when he was both interested and puzzled, immediately shot back, "The two living men who've had the most intellectual influence on you?" Then that pause again, followed by a thrust: "Okay, I'll accept that. One of us for good and one bad." Hutchins, no slouch at such verbal fencing, responded without a moment's hesitation, "You're right, Harry, and we each know who was the good influence and who was the bad."

Actually, it has always been a toss-up. One pulled me when I was young toward abstract philosophy, more suitable for reflection than action. Ideas were king; everything else, vocationalism. The other led me down a different route, inquiry into everything on earth, with a dazzling array of resources that took me—and the reporters who worked with me—every-place to ask anything. Hutchins' methods unseated me from a collection of firmly held but innocently arrived at views. Luce's pulled me back onto an energizing platform in the center of world affairs, from there to pursue my own secular god, journalism. I never believed it produced The Truth or even the truth. For me it always had a more limited objective. To find out what was happening, to report it and explain it if *we* could, so *they* could understand better, if they could. A different quest from my two mentors.

I respectfully disagreed with both of them about many other things. For Hutchins, that was exactly the kind of combat he relished. For Luce, it was different. He enjoyed interrogatory conversation more than anything but in the end he wanted conclusions. It was not enough for him just to express his opinions. He wanted to be involved in affairs of state and often was. Although his manner suggested otherwise, he liked to have a few dissenters around him—very few. Luce affectionately viewed me as one. But in the house he built, he never disparaged—or, of course, completely accepted—my view that journalists should behave purely as observers, nor my deviant inclinations (Democratic-leaning, Jewish agnostic, ideolog-ically uncommitted). That never kept me from rising to the upper reaches of his pantheon. As was his style, he advanced me in grand sweeps.

Right after World War II, with a year more to complete college, I went first to *Commentary* magazine, which was only slightly less highbrow than my university quarterly. When I moved to *Time,* three years later, I was the writer and reporter of the Press section, then one of the very few places where the press itself was regularly reported and criticized. It was a long jump from *Commentary* to *Time,* even further than from Hutchins to Luce. My first week there, Irving Howe, a reigning socialist intellectual who had been at the center of the *Commentary* world, but who got better pay by anonymously reviewing books for *Time,* spotted me in my closet-sized office. "What are *you* doing here?" he asked with genuine surprise. When I explained that I now worked for *Time,* he made a moral distinction that eluded even him after he sputtered: "You don't mean *full-time,* do you?"

Six years later, at thirty-one, I left *Time* to become editorial director of Alicia Patterson's *Newsday,* Long Island's thriving daily tabloid, which she had started. "You have the brains and I have the instinct," she had said to me. "We'll make quite a combination." We did until I returned three years later to *Time,* where I quickly became chief of the magazine's North American correspondents. Then one day when Luce had decided to end the abrasive division between foreign and domestic coverage for his magazines, he telephoned me in the Caribbean, where I was vacationing.

"How would you like to have the whole world?" he said without further explanation. I understood his bursts of spoken shorthand and said that sounded good to me. "Stay there and I'll arrange it," he announced and that was it. When I returned to New York a week later, I was put in charge, for the next decade, of the combined new Time-Life News Service. At the time it was not only the largest but generally acknowledged to be the most talented of all the worldwide publishing and broadcast news gathering operations.

We always had one gnawing problem. Our correspondents, at home and abroad, reported from the scene. The editors and writers rewrote and interpreted them in New York. That was—and is—the news magazine system. Although Luce had a lifelong energetic romance with his reporters, he loved his magazines and advanced his views with even more ardor. This tense marriage between high-strung reporters in the field and instructed editors at home produced many divorces and one of the most accomplished alumni groups in journalism. Among other, more gratifying duties, I was often my staff's professional counselor in this stormy union, or the broker for their remarriage elsewhere to other forms of journalism.

In those days, before the impact of network television and national newspapers, *Time* and *Life* were the most powerful single press voice in the country. If you worked for them then, you often found yourself in the salons and streets of the world, answering for their artfully crafted views. Irwin Shaw, the spirited, popular novelist whose books had repeatedly been murdered in *Time*'s book reviews, had that special reason for his animus toward the magazine, besides his dislike of its political views. He said tipsily to me late one night: "Dick, I've got a question. You've got the most interesting, intelligent bunch of people around the world working for you I've ever met in any outfit. I love to eat with them, drink with them, talk to them every place I meet them—in Rome, Paris, Los Angeles, New York, Switzerland." "Thanks," I replied, glowing at the unsolicited accolade, "but what's your question?" "Why is the magazine so shitty?" he thundered triumphantly. It wasn't but—in less graphic language—"why does *Time* slant the news?" was a question that those who disagreed with *Time*'s tendentious journalism asked people like me wherever we went.

Within the walls of our New York office and on the cables that connected us around the world, we "Time-incers" (rhymes with "blinkers," as *Time* would say) had many outspoken pitched battles over politics, the war in

Vietnam, China, the American Century (Luce's dream), foreign policy, who and what to applaud or damn—everything. Luce liked it that way, enjoyed pitting his feisty staff against one another. He resolved it his way in the end, invoking the unchallenged right of a press proprietor. More than half a dozen novels and an equal number of mostly non-fiction books were written about the atmosphere he created, a few admiring, more deploring. His overbearing ways angered many, disaffected others.

At one of the first senior editorial lunches I ever attended, Luce mildly wondered aloud whether perhaps *Time* was being too uncritical of President Dwight Eisenhower. The editors disagreed, defending every word they had put in print. So Luce, a strong supporter of Eisenhower, relented and went on to other subjects. The week following, *Time*—to Luce's dismay—turned around and harshly attacked Ike and his administration. As one Chicago *Tribune* editor said of his own autocratic boss, Colonel Robert R. McCormick: "When the colonel asks for a drink of water, we turn the fire hose on him."

Luce was full of quirks. He was said by one woman "to have the worst natural bad manners" of any man she had ever met. He hated air-conditioning, was oblivious to food, rarely carried any cash or even change and insisted on summoning his staffers himself rather than through his secretary. The old-fashioned black telephone (no dial, no buttons) on his sleek modern desk flashed a special red light and set off a clanging bell at the Time-Life switchboard whenever Luce picked it up in his thirty-fourth floor New York office.

"Get me Clurman," he barked into that phone early one morning. A moment later, the operator's voice announced: "Mr. Clurman, Mr. Luce is on the line." In seconds Luce came on and said brusquely, "Can you come up." "Well, Harry, I'm in Mexico City," I replied. "Oh, never mind then," he said and hung up.

I found him more stimulating than intimidating, his unending curiosity more important to me than his unyielding conclusions. He also attracted a large pool of incomparably talented colleagues of every stripe and coloration. As for my dissenting views, I would have had as many on, say, the *New Republic*, or even more on the *National Review*, without such broad companionship and the opportunities to cover the world that Luce's place offered. We were rarely evenhanded and too often one-sided—a serious short-circuit in what was then the most electric and stimulating journalistic process anywhere. If we blew our fuses and burned our readers more often than we should have done, so did many others. But in those days ours gave off bigger sparks.

Is that a cop-out to justify the golden chains and high level of excitement that bound us so closely together? A fair question. I thought not then, nor do I think so now. Today, in a different period, I would find such views of our responsibilities unacceptable, a much too self-indulgent attitude for journalists to have toward their readers and viewers. Most of my friends who are still at Time Inc., under different leadership, would agree.

My tenure at Time Inc. began when television was an infant. My final task—after I had been elevated to the formally higher but much less engaging job of editorial vice president—was to grapple with a fully grown television giant. By then Luce was gone, struck down by a heart attack as swiftly as he had lived. One of his mistaken legacies was to decide in the 1950s that he was a print man—none of this new communications stuff for him. It was a classic parallel to the famous business school case of the railroads thinking of themselves as the train rather than the transportation business. As chairman of Time-Life Broadcast, I headed a lively group to map out the strategy for Time Inc.'s huge new financial commitment to cable, the second generation of television. "Narrowcasting" we christened it—and the term stuck.

In a report for the Time Inc. board of directors, I wrote:

> Investing in cable systems, for all its financial and managerial *angst,* is a sound long-term investment. The real interest that Time Inc. should have in cable TV is in its content, which will have a tremendous impact on American life—and also could ultimately be the largest source of profit. In the long run the kind of programming Time Inc. should develop has to do with narrowcasting and pay TV as opposed to television mass-network broadcasting, i.e. providing higher quality information, entertainment, illumination, self-help, culture and the whole range of subjects that now interest us most in print.

It never happened. Instead, Time Inc. made a fortune in cable systems and by showing movies on Home Box Office. Luce would have loved the profits—but hated the stale product.

Although I have done a number of other things—in government, the performing arts, public service, as a public policy adviser—almost everything except press relations or pure business—whatever else I did, my basic perspective has always been that of a journalist. With no disrespect to friends and acquaintances in any other occupations, I still prefer the company of journalists to any other single occupational group. Some might call it an addiction, a standing apart. I consider myself lucky. But more important you should know that most journalists feel just the way I do. Others today now call that élitism, or worse, arrogance.

We journalists, in the early 1960s, had an answer to most questions. Not that the times were easier. The Vietnam War had just begun in earnest and in 1962 I made my first of thirteen trips to its fields of anguish. We were at the edge of the turbulent 60s social revolution. As chief of foreign and domestic correspondents of *Time* and *Life* publications, I was in touch minute by minute with all of it. I was also there. At the time, I must have held the course record for worldwide air travel.

Despite the deafening uproar of change, most journalists comfortably dealt with the clichés of criticism that surrounded us: Why do you emphasize so much bad news? Why are you so negative? Whenever I read something I know about, why is it wrong, misinformed, naive or all of the above? How dare you tell us what to think? Why is that any of your business? Why are reporters so biased, so left-wing, so anti-establishment? Who elected you?

The critics never seemed equal to the answers we so trippingly gave to all those questions. True, among ourselves, as in most trade associations, we felt we really knew better than outsiders what our deeper faults were. And although I gave the *pro forma* answers to critics, there is plenty of evidence that I was especially aware of our sins and shortfalls, not to say just plain embarrassments, in both our behavior and the results of our work. One example:

In 1959—a long time ago—I wrote a memo to Luce and his then deputy, later to be successor, Hedley Donovan. It was on what was then an arcane subject. Perhaps my Hutchins background was coming to the fore. It said:

> Journalistic ethics are in terrible shape. There are, of course, no laws or serious codified rules (as in law or medicine) and the state of common law (as in table manners or marriage) in journalistic practice is so chaotic as to be useless. There are some flinty guys operating alone by their own rules, but that's all. As a result, the American press under the kind of scrutiny the TV industry has just had [in the "$64,000 Question" quiz show scandal] would be slaughtered. It would be much worse than TV since journalism is supposed to be related to the pursuit of information and truth—not alone entertainment.

> The problem: the U.S. press, freed by law (Article I of the Bill of Rights), has never made up any rules or even developed by tradition practices which indicate to journalists what they should and should not do. At its most serious this negative restraint allows anyone to print what he wants (which cannot and should not be remedied); less seriously, but more pertinently, this freedom creates an atmosphere of unlicensed, wild and often unethical journalistic practices (which can and should be controlled by tradition).

> Let's leave out a detailed indictment. Enough to say that it would not be at all difficult at this moment to write a story quite printable in *Time* on the journalistic malpractices of staffers on, say, the New York *Times,* which would enormously embarrass even the holy *Times* and cause it overnight to write a set of rules. If this is true of the *Times,* it is at least as true of Time Inc. I have thought—and said—for years that we should do something about it. I still think so.

I offer that now not to indulge myself by reprinting my old memos or to suggest some prescient early wisdom. But only as a small demonstration that the subject of this book is a long-standing preoccupation of mine, as much an obsession with me as journalism itself.

It is not easy to report fairly and accurately about the house where you live, occupied by many of your press family and friends. The least obvious but most entangling alliances that journalists have are their sympathies and understanding for people they write about whom they know better than others. To avoid some of those inevitable biases, I have adopted an unusual—as well as deplored by many journalists—procedure.

When the manuscript of this book was in its final stages, I sent the following self-explanatory memo to twelve of the leading principals I report on:

> Forgive the impersonal formality of this but it is an effort to be journalistically even-handed in the process, if not in my conclusions, when dealing with a variety of people:
>
> I am sending this same memo with varying attachments to the key principals in the Westmoreland and Sharon trials and other major figures in the text. In my forthcoming book, one half of the total book is devoted to what I consider to be some of the lessons learned from these trials.
>
> Since there is time, and it is reporting and opinion of my own, as well as gleaned from many other sources, it seems fair to me to let the key principals or their representatives have an opportunity to read relevant sections at this pre-publication stage.
>
> In so doing, I have several objectives in mind:
>
>> 1. I would like to be factually as accurate as I possibly can. To that end I invite you to suggest any factual corrections on the manuscript in areas where you are specially informed.
>>
>> 2. I would also be interested in your contrary views of opinions and judgments I make if you feel they either distort or are unfair to positions you hold yourself or motives ascribed to you.
>>
>> 3. If there is any material or quotations you find that you feel misrepresent or were acquired in a manner you object to, I would like you to express those views.
>
> It would be helpful if you could confine any or all of these comments to writing on the pages attached—or on the back of the facing pages. I will be happy to discuss any points with you on the phone or in person, or, of course, you may wish to write me more extensively than manuscript comments may allow.
>
> I recognize this is an unusual procedure. But since this is a book whose intent is to comment on good and bad standards of journalism plus the public and

government's relationship with the news media, I think this final step in my reporting and checking important, although not an obligation in journalism.

I'm sure you understand that while I welcome and even seek your comments in all the areas I describe, in the end the judgment of what I respond to by changing facts or passages, will be mine alone. In sum, I will listen with respect and then decide.

I only impose this burden on you because I think you would welcome it now instead of later coming upon page proofs or when the book is actually published. For the lawyers among you, in the unlikely event you are moved formally to put me on notice for malice or to seek a temporary restraining order, please don't. (It wouldn't work and would discourage in the future what I consider an honest, open effort at further inquiry before publishing.)

If you choose not to respond, I will attach no significance to your silence.

Thanks very much.

There is a long-standing rule in journalism that the subjects of stories should not be told, even in paraphrase, what the story says until it is in print or broadcast. It is a firing offense in some of the best newspapers, magazines and broadcast organizations to read or tell the principal sources their part in a story before it goes to press or on the air. The rule is let them read it or see it as everybody else will when it comes out.

After having observed and enforced that rule myself in the past, I now know of only three reasons when it should be perpetuated: 1) in daily journalism, when there is quite simply not enough time; 2) when there are a number of sources and if you did not afford them all the same opportunity, it would give one unfair advantage over another; 3) when the subject of a story is so demonstrably venal or crooked, that nothing said could be believed anyway.

Apart from those three big exceptions, I have the heretical view that letting the main subjects of a story know more often what is about to be said before it is published or broadcast, can only help improve the report. It can be the final step in reporting to test interpretations, facts and conjectures with those about whom the journalist is writing.

Such advance disclosure usually produces howls of objections from reporters, editors and some lawyers. The lawyers are the easiest to deal with. American courts do not grant injunctions in restraint of publishing (i.e., print or broadcasting). So the objecting source cannot stop the story from being printed or shown. But, say the lawyers, the publication will be put on notice that it is about to say something that it has been warned not to in advance. That could create grounds for a libel suit based on actual malice. Not likely, since the story must in fact be wrong to lose a libel suit. If the story is incorrect, it should not have been published in the first place. Libel suits are more easily won in the newsroom than in the courtroom.

As for reporters and editors, they find such a checkback process too much trouble, unnecessary "censorship," or "letting people edit our copy, which is *our* job." Not so. The people about whom the story is written or broadcast have only arguing rights, not editing rights. If there is time, why wait until the story has been published or broadcast to hear complaints about it? Hearing in advance could enrich the story and further assure its accuracy as well as its fairness.

In this case, interesting and useful responses were received from almost all of the twelve to whom the manuscript was sent, or from their representatives. Many, indeed most, of their corrections and objections influenced me and caused me to make changes. Some disagreements were fundamental and were considered but not used. Not one made any threats—legal or otherwise. The fact of their responses should not, of course, be taken as an endorsement of my views or my reporting.

But from my experience in this instance, it is a process that I commend to others, when there is time. Rather than being a violation of journalists' rights or a threat to their independence, it can result in many appropriate instances—and certainly did for me—in new illuminations and nuances that otherwise would have escaped even careful reporting and checking.

"He has a very interesting mind until it's made up," the editor of the Manchester *Guardian* once said of one of his editorial writers. Mine is not made up on many subjects. But it is made up on the overall conclusions of this book. You should know them even before I unravel the reportorial evidence. They are fivefold:

- The American press lives by a tradition of freedom established two hundred years ago in the Constitution's First Amendment—"Congress shall make no law . . . abridging the freedom of speech, or of the press"—and elaborated by the courts ever since (no doubt about that).

- In the twenty years from the 1960s through the 1970s, that press was transformed, in its shape and power, by television and electronics of all kinds, a more dramatic change than in any other period in our history (not much doubt about that).

- By the 1980s, the new force and *impact* of that transformation created such friction among the press, the public and the government that changes in many news media practices were demanded and became a necessity (to be demonstrated, in part, through the magnifying glass of two historic trials in 1984–85).

- At the same time, the economics of broadcasting and publishing went through a change that brought in new owners whose pitch, unlike that of their predecessors, was more attuned to the judgments of Wall Street than Main Street (to be described).

- As a result, the news media, transformed by technology, finance and public opinion have started to realize—as they had better—that they must revise many of their most cherished practices, traditions and attitudes. It is a process of self-examination unparalleled in two hundred years, although its effect has barely begun to be translated into action (to be reported and argued).

Withal, I believe that American journalism has its mind set in old theory, despite a wholly different climate of public opinion and economics. Relying too much on the past, the media turn out new products with such high impact that the basic principles of an unbridled press are being challenged. As has repeatedly been said, the First Amendment was written not for the press alone, and certainly not for commercial advantage, but primarily for the people.

All this against the fact—yes, the fact—that the U.S. press, publication for publication, network for network, is still the best and the freest in the world. The most influential newspapers and news services are better than they've ever been. So too, in my opinion, are the quality and variety of information on network television and in news magazines (including, among others, CBS and *Time,* which are sternly criticized in what follows). But that is not good enough. Like an errant child grown to maturity, the media are now too big and too powerful to be so bad—even though they remain the best. "The University of Chicago," Hutchins used to say, "is *not* a very good university. It's just the best in the world."

Why another book about the press now? It is true, by definition alone, that in a twenty year period what was once simply called the press has become the national news media.

We have not invented a word—except something crazy like mediacracy, or metaphoric like the Fourth Estate—to describe adequately its new incarnation. It is a press whose ownership silhouette and economics have changed almost as much as its power and its new technology. We now use the terms press and news media interchangeably. Neither the Supreme Court nor the framers of the Constitution did. James Madison could never have imagined the transformation of what was quite simply called "the press" in the Bill of Rights. Justice Potter Stewart suggested in a 1974 speech that the First Amendment could stand revision to read: "Congress shall make no law abridging the freedom of speech or *of the news media.*"

"Media is a word," acknowledged columnist Anthony Lewis, "ordinarily to be avoided in civilized discourse but alas there is no way to escape its use." (Comedian Fred Allen cracked that television was called a "medium because it was seldom well done" and columnist Jimmy Breslin added that "media is the plural of mediocre.") By the early 70s, the word press, laminated into reporters' credentials, was being replaced by media. It was much more than a change in terminology.

With that transformation, the news media are more a target than ever for the same kind of skeptical criticism they once applied only to others. It takes no poll or survey (although there are plenty of them) to prove the change. One certain piece of evidence is that I have never told anyone— butcher, baker or missile maker—that I am writing a book about why people have come to look so critically at the press without unfailingly provoking a reaction something like "We must get together and talk. I want to tell you about the time I . . ."

Fortunately, George Orwell was wrong about the year he described in his classic book, *1984*. Big Brother has not taken over in the part of the world that could be called free. In the forty years since he wrote *1984* there certainly have been life-changing transformations in technology, science, medicine, social attitudes, governance, economics and international affairs. They have happened at a faster pace than at any time in world history. One of the biggest changes of all has taken place in the news media ganglia that linked and accelerated all the other changes.

A Golem has arrived in our midst, a gigantic doubting machine, raising more questions than it answers, bringing more bad news than good, prying into everyone's affairs. The signs of the change are everywhere. The cry for fairness and responsibility as the price of success and press freedom is louder than ever. The conflict between personal privacy and media privilege has shaken the confidence of both journalists and the public. One judge, hearing a group of journalists discuss their role, had about enough. "Who died and made you God?" he exploded. It seemed like a strange but understandable complaint from a judge, of all people.

This is a book about that problem.

"Book One: The News Media on Trial" is very selective and opinionated reporting mostly on two trials that pointedly symbolized many of the tensions in the press-public-government triangle. "Book Two: The News Media at Work" examines those tensions outside the courtroom, in other closely related practices and problems that have more to do with who owns the news media and the way journalists work and behave than with formal trials and law.

I visited a close family friend, New York's Senator Jacob K. Javits, ten days before he died in early 1986. His valor as his body slowly deteriorated from a degenerative disease over five years was even more inspiring than his lifetime legislative record. From his wheelchair, in his most avuncular fashion, he had some words of advice for me that last time I ever saw him. "You have been an observer and a professional spectator for most of your life," he said. "Don't ignore your passions."

I will not here.

In journalism, if you intend to be very free with your opinions, you'd better set your facts out first. On to the facts.

Prelude

Political journalism is not a way of satisfying the random curiosity or the voyeuristic inclinations of reporters or readers.
—Columnist David S. Broder, 1987

In the language of comic strips, "POW!!!" is the ultimate punctuation mark. You won't find it in print or broadcast journalism, or as a category in public opinion polls. But in the recent history of journalism, twelve months in 1986–87 alone produced—among other attention-getting stories—these familiar POW!!!'s, one after the other:

- A tiny Beirut weekly revealed, in a planted story, that the U.S. was trying to trade arms with Iran for hostages. The news instantly ricocheted around the world, followed shortly thereafter by the revelation that profit from the two-faced dealing was being used covertly to finance arms for the contras fighting in Nicaragua. President Reagan at first blamed the year's biggest uproar on the media "sharks circling" around him. In the televised congressional hearings that followed, the name of Marine Lieutenant Colonel Oliver North became momentarily as well known for derring-do as Rambo. So did his White House secretary, Fawn Hall, whose celebrity and beauteous competence fleetingly gave her the fame of a Diane Sawyer.

- The Miami *Herald* accepted the challenge made by presidential candidate Gary Hart to the New York *Times* to prove the whispered charges about his philandering ("If anybody wants to put a tail on me go ahead"). The *Herald* staked out a Washington town house where Hart was caught weekending with a woman whom the paper had been tipped, Hart had been photographed nuzzling aboard a Florida fishing yacht, appropriately named—it was too good to believe but true—*Monkey Business*. The stakeout was sloppy, but circumstantial proof enough so that when the Washington *Post* told Hart it was ready to go from a

15

confirmed private detective's report with another such incident involving Hart, he bitterly withdrew his candidacy, blaming his fall from national grace on "misleading and false" stories in the press. He got instant support from Richard Nixon who wrote him, "What you said about the media needed saying." Seven months later in an astonishing reversal Hart reentered the race. This time he began by aiming his campaign guns not at the Republicans or other candidates but squarely at the press, who he said, with tears in his eyes, "has a need to destroy me." His new slogan: "Let the people decide" about what he called his "damned fool mistake." They promptly did—against him.

- Far from the Washington Beltway, the Atlanta *Journal and Constitution* published the charge that the Georgia politician and civil rights activist, Julian Bond, regularly used cocaine. Local television and the national news media picked up the charge, finally dismissed by a grand jury. "Everyone," said Bond, "is fair game [to the press] in a foul game with no standards and no rules." In Cleveland, the *Plain Dealer* decided to refute Ohio's Governor Richard Celeste's claim that he didn't have a "Hart-type personal problem" by reporting that in recent years he had been involved with three women while married. The paper said it broke the story because he was a "potential" presidential candidate. Evangelists Jim and Tammy Faye Bakker were exposed, by the Charlotte (N.C.) *Observer* of sexual shenanigans and financial fraud. One of their accusers, the Reverend Jerry Falwell, appeared for three nights on Ted Koppel's "Nightline," in programs that outrated Johnny Carson. (The paper won the 1988 Pulitzer Prize For Public Service.)

- In the middle of the televised hearings that so damaged Judge Robert Bork's nomination to the U.S. Supreme Court, the Senate Judiciary Committee's chairman, Delaware's Senator Joseph Biden, was forced to withdraw from the Democratic presidential sweepstakes. The New York *Times* and Des Moines *Register* reported from, and then NBC and the other networks showed, the videotape of a plagiarized campaign speech. *Newsweek* followed with the revelation—also on videotape— that he had exaggerated his academic accomplishments. None of the news media that exposed him mentioned its anonymous source for the first and most damaging videotape. When *Time* magazine, not bound by the pledge of confidentiality, said the source of the "attack video" was campaign aides of another presidential candidate, Massachusetts Governor Michael Dukakis, his campaign manager promptly resigned. Dukakis' "character"—the new buzzword in politics—was deemed undamaged, although his management abilities were thrown into question. Bork also was rejected by the full Senate for a seat on the highest court in the U.S., as much for his unprepossessing presence on national television before Biden's committee as for his intricate views on key constitutional issues. All together, a triple-header.

• Washington *Post* reporter-editor Bob Woodward had repeatedly led the entire world press on revelations about CIA secret operations. It turned out that while he had provided more than seventy stories for the *Post* on the CIA, he had saved some of his most important stuff for a book about the CIA under Director William Casey, who died before publication of Woodward's best-seller, *Veil*. But *U.S. News & World Report* managed to get galley proofs of the secret book and released its juiciest news before either the *Post* or *Newsweek* could serialize it in their pages, featuring what some of the press headlined as Casey's "death-bed confession." Although Woodward received accolades and a vote of confidence from other reporters and editors based on his past record, much of the public believed Woodward had made up at least his last four-minute Casey interview. And some of Woodward's supporters still wondered why he and his editors had waited to publish his much more startling news-making reporting in the book when they all worked for a daily newspaper that had led the fight in the courts for the right not to withhold even for a day stories they thought important.

• The *Wall Street Journal* profiled Pat Robertson after he resigned his ministry and became a Republican presidential candidate. A Washington *Post* Robertson-watcher noticed in the profile that Robertson had changed his wedding date to conceal the fact that his son was born only ten weeks after Robertson was married thirty-three years ago. The *Post* made a front-page story out of what Robertson said was only an attempt "to protect his family." He called the press coverage "outrageous" and a "reprehensible" invasion of privacy. *Newsday* columnist Murray Kempton acidly damned the *Post's* hypocrisy in coming out against Judge Bork's nomination because the *Post* charged he was, among other things, wishy-washy on constitutional "privacy," while the *Post* had not the slightest compunction about violating Robertson's privacy. The *Post's* ombudsman, Joseph Laitin, slammed his own paper even harder. "The press is hounding him," Laitin wrote, "and the *Post* is leading the pack. God would forgive [such] a lie, but I'm not so sure about the Washington press." Never mind the Washington press. The Atlanta *Journal and Constitution* followed by reporting that the wife of the only other cleric running for the presidency, Jesse Jackson, was pregnant on the day he married her twenty-five years earlier.

• By most reckonings, the media did an impressive job reporting, not making worse, the heart attack the stock market suffered in October 1987. Not to the U.S. secretary of the treasury, James Baker. In a howl of self-defensive anger he complained: "What triggered it was not my remarks but a front-page story in one of our major newspapers [the New York *Times*.]"

• National Public Radio's Nina Totenberg discovered that Judge Douglas Ginsburg, forty-one, President Reagan's follow-up nominee, after the rejection of Bork for the Supreme Court, had smoked a little marijuana in college and while teaching at the Harvard Law School eight years ago. The White House summarily dumped him, not for his all but invisible qualifications but because fake national piety demanded that anyone who ever smoked pot, which included a high percentage of the 60s generation, was unfit to dispense justice. Reporters promptly asked every candidate the new "M" question: Do you now or have you ever . . .?

- When more than 6,000 press converged on Washington for the Reagan-Gorbachev summit, the two superpower leaders had more in common than their desire to sign a nuclear treaty. Both were mad at the press. In a numbing "press conference" that lasted more than two hours in which Gorbachev did most of the talking, he angrily responded to his questioners: "The press tries to drive politicians into a corner. Is that a dialogue? Is that an interview?" Reagan offered his sympathies: "I just told him what Lyndon Johnson once said. LBJ claimed that if one morning he walked on top of the water across the Potomac River, the headline that afternoon would read, 'PRESIDENT CAN'T SWIM' "

- Israel, confronting its worst violent Arab protest on the West Bank and in the Gaza in the past twenty years (an "all-stick-and-no-carrot approach," one reporter called Israel's tactics), once again blamed much of its troubles not on the unresolved, long-simmering dispute but on the American press, which reports "only those things that give Israel a negative image."

- For one whole week the biggest issue in the presidential campaign became not who was ahead in the polls or what the issues really were but who won in the evening news battle between candidate George Bush and anchorman Dan Rather. When Vice President Bush angrily refused to answer Rather's overheated questions about the Iranian hostage exchange, the aftermath produced more analysis, commentary, replays and locker room reports than a championship heavyweight fight or bruising Super Bowl game. "Using the news media as a foil," said political strategist David Sawyer, "is excellent because people think of the news media as manipulative and arrogant." The Washington *Post* editorialized: The candidates "are running against the media capitalizing on the public's fed-upness with the press—its pushy ways, its occasional dirty pool and its generally enormous power." And *Newsweek* summed up the 1988 campaign: "This year, bashing the press has become a popular blood sport in both parties."

Each of these stories produced a raw backlash blaming the press or at minimum wondering where all this media intensity and prying was leading. Could we ever elect a president or confirm a nominee in today's all-seeing media climate who was more than a bland, lumpless bowl of cream of wheat? At another time didn't some of our most accomplished leaders (Roosevelt, Eisenhower, Kennedy, Martin Luther King) have unreported private lives that would have disqualified them from national leadership today? Was it possible altogether with today's omnipresent media to conduct the public's business without the media messing it up?

As for the journalists themselves, by this time many were worrying more about their power and their *ad hoc* standards than crowing over their triumphs. The crown of avenging angels fit uncomfortably on their gnarled heads.

Was all the public criticism and press self-examination something new? Certainly not. But the questions had never—not even during Vietnam or Watergate—been asked outside and inside the media with such intensity and so few convincing or even resolute answers (see page 30). If it wasn't a new milestone, was it the beginning of a new era—or at the very least a new period? Not likely.

Some beginnings are easy to describe. The builder of a skyscraper begins with a hole in the ground. An artist with a clean canvas or an unmolded piece of clay. A writer with a blank sheet of paper (or a blank word processing screen). The precise beginnings of periods of social, political and cultural change are usually harder to fix in time. Did the nuclear era start with Albert Einstein or J. Robert Oppenheimer? Did modern popular music begin with Elvis Presley or the Beatles? Changes in life patterns are more often a string of events than a singular moment. When did these years of media power accompanied by floods of resentment and anguish really overflow? In its modern incarnation, of course, there *were* Vietnam and Watergate.

But for the sake of example, not of argument, go back to a more recent high watermark: the winter of 1984.

1

A Very Cold Winter

*The American press is a wonderful target right
now for both criticism and constructive abuse.*
—Columnist Russell Baker

The selection process gave exact definition to a much abused cliché. It was truly a matter of life and death.

In the winter of 1984, hundreds of dying patients applied for a unique lifesaving device. They were suffering from terminal cardiomyopathy, a progressive weakening of the heart muscle. It was the time of the latest medical wonder: the Jarvik-7 Total Artificial Heart. It might rescue a body, at least for a while, from certain death.

The panel that decided who would get the Jarvik-7 used no euphemisms about the patients' grim condition. Candidates for the artificial heart, which was still in very limited supply, were required to sign a statement. It made them face the reality that "it is probable I will die" without the operation. Then it added a vividly modern question. Were the patient and the patient's family prepared to deal with the news media? The precise words were as plain as a poison label: "I am fully aware of the considerable public interest anticipated in my story in newspaper, magazine articles, television, radio broadcasts, movies or any other media."

At the Humana Hospital-Audubon, in Louisville (Ky.), one surviving implant patient faced that reality more jauntily than most. When he regained some composure after the surgery he asked, "Would you please turn on the television? I would like to see if I'm alive and how I'm doing."

Whether we are alive, how and what we are doing is not a bad definition of what journalism is all about. By the 1980s, as the Jarvik-7 candidates were made to realize, journalism had become something different.

The modern national news media were born in the 50s, revealed their strength in the 60s, asserted it in the 70s and were hammered for it in the

80s. Television alone was not the source of the change, but it was the main engine. The media in those years became as different from the press, in Mark Twain's phrase, as lightning is from a lightning bug.

Perversely, one of the least likely places to find reports of the transformation was in the press itself. The press is the only major institution in the world that the press barely covers. The news media tend to look outward and around rather than at themselves. They are mostly spectators of the life and times of others. "We are simply, I'm afraid," the pioneer television commentator, Eric Sevareid, said in 1984, "disliked by far too many—perceived by them as not only smug but arrogant and as critics of everybody but ourselves."

By the winter of 1984–85, however, what and how the press was doing was a big story itself. In fact, the subject had become what journalists are fond of calling a "Topic A," when they refer to other major uproars.

It was a very cold winter.

For the first time in history, snow fell in forty-nine of the fifty states, even including the Mojave Desert—sparing only the flatlands of Hawaii. Record low temperatures afflicted more than fifty-eight cities. And in freezing Washington, the fortieth president of the United States began his second term after what was scornfully derided as an "electivision."

At the Democratic convention in San Francisco and at the Dallas convention where Ronald Reagan was nominated, 13,000 members of the press outnumbered the delegates and alternates by close to 3 to 1. "The convention does not decide and it does not debate," complained New York's Senator Daniel Patrick Moynihan, "we have to make up our arguments to have on the floor so that television will have something to cover." Political convention halls were no longer the biggest smoke-filled rooms in America. They were multimillion-dollar television studios whose journalistic stars were more recognizable to the public than all but a very few of the politicians they were covering.

On election day, six hours before the polls closed anywhere—when only 2 percent of the nation had voted—exit polling data fed into network computers could have called the outcome. Under heavy public pressure, the news media slightly restrained themselves. But not for very long. CBS projected (then so did ABC and NBC) and announced the final results less than one minute after the East Coast polls closed, but long before many had even voted in the thirty states where the polls were still open. "Walter Mondale," said CBS anchor Dan Rather while West Coasters were still waiting on line to vote, "has seen the light at the end of the tunnel—and it's out."

A weary Mondale delivered his own verdict. "Modern politics today," he said, "requires a mastery of television. I've never really warmed up to television and, in fairness, it's never warmed up to me. Sometimes I felt it was an election between two advertising agencies." Of course it was not. He lost for more profound reasons. But neither was his postmortem entirely a loser's fantasy. More and more, the traditional two-party system is dominated by three parties that never appear on any ballot: ABC, CBS and NBC.

President Reagan was sworn in privately on a Sunday to satisfy the law, without distracting more than 100 million Americans who were watching the San Francisco 49ers beat the Miami Dolphins in the Super Bowl (advertisers paid half-a-million-dollars for a thirty-second ad spot).

Like everybody else Reagan focused on the game. Or if he was not actually watching, he at least acknowledged the nation's priorities by appearing briefly on the screen by satellite from the White House to toss the coin for the opening kickoff. "After all," Reagan had said, "I came from an industry where ham is a basic ingredient."

It was so cold in Washington the next day that outdoor inaugural activities were canceled. The world watched the impressive but small repetition of the White House ceremony on television. This event put Dan Rather in a more reflective mood. Interrupting his own and the other CBS reporters' coverage, he said: "One of the things television does best is to take people places, so let's just watch."

No traditional swearing-in took place on the steps of the Capitol and no stirring inaugural parade marched down Pennsylvania Avenue. Just as well. The president had decided not to risk exposing waiting crowds and marchers to a wind-chill factor of minus ten degrees. They could witness history, as they more and more often did, from the warmth of their own living rooms.

It was also a chilling year for the news media.

On Manhattan's Foley Square, under the roof of one courthouse, three press trials were under way at the same time in the same building. Each brought to the bar of federal justice, separately but simultaneously, the country's leading television news network, largest news magazine and most widely circulated daily newspaper—a clean sweep of the biggest giants in the American news media menagerie. For once, the only transportation reporters needed to cover three different front-page stories was an elevator.

The first case, Westmoreland v. CBS Inc., was viewed as a question of fairness, interpretation, news media practices and history. Tried before a packed house, it was brought by the highest public official in the United

States ever to sue for libel before a jury in a federal court over his official conduct. Two floors below, an equally crowded courtroom heard *Sharon v. Time Inc.*, a question of accuracy and sources. It was the first time that high a foreign government official had gone to trial with a libel suit in a U.S. court, this one to try to salvage his damaged political reputation back home in Israel.[1]

Two of the trials reached conclusions that neither the public nor the news media would easily forget. The third, on the thirteenth floor, was simpler. Another federal judge heard criminal charges against a *Wall Street Journal* writer, R. Foster Winans, accused of leaking valuable information and profiting from stock tips on stories he wrote. The *Journal* fully reported his misdeeds and its own editorial culpability, before the writer was found guilty and sentenced to 18 months in prison, a conviction upheld by the Supreme Court on the charges of securities, mail and wire fraud.

A smoldering friction between the American press and the public has ignited bursts of flame throughout American history. As the Westmoreland and Sharon cases were moving toward trial, the friction suddenly erupted into a firestorm. The spark that ignited it this time seemed trivial at first. The aftermath did not.

When U.S. troops invaded the Caribbean island of Grenada, the news media for the first time were barred from covering the operation as the troops landed. From the puniest to the most prestigious, they unanimously cried "foul." They confidently asserted what they thought were their historic rights, certain that the American public wanted to know about Grenada from the first shot-and-shell. Some seriously considered bringing a lawsuit asserting a right of access under the First Amendment. It was just assumed *everyone* knew that without an ungoverned, inquiring free press there could be no true democracy.

Journalists were flabbergasted to discover that the public widely supported excluding them until the invasion was secure. NBC commentator John Chancellor, who led the early news media protest, was astonished by an avalanche of mail opposing his view, characterized by one note that said, "Well, you dumb bastard. What do you think we elected Reagan for? It's damn sure *you* were never elected." Or a Methodist minister in the South who wrote, "I was sure that no one would take offense if in a

1. Well, not quite, if you include the president of the South Pacific Republic of Nauru (pop. 8,000), who sued Guam's *Pacific Daily News* (circ. 18,076) for $40 million over a "secret, illegal" loan in which the paper said he had been involved. In 1985, the jury decided against him.

sermon I defended the Constitution and its guarantee of freedom of the press. I was wrong."

The media clutched at some public-opinion polling evidence that narrowly appeared to support them. But the questions and replies were couched in unconvincing language. The public, it was obvious, overwhelmingly favored keeping news media eyes and ears out for reasons of security until the government decided it was militarily and politically safe for them to bear witness. "It was sometimes difficult to tell which the American people enjoyed more," said former White House press secretary Jody Powell, "seeing the president kick hell out of the Cubans [on Grenada] or the press."

Another invasion—the invasion of privacy by the media—was as galling a topic with the public.

Everybody had his or her own deplorable example, but the one then most indelibly etched on the national conscience came in the aftermath of the terrorist bombing of U.S. Marines barracks in Lebanon. Television crews and print reporters stood vigil outside the homes and in the living rooms of parents who were waiting to find out whether their sons were among the 241 killed. Several journalists got exactly the story they wanted when they were on hand to record the shrieks and weeping of families just as they received the tragic news. What luck. They didn't even have to ask the mourners that most absurd and offensive question: "How do you feel?" The answer was tearfully obvious, on video and audio tape, and in print.

But isn't that the journalist's job—to tell it and show it as it is? It always has been. Still, there was something ghoulish about the intrusive presence of swarms of professional spectators, with their minicams, tape recorders and microphones, sending intimate sorrow instantaneously to millions around the world. There was every traditional argument in favor of the press's role to report life firsthand and first. But did journalists really have to be there at that very moment? "Vultures," "animals," "voyeurs," were some of the milder epithets used to describe them.

To add it all up, *Time* ran a ten-page cover story titled "Accusing the Press. What Are Its Sins?" The article warned that public complaints of unfairness, arrogance, irresponsibility and inaccuracy had reached alarming proportions. Pent-up hostility seemed to be uncorked. The public often views journalists as:

> Rude and accusatory, cynical and almost unpatriotic. They twist facts. They meddle in politics, harass business, invade people's privacy, and then walk off without regard to the pain and chaos they leave behind. To top if off, they claim that their behavior is sanctioned, indeed sanctified, by the U.S. Constitution.

Time, it would turn out, was a fine one to talk.

"The power of the press" once had an honorable ring to it. "Power of the media" has a different, darker resonance. A mammoth new apparatus, electronically propelled, spewed both print and television into every American home—reporting, viewing, prying, judging, overwhelming.

Press power had never been an abstraction. Not a single American president, from George Washington on, was deaf to its thundering—or failed to denounce it. Governments, their leaders and candidates for public office became known publicly only by the way they were reported and interpreted—or exposed—in the news media. The dollar plunges and rises on international currency markets partly as the result of behind-the-scenes stories on U.S. fiscal policy. Outside political life, the media have grown to be the great makers and destroyers of reputation. Businesses, their leaders and their products, have been raised up and then slammed down. Actors, writers, musicians, athletes, performers of all kinds—including chefs—can have their work celebrated or broken by the reception they get from media critics. Heroes (some inadvertent) are raised to unreal heights; villains (some innocent) are consigned to the depths. What the media build up they even more enthusiastically tear down.

David Halberstam, in his best-seller chronicling their rise, gave a name to the media: *The Powers That Be.* Journalist-historian Theodore H. White has summarized their modern impact:

> The power of the press in America is a primordial one. It sets the agenda of public discussion; and this sweeping power is unrestrained. It determines what people will talk about and think about—an authority that in other nations is reserved for tyrants, priests, parties and mandarins.

In barely twenty years, the new media mandarins had led us out of two divisive wars (Vietnam and Lebanon); recorded and accelerated the biggest social upheavals in the U.S. since the Civil War and the Great Depression (the 60s revolution); exposed one president who was forced to resign from office (Nixon); heightened national anxiety about events and personalities that made it impossible for two other presidents to have second terms (Ford and Carter). The media also introduced us to previously unknown environmental hazards on the ground (dioxin and pesticides), in the air (acid rain and radiation); in the ozone (from aerosol hairspray and shaving-cream cans). And in the years following, recanted many of the glowing reviews on the popular performance of the next president's first six years (Reagan); drove potential candidates and appointees off the hustings and out of office.

By the mid-80s, the media had made themselves the cop on every beat, the umpire and unofficial scorer of the biggest game going—the affairs of the world. Too often journalists played that game, as one of them said, as if it were "all pitch and no catch."

When the Constitution was written, the framers did not reckon with today's conversion of the press into the news media. The Federalist Papers made no mention of the media's compulsion to be first, to be fastest, to get the most attention. The Founding Fathers created a system of checks and balances for bringing conflicting objectives into harmony. When the nation was young, adjustments and resolutions were slower and more reflectively made. The modern news media, with their instant, worldwide reach, have moved the process into such high gear that bigger clashes became inevitable. The Founders had a different press in mind, not one with an unforeseen technology that could overwhelm with incredible speed and sweep virtually any individual or institution.

Journalism—unlike law, medicine or science—is a process, not a body of knowledge.

It is an unruly process on the inside; unruled from the outside. To tame it by trying formally to restrict the press is more hazardous to democracy than letting it run free. But when it runs wild or becomes overbearing, so does the temptation to rein it in, or at least to yell like hell. Giving bigmouths their comeuppance is a good old American tradition.

The media leviathan is a vulnerable target. Skeptics in the midst of achievers (good and bad) are rarely popular. Journalists are raised to be skeptics. An old Chicago newspaper maxim goes: "Does your mother say she loves you? Check it out." Doubting and questioning are the guiding principles of journalists' work. If they are good at it, they are neither cheerleaders nor cynics—although at their most irreverent no one would ever doubt which way they lean. Reagan's press secretary announced that the president had received more than 4,000 letters in the hospital after the assassination attempt. "For or against?" a newsman at the briefing shouted.

Most journalists try to behave as if they really believed that corn belongs on the cob, not in their copy or on their airwaves. Yes, they feel like an élite, with special access and immunities. They consider themselves on the "inside" of events that move the world. When confronted with what sounds like piety, pomposity, or stuffiness, they reach for their hatchets. They stand in awe of no one because they have reported on everyone, saints and sinners, the high and the mighty, the falling and the rising. They are more competitive than the hungry business people they often disparage. They are constantly on guard against the wiles of self-servers, yet in pursuit of a story they often manipulate their sources with the guile of a Ponzi.

A popular song titled, "Dirty Laundry," never made it to the top of the charts, but in 1985 television's Robert MacNeil pointedly repeated the lyrics to a gathering of journalists:

> Dirty little secrets
> Dirty little lies
> We got our dirty little fingers
> In everybody's pie.
> We love to cut you down to size.

And then in the refrain:

> Kick 'em when they're up
> Kick 'em when they're down.

By the cold winter of 1984–85, "Why do they hate us?" became a refrain that many journalists no longer considered entirely paranoid. At the extreme, there had been enough pure fraud and callousness to justify the question.

The decade's first big revelation of outright fraud came in 1981 when a Washington *Post* reporter, Janet Cooke, invented an eight-year-old heroin addict so convincingly that she won the Pulitzer Prize, until her fiction was exposed and the prize revoked. In the aftermath of the "new journalism," reporters at times created characters and events instead of reporting them. A young New York *Daily News* reporter was fired for making up parts of a vivid account, complete with dialogue, of British troops in Northern Ireland. "Faction" some called it. Even the *New Yorker,* much admired for its punctilious fact-checking, was forced to acknowledge that one of its regular contributing reporters had created composite characters, quotations and scenes when it suited his purpose. Lamely, he justified his fakery on the grounds that "in reporting, at times we have to go much further than the strictly factual."

The New York *Times Magazine* abjectly apologized after a free-lance writer wrote an intimate eyewitness account of modern Cambodia without ever leaving his apartment in Spain. He compounded his deception with a theft. The piece included an eloquent passage stolen from a book written fifty-one years before by André Malraux.[2]

Newsweek gave cover treatment to what quickly turned out to be fake Hitler diaries, with the mind-boggling explanation that "genuine or not, it almost doesn't matter in the end." Rupert Murdoch, whose London *Sunday Times* originally bought and syndicated the "diaries," had an even more cavalier view: "Nothing ventured nothing gained. After all, we are in the entertainment business."

The callousness—as well as callowness—prize went to two young television men in Anniston, Alabama. They covered the protest of an unemployed roofer so depressed or depraved that he showed up in a public square, doused himself with lighter fluid and ignited it. Only after the television crew let the camera roll as he went up in flames, did one of them decide belatedly he should try to put out the pyre. (The badly burned, and morally chaotic, victim later reversed himself and said he would sue them for putting their pictures on a higher plane than his life.)

Few journalists themselves turned up so very harshly in the news. But when they did, they usually were as thin-skinned and echoed the same complaints as the people they reported. ("Journalists don't have thin skins," Edward R. Murrow once said, "they have no skins.") NBC newsman Roger Mudd moaned that "until I was covered myself, I didn't know what it was like." Neither did CBS's jovial Charles Kuralt, after he had been picked up by a cop for being on the road slightly loaded. Journalists, especially news executives, were often the least available subjects of all when reporters tried to interview them. They knew the hazards.

An era of "contemplative self-assessment" one editor grandly called it.

The *Wall Street Journal,* in its year-end report to readers, had as its central theme "this age of widespread criticism of the press." Van Gordon Sauter, then president of CBS News, called it the time "when the media

2. The *Times Magazine* seemed plagued by imposters. In the years following, the *Times* again apologized for an article by an unknown secretary from New Jersey describing her rise to success in her first novel without any help or experience in the literary marketplace. It turned out she had considerable, and unmentioned, experience as well as connections in the literary world and on the *Magazine* itself. Not long after the Sunday paper confessed to two other embarrassments: a full-color picture it bought and ran across two pages of the *Magazine* accompanying an article on Miami's problems was both old and posed; and in another issue, a photo that turned out to be a composite was unknowingly used on the cover.

has discovered the media—the veils have vanished.'' His second-in-command at the time, Howard Stringer, had a more pained description of CBS's year of Westmoreland and the corporate uproar that came months later: "I don't think you should underestimate the impact of that troubling year upon people's lives. It's hard to look back on that year and see anything but struggle. God, if struggle makes you wiser and stronger, we sure have had a dose of it." (Stringer would later discover he would need even more strength and wisdom.) Osborn Elliott, then dean of Columbia University's Graduate School of Journalism and once editor-in-chief of *Newsweek,* assessed the mood in 1985: "I don't think there is any industry in the country that has done as much soul searching over the past few years."

The search took many forms. Sigma Delta Chi, the national professional journalists' society, launched "Project Watchdog," a two-year "public-awareness" campaign to trumpet the importance of the First Amendment. The program's director was the Washington public relations man for General Motors. At the same time, SDX began considering—but after years of debate, ultimately rejected—a hotly contested enforcement provision for its old voluntary ethics code. Later it launched a national ad campaign in magazines, newspapers and on radio and television with the slogan "If the press didn't tell us, who would?"

The American Society of Newspaper Editors (ASNE) declared a "Blue Press Alert" ("red" perhaps reserved for Armageddon) to defend the press's freedom. After commissioning a study on press credibility, the editors concluded: "Three-fourths of all adults have some problem with the credibility of the media, and they question newspapers as much as they question television."

ASNE also filled its in-house *Bulletin* with dozens of articles on the problem, including suggestions for everything from the appointment of a committee on credibility to a massive public relations campaign for improving the press's "image." Obviously, the editors felt so strongly that they fell into the trap of using the palliative jargon they deplored when those they covered sought to improve their reputation with the same "image-changing" remedies.

Louis Boccardi, the new head of the Associated Press, the biggest distributor of basic information for the Western world, thought the reality was as important as the reputation. He said in a speech: "Isn't it possible that the problem is not that we don't explain ourselves enough to the public but rather that having heard our explanation, the society is increasingly saying to us: 'No, that may be what you want but it does not serve our interests.' Or, put still another way, have we not reached a point where we must recognize an obligation not to do some of the things the First

Amendment gives us every right to do. Have we acquired habits that need to be broken?"

To find out what was really wrong, more seminars, conferences, surveys and committees of inquiry were appointed than at a plenary session of the United Nations. Self-conscious that he not sound too academic in establishing a study center, one publisher called his "not a think tank but a hot tub." At one media inquiry into the coverage of terrorist hostage-taking, another journalist pointed out that it was the third meeting on such subjects he had attended in three weeks in three different cities.

A public-spirited group calling itself Citizens' Choice concluded its lengthy and thoughtful report on news media performance in 1985: "Everyone agrees on two propositions: 1) The press is free enough to perform its function in a democratic society 2) The press is not responsible enough."

Responsible to whom, the press has asked? Certainly not to the government. That would undercut the very foundation of press freedom. To the public? Yes, say journalists; their readers and viewers can chastise them simply by turning to another program or not buying their product, whether a newspaper or magazine. The news media, journalists argued, should be responsible to themselves and their own consciences, other than the limitations imposed by libel laws. That is the American free press tradition, they reminded those who wanted more formal remedies. But they were saying it more softly and with less confidence than they ever had before.

With more than 800,000 lawyers in the U.S. and 130,000 journalists working in the news media, no less an eminence than Chief Justice Warren Burger chastised a convention of lawyers by telling them that in public esteem the legal profession ranked along with journalists "near the bottom of the barrel." Perhaps neither, he said, "likes the company they find themselves in." His barb found some statistical confirmation in the ASNE survey of how the public viewed the press's standards of honesty and ethics. Journalists were close to the bottom of the list, only two notches above used-car salesmen, and one above advertising executives. One newspaper headlined its column on the survey, "Would You Buy a Used Typewriter from a Journalist?"

There were dozens of new polls by and about the press.

The appetite for quantification was so strong that studies of the studies came pouring out. You could find numbers for virtually any point of view. Some of the polls were plainly self-serving, for or against the news media. All were underwhelming either way. Most showed a decline in respect and admiration for journalists and the big institutions that employed them. At first the print people blamed it on television. Then the television journalists blamed print. Finally most in both groups sensibly decided they were in the same leaky boat together.

"The harshest critics of the media," said Irving Shapiro, former chairman of Du Pont, "are not outsiders but in the media themselves." He labeled it with his own neologism: "Media culpa." Many in the media argued forcefully, as expected, that American journalists had always had such problems and that the handwringing had gone too far. They should just tough it out. "The press today," said Howard Simons, curator of the Neiman Foundation at Harvard and managing editor of the Washington *Post* during its Watergate days, "is agonizing too much about its role and how it's viewed and accepted." He was so heatedly disputed that he at least demonstrated he was right about the agony. Simon's former boss, Washington *Post* executive editor Ben Bradlee thought the press had "panicked": "There is a tendency to cater to our critics and I don't like it."

Editor & Publisher, which bills itself as the trade publication of "The Fourth Estate," rarely concedes anything to critics of the press, but it concluded in its annual "Status of the Press—1985": "The critics are tarring all reporters, all editors, all media—the press—with the brush of irresponsibility, a lack of ethics, disregard of facts, designed to 'prove' that the press does not care about the public interest but is concerned only with getting a sensational story."

New York *Times* publisher Arthur O. Sulzberger told a Yale audience that "there seems to be a growing feeling that our free press is not consistently enough a responsible press and that both regulation and punishment are called for." A leading First Amendment lawyer, Floyd Abrams, added, "I really don't believe that after more than two hundred years of a free press that the public understands it."

What the public felt but barely understood was that as the press grew into the news media in the second half of the twentieth century, they overwhelmed other conventional centers of American power. To politicians and public officials on every level—from president to alderman—it was how the media reported and commented on them that determined their fate. The same was true of people in business or anyone who wandered into public view. What the press said and did not say was fateful. It became the most important constituency those in public life had because it was the way everybody else knew what and how they were doing. The media, more than any other group, became the leaders and dominators of our culture.

Technology had made the media the American Bigmouth—resented, used, feared and abused. What had gone wrong? Was it the public and those who represented the public or the news media who were going to hell? Most likely neither, although you did have to wonder when, on a single day, Lloyds of London and the Salvation Army were reported as being investigated for fraud.

Quite a year!

And it continued. Three years later, journalist turned novelist, Tom Wolfe, in his *Bonfire of the Vanities,* used a new metaphor from the lips of a character afflicted by the press:

"Welcome to the legion of the damned now that you've been properly devoured by the fruit flies." "The fruit flies?" "The press. I'm amused by all the soul-searching these insects do. 'Are we too aggressive, too cold-blooded, too heartless?'—as if the press were a rapacious beast, a tiger. I think they'd like to be thought of as bloodthirsty. That's what I call praise by faint damnation. They've got the wrong animal. In fact, they're fruit flies. Once they get the scent, they hover, they swarm. If you swing your hand at them, they don't bite it, they dart for cover, and as soon as your head is turned, they're back again."

2

Battleground

Libel suits have become a growth industry.
—Columnist Nat Hentoff, in
the Washington *Post*, 1985.

Tensions, angers and frustrations always seek an outlet. Pressure cookers pop their safety valves before they explode. Smoke alarms whine before the house burns up. Nuclear reactors are supposed to shut down before they melt down. By the mid-1980s, the rising tension between the public and the news media was symbolized in a burst of the biggest libel suits in history. The battlegrounds were the courthouses of the U.S., none the site of greater siege than one in lower Manhattan.

Few U.S. government buildings are richer in modern drama than the granite and marble Southern District Court on Foley Square. It is the largest federal district courthouse in the country.

Libel suits were hardly its best known business. Through the portals of the neoclassical building came the Rosenbergs to be sent to their death, the only Americans ever executed for espionage in peacetime. Here Alger Hiss was adjudged a perjurer and sentenced to prison, after one of the most reverberating political trials of the era. Mafiosi were dispatched to prison or lost their citizenship and were deported to Sicily. Hard by, the S.S. *Andrea Doria* collided in the fog of admiralty law with the M/V *Stockholm,* as they had in the sea off Nantucket Island. Nicky Barnes, the drug lord, and the Reverend Sun Myung Moon, his own lord, both had painful reason to remember the thirty-story building's handsome, magisterial chambers—from their cells.

Many—from the biggest investment bankers, corporations and media stars to the noisiest American Communists, conmen and crooks—had entered its hundred-foot-wide columned entrance to meet their makers and unmakers. The building, on the edge of Chinatown, has its ups as well as its downs, its lighter moments alongside its solemnities.

34

On the morning of October 9, 1984, more than two hundred joyful immigrants of every hue and accent, filled with emotion and chattering expectantly, lined up to raise their right hands and become U.S. citizens. On that October day also—as every day—most refrains of American life echoed in the court's wide hallways. Outside, on the street facing the court's Corinthian portico, a sapphire-blue Rolls Royce Corniche coupe, with a smiling, rotund lawyer behind the wheel, made its way through the traffic. On its front and rear bumpers were the black-and-yellow letters of a New York license plate, "ACQUITAL" (the misspelling conformed to the rule allowing only eight letters on special "vanity" plates.

In the slow-moving elevators, potential jurors, lawyers, clerks, defendants, plaintiffs, many carrying morning coffee containers or plastic breakfast trays, all crowded in side by side with manacled and shackled prisoners under the watchful eyes of federal marshals. On the courthouse's broad front steps, more than a hundred television, radio and print reporters waited with their tangle of equipment. And at a side entrance another small gaggle staked out the territory for that one possible picture, or the shouted question that could make the evening news or the next day's paper.

Up on the third floor, General William Childs Westmoreland, seventy, his head thrown back, chin out, his silver hair in perfect place, strode uncertainly down the corridor to courtroom 318.

It was the first day—jury selection—for his much-heralded lawsuit. "The libel trial of the century," it had been called. Despite his confident mien, Westmoreland was obviously nervous. He was out of his lifelong environment, now accompanied by one of his band of lawyers instead of the polished military aides who had attended him before his retirement from active duty.

I hadn't seen him in fifteen years. But when I approached with a greeting, he feigned recognition in the polite manner of well-trained celebrities. For a few moments we chatted amiably about old times in Vietnam— and about nothing in particular. It was hardly a time for questions and weighty talk.

Suddenly a middle-aged man, rumpled and lean, with watery, darting eyes, ran up carrying a pile of press releases and documents. He thrust one at the general. At the same time the stranger blurted out, so hurriedly that he could barely be understood, "You knew you were not telling the truth when you spoke to Congress." A startled Westmoreland recoiled and his lawyer wordlessly shooed the intruder away. "That was Daniel Ellsberg," I said to Westmoreland, "the Pentagon Papers guy. He seems rather agitated." Westmoreland looked puzzled and distracted.

Next day the New York *Daily News,* the second largest newspaper in the country at the time, headlined at the top of the page: "ELLSBERG TO WESTY: 'LIAR!' COURTHOUSE CONFRONTATION AS CBS TRIAL JURY IS SELECTED." The story reported that Ellsberg "branded" Westmoreland "a liar" after he "accosted" him outside the courtroom.

As in so many hyped-up incidents created for media consumption, the story was mostly factually true—and as wrong as it could be. There had been no "confrontation"; just a hit and run. After seeing the paper, Westmoreland said plaintively to me in the same corridor, "You were there. I never even spoke to him. I didn't even know who he was until you told me. Some journalists are incredible."

Plainly not only an American general, an Israeli foreign minister, or CBS and *Time* were on trial. All the American news media were— broadcast and print.

The courtroom is a convoluted forum for understanding the real world outside. Then why begin by examining the media's problems with the public and the government at the birth of two libel suits?

The reasons are compelling. The arguments and angers between the press and its publics can easily get mired in rushes of generalizations and moralizing attacks on one side, or stand-pat defenses and excuses on the other. The amphitheater of the courtroom offers a more clinical view. In medicine, neurologists call some serious emotional disorders "insults to the central nervous system." Some libel suits peel back the skin covering the news media's nervous system and allow a diagnosis of many of the "insults."

These two trials exposed many of the raw nerves: the embattled adversaries from the press, the government and the public; the abrasive collision between legal rights and public expectations; the conflict between the methods and mores of journalists pitted against the interests of their subjects; the erratic press coverage of the trials themselves; and the lessons learned by the reporters who covered them.

The Westmoreland and Sharon trials are emblematic of one of the great dilemmas of the 1980s: how the threefold interests of the press, the government and the people of a democratic United States can be accommodated without inflicting near mortal wounds on one another.

Start with the Westmoreland and Sharon trials before moving on to other disorders.

Book One:

THE NEWS MEDIA ON TRIAL

3

The General

*Newsmen are supposed to report events, not
influence or precipitate them. Military men are
trained to regard their efforts positively. Still,
journalists might have appreciated that the
military has no obligation to make itself look bad
and that optimism is in itself no sin.*
—General William C. Westmoreland, 1976

In journalism as in life, courtroom trials are not the beginning of a story.
They are the end. The beginning is a person, a deed, or an event.

For me the story of the Westmoreland–CBS trial began one hot night in
Saigon in December 1967, on the screened-in veranda at the quarters of
that acronymic modern war chief, COMUSMACV (Commander United
States Military Assistance Command–Vietnam). By name, General William
C. Westmoreland. Under him were a half million U.S. troops nearly
10,000 miles from home, embattled in a country not much larger than the
state of Florida. The eyes of the world were on him.

He had returned from Washington just a few weeks earlier. Westmoreland said he had not wanted to go there. He considered such trips being
"thrust on the political scene." He was more comfortable directing foreign
battles than playing domestic politics. But a military man—unless he is
Douglas MacArthur—does not ignore an order from his commander in
chief, especially if that president happens to be Lyndon B. Johnson, facing
an election year and a rising challenge from within his own party.

At that moment the president needed him more at home than in the
field. All over the country there were protests against the war. Congress
was balking at continuing the effort, much less escalating it. Even within
LBJ's own government, opposition was rising. Mocking disbelief greeted
such florid presidential rhetoric as "Our spirit is sharp. Our cause is just,
and it is backed by strength. Our cause will succeed." LBJ desperately
wanted Westmoreland to reassure Congress and, through the news media,
to put out or at least stamp down the fires of protest.

Westmoreland's stateside public appearances on his visits that year were carefully planned by the White House for maximum media coverage. In full military dress, a salad bar of battle ribbons and decorations on his chest, he was poster-perfect, the very model of confidence and command. He sounded as good as he looked. His words were simple, his tone oratorical. Before a special joint session of Congress—the first battlefield commander in the middle of a war ever to make such an appearance—he got a hero's ovation when he said: "Backed at home by resolve, confidence, patience, determination, we will prevail in Vietnam over the Communist aggressor." He responded to the standing ovation with a snappy, gratified salute.

On NBC's "Meet the Press," then the prime television-interview show, he explained that "we are winning a war of attrition now." At the National Press Club, he was even more confident: "I am absolutely certain that whereas in 1965 the enemy was winning, today he is certainly losing and sees the strength of his forces declining. We have reached an important point when the end begins to come into view."

With understandable self-satisfaction at the apparent success of his latest trip, he sent a top-secret cable to his deputy in Saigon, General Creighton Abrams. Westmoreland said he had reported to the "Highest Authority" (militarese for *The* president), secretary of defense and Joint Chiefs of Staff that "we are grinding down the enemy." The administration could now portray "to the American people 'some light at the end of the tunnel.' "

The night that I saw him, at his quarters in a Saigon villa at 60 Tran Quy Cap, he was exhilarated by his Washington reception and his day in the field visiting his troops. He received me with cordial familiarity. Not surprising; it was my ninth visit to Vietnam since 12,000 American advisers were sent there in 1962, and I had seen Westmoreland on every trip after his arrival in 1964. I had met with him in his "Pentagon East" headquarters, taken dinner at his residence and flown all over the country with him in his command airplane and helicopter.

In print, *Time* and *Life* had been ardent supporters of the war. *Time* chose Westmoreland as its 1965 "Man of the Year," even though by then our correspondents and I had very different views from our editors about how the war was going. So "Westy," as he was always referred to and occasionally addressed, was at least as comfortable with me as he ever was with the press. Hai, his Vietnamese number-one houseboy, served us iced tea. It was as strong a drink as either of us needed at ease on his moonlit porch.

We talked about his Washington trips. He explained that he had not meant to sound too optimistic. Then he asked me, as he and his predecessor always did in one form or another, the question that really bugged him. "Why do the media and the government see this war so differently? I don't mean *you,*" he interjected, with his characteristic politeness to any journalist who displayed no personal hostility toward him or his men, "but why are *they* so pessimistic?"

As in the past, I again made a brief pass at explaining the difference between commanding and reporting, keeping it short and vague, because I was more interested in hearing his views than in expressing mine. We continued on other subjects and when we finished, I had one final question—the kind of catchall wrap-up that reporters ask when they want to make sure they haven't missed anything. Whenever I leave Vietnam, I said, wherever I go—New York, Tokyo, Washington, Paris—everybody immediately asks me, "What's new in Vietnam?" If he were I, how would *he* answer that question this time?

He was pleased at the softball I lobbed up to him. "There is something *very* different," he replied, rising to an easel and uncovering a sheaf of tactical maps. "We have a long way to go yet. But there's a big change. We have broken the enemy's infrastructure, his communications and supply lines. He can still hurt us but he can only really attack us in hit-and-run sorties from sanctuaries across the border from Laos, Cambodia or the north. The enemy has lost his ability to launch a coordinated attack."

I have never had any doubt that Westmoreland honestly believed what he was saying.[1] It was not an effort to con me or fool himself. His military analysis was credible—with one catastrophic exception.

In our New York office as well as our outposts around the world, *Time-Life,* like all of America, was divided by conflicting views of the war.

Most journalists started out believing that it was a "good" war to prevent Chinese communism from expanding in the 60s the way Hitler's Germany had, unopposed, in the 30s. "Containment" of communism, in Asia as well as in Europe, was widely accepted U.S. policy since the end of World War II. None of us seriously believed in the knee-jerk charge of "American imperialism." Of course, the United States went into Vietnam originally

---

1. Nor was he saying it for the first time. Like most people at the center of public life, he was repeating, in only slightly different words, what he had already said in a public speech two weeks earlier. It was also the official military position. One of Westmoreland's bosses, the army's chief of staff, General Harold K. Johnson, was saying at the same time that "the major forces of the enemy have already been largely broken up. They will have an occasional ability to mount an attack but this will be periodic and somewhat spasmodic."

out of national self-interest. That is what foreign policy is all about. But we also had a measure of that uniquely American spirit of evangelical optimism and idealism. Gradually, as the war changed, most us changed our minds about what the effort could accomplish and what it could not. My own changed—late, to be sure, but conclusively—after that very visit in December 1967.

In Saigon I had seen Westmoreland, the U.S. ambassador to Vietnam, Ellsworth Bunker, and other American and Vietnamese officials. More important, I had been out in the field for days and nights with U.S. and Vietnamese troops. And I talked to dozens of reporters, many of the best and a few of the worst.

On the airplane going home just before Christmas, I typed what seemed to me the most important dispatch I had ever written. It was dated December 18, 1967, and was slugged "Vietnam: A Conclusion." It began:

> In making new judgments on old subjects, Montaigne once said, you can only repeat yourself or contradict yourself. The truth is that the result of visiting Vietnam over the past six years is mostly an inconclusive blur of often contradictory if always memorable experiences. But this time—for the first time—it was different. There was something really new: we have won the battle against a Communist military takeover of the central government and paradoxically in so doing made it impossible for us really to win the war.

> Pause a moment—if you haven't already—and beware. The war in Vietnam produces unique rhetorical opportunities. One can find facts, evidence or anecdotes to prove almost any conclusion. That's why the argument rages and frustration rises. My discouraging conclusion is not only new for me but unwanted. While I will describe in detail the evidence that cannot be ignored, I will also try to explain (as I must to myself) how a contrary view could be held by such honorable, decent and well-informed advocates as General Westmoreland.

Never mind the evidence I reported. It was made up of tragic and disheartening little snapshots enlarged into hopeless big pictures. Together they finally proved to me—and helped change Time-Life's editorial views of the war—that we were inadvertently destroying the country and its people in the process of trying to save them. It was a dispiriting cause that Americans rightly would not continue to support. In the end it was destroying us.

David Greenway, an experienced *Time* combat correspondent, had often been my battlefield guide. When he saw my dispatch he sent me a message from Saigon saying that he thought my reporting and the conclusions were right, but he disagreed with the Westmoreland quote I had uncritically passed on. Greenway wrote me: "I think Westmoreland overstates the case when he says the enemy will only fight us from sanctuaries. It's a trend, but they still have powerful forces in the country."

Greenway's caveat—shared by many other reporters on the scene—and my conclusion that the U.S. objective was unachievable needed only a clincher. It came straight from Vietnam 42 two days later.

In the midafternoon of January 30, 1968, I was called to the *Time-Life* cable room in New York for an urgent 4:06 A.M. message on the direct teletype line from our Saigon bureau. The new chief of the bureau was at the Saigon keyboard: "DICK. BILL HERE. DON'T RING THE TELEX BELL. WE MUST KEEP SILENT. PLEASE DO NOT TURN ON YOUR MACHINE. WE WILL CALL YOU. THERE'S BOOM BOOM NOT FAR FROM DOOR. EYE PREFER TO WAIT UNTIL ALL QUIET TO TALK."

It was the opening of the enemy's countrywide Tet (Vietnamese New Year) offensive. Remarkably and with complete surprise during the holiday period, the Viet Cong had simultaneously attacked forty of the country's forty-four provincial capitals. Westmoreland's own massive headquarters near the Saigon airport was hit. On television, the Viet Cong could be seen battling within the walls of the U.S. embassy.

Tet marked the beginning of the end of the war. For us, from then on, it was all winding down, finding a way to get out—even though it took seven more years for the last American to fly out, with panicked Vietnamese trying to cling to the skids of the last departing helicopter.

More than five thousand books and monographs have been written about the Vietnam War—most of them with some evaluation of the Tet offensive. This is not one of them. Here I am not dealing with who was right or who was wrong, whether it was actually a victory for the United States or a disastrous defeat, even whether the news media assessed its importance correctly at the time.

Years later, an American colonel met his Vietnamese counterpart in Hanoi. "You know you never defeated us on the battlefield," the American said proudly." "That may be so," the Vietnamese answered, "but it is also irrelevant." Nothing was irrelevant or ever disputed about the impact of Tet.

In the White House that day television sets were on as they were in millions of homes all over the U.S. Harry Mc Pherson, presidential confidant and speechwriter, recalled the moment: "I watched the invasion of the American Embassy compound. I put aside the confidential cables. I was more persuaded by the tube and by the newspapers. I was fed up with the optimism that seemed to flow without stopping from Saigon." He was not alone. The entire Johnson administration was devastated. The Pentagon Papers later said that "coming on the heels of optimistic reports from the field commands, this offensive caught official Washington off guard and stunned both the Administration and the American public."

Even General Maxwell Taylor, a stouthearted and vocal defender of Westmoreland, acknowledged the effect of Tet: "While the enemy was losing the war on the battlefield, he was gaining a valuable psychological victory in the United States and in large parts of the world. The general public was shocked by the unexpected vitality shown by an enemy whom many had supposed to be on its last legs."

It was impossible to tell whether LBJ, often manic in public and depressed in private, was more disappointed or angry. Against the background of the countrywide Tet assaults, Westmoreland's upbeat pronouncements were an unconvincing failure. Day after day, commentators, editorial writers and media organizations that had supported the war now turned against it. The hawkish *Wall Street Journal* wrote: "The American people should be getting ready to accept, if they haven't already, the prospect that the whole Vietnam effort may be doomed." Walter Cronkite, in the only on-air editorial he had ever delivered, urged that we find a way out: "It seems now more certain than ever that the bloody experience of Vietnam is to end in a stalemate." Even *Time* and *Life* eventually said "enough."

LBJ, taunted with such slogans as "Hey, hey, LBJ, how many kids did you kill today," named a new secretary of defense (Clark Clifford, to replace Robert McNamara). He called on his prestigious task force of "Wise Men" to reassess the American commitment. From hawk to dove their consensus was that the time had come to call a halt. "The majority of us," wrote McGeorge Bundy, the group's rapporteur, "were in agreement with Dean Acheson[2] that we could no longer do the job we set out to do in the time that American opinion would permit us, so that we must begin to take steps to disengage."

The political fallout was everywhere. Robert Kennedy, seizing the moment, decided to run for the presidency. Protests spread on the campuses. Two months to the day after Tet, amidst the catastrophic domestic and foreign debris of our Vietnam involvement, Lyndon Johnson startled the nation by announcing he would not run again.[3]

---

2. Who in a letter to his daughter, described LBJ as "a real centaur—part man, part horse's ass."
3. Westmoreland said he had had advance word of LBJ's intention. In his pretrial examination, Westmoreland recalled: "Mr. Johnson told me, I believe it was in November, that he was seriously thinking in terms of not running for re-election and he explained why but he asked me not to mention it to anybody, which I did not." LBJ at the time had been ascribing his indecision not to Vietnam but to his health. He told his wife, Lady Bird, Westmoreland, Dean Rusk and a very few others that he did not want to end up a sick, ineffectual, old second-term president.

At the Democratic convention in Chicago that August, on streets clouded with tear gas and in the uproar of the convention hall, Vietnam was the only real subject. Hubert Humphrey humiliated himself and later lost the election to Richard Nixon partly because he at first heeled rather than ran at his own gait on Vietnam. In his memoirs written years later, Henry Kissinger summarized the period: U.S. entry into Vietnam "had begun openly, and with nearly unanimous congressional, public and media approval. But by 1969 the comity by which a democratic society must live had broken down."

By July in the year of Tet, Westmoreland was in Washington for his new assignment as chief of staff of the army, a post ordinarily considered a promotion. Not this time. It was widely interpreted as a kick upstairs. "WESTY SULKS," said a headline in the Washington *Post*.

In the decade thereafter, there were no Vietnam heroes—least of all Westmoreland. He was burned in effigy, abused, vilified in print and in person, called a "murderer," "a liar," a "war criminal," responsible for "another Pearl Harbor." His face adorned the dart boards of American anger and disappointment. Even Ngyuyen Cao Ky, of all people, his former junior ally, the onetime Vietnamese fighter pilot and prime minister, inveighed against the Westmoreland command's "squalid deception." In the words of Ky's ghost writer: "It was clear that some American leaders in Saigon deliberately issued a string of lies to the White House, in an effort to maintain the impression that the Americans were getting on top of the Viet Cong."

The House Select Committee on Intelligence (the Pike Committee) accused Westmoreland's command of doctoring discouraging intelligence reports. (Westmoreland himself was not asked to testify but sent a letter to the committee for the record.) The committee launched its investigation four months after a May 1975 cover story in *Harper's* magazine. Written by a former CIA analyst, Samuel A. Adams, it was titled "Vietnam Cover-Up: Playing War With Numbers—A CIA Conspiracy Against Its Own Intelligence." The article charged that the military's reports from Vietnam were based on "fabricated" enemy strength estimates. The editor of the piece was a young journalist named George Crile. In the next ten years the duo of Crile and Adams was destined to play a central role in Westmoreland's life.

Westmoreland rarely publicly complained or answered back. "The soldier," he said, "must be prepared to cope with the hardships of war and bear its scars."

After his formal retirement in 1972, he had gone home to South Carolina, the state where he was born. In his forty years of military service he and his wife, "Kitsy," (née Katherine Van Deusen) had had 33 different homes. Now they lived on one of Charleston's quiet, venerable streets, in a well-landscaped, pale-pink stucco house, with a small building in the back that was used by the general as his study. He served on a number of out-of-state business and charitable boards, frequently making speeches around the U.S. and the world.

At home they led a quiet, neighborhood life, helping local community groups and dining occasionally at the unpretentious local yacht club. "He is a man who likes to focus on things and pursue them," his son Rip said. "That was certainly missing through those years" of retirement. They were "good neighbors," "nice people." "Westy's a real gentleman," everybody said. He was a local celebrity, even a hero, but oh, so local. *Who's Who in America* dropped him from its new edition, waiting to consign him to its companion volume, *Who Was Who*.

In 1976 he published his autobiography, *A Soldier Reports*. It was a stolid, proud book destined for the military history shelves of libraries rather than the best-seller lists. Two years earlier he had run for the Republican nomination as governor of South Carolina. But he was right when, years before, he had said he was no politician. He lost. It went unrecorded in his book. It was not really part of this soldier's much bigger story.

How does a journalist tell the "truth" about such a soldier? Does the private man really matter or only the way he performs his public role? Should he be judged with Old Testament severity or New Testament charity? Do his feelings and motives really matter when larger issues are at stake?

First take the man himself. Westmoreland presents a special problem for most reporters. By training they are a suspicious lot. In their irreverent ways, they rightly refuse to take anybody or anything at face value. Compare news people as a group to such a straight arrow as the guileless Westmoreland. His very bearing and appearance invoke images of Mt. Rushmore. He commanded troops in three wars (World War II, Korea and Vietnam). When asked what moral dilemmas he had faced as an Army officer, he reflected, then answered, from his depths that he could think of absolutely none. Had he ever done anything that brought a reprimand? Well . . . he did remember being "dressed down" and losing the use of his car for a month for driving at 20 in a 10 mph zone at Hawaii's Schofield Barracks; receiving a "letter of censure" for paying his commissary bill five days late at Fort Sill, Oklahoma; and being gigged at West Point for having an illegal radio in his room. Once during his libel suit against CBS, when pressed to explain how he could be so certain that he would have known if officers under him had been improperly pressured, Westmoreland gave an answer that would have made any ex-GI guffaw: "I'm sure my chaplain would have heard about it."

As a boy in Spartanburg County, he had, not surprisingly, been an Eagle Scout. He remembers that his father, the manager of the local cotton mill village, was "a man of strong character, industrious, thrifty, scrupulously honest, intolerant of unreliability and immorality." His higher education started as a cadet at the Citadel, the military college of the South. His father wanted him to be a lawyer, but he decided he not only liked the discipline of the military life but "wanted to see the world." So he sought and received appointment to West Point, where the experience "most rewarding of all was the respect I gained for the code of ethics."

Although he struggled with English grammar and composition, that didn't prevent him from becoming first captain of the corps, just as Generals Pershing and MacArthur had been before him. Westmoreland's classmates called him the "inevitable general." He recalls two of the most exciting moments of his four years at the Point, the first when he was a plebe and MacArthur orated on the military code of honor at commencement. The other was an aging Pershing's words that Westmoreland remembered from his own graduation: "Maintain your own morals at a high level and you will find them reflected in the morals of your men."

He fought Rommel in North Africa, saw combat in Sicily, was a full colonel at thirty, fought at the Battle of the Bulge. In Korea, he won a battlefield promotion to brigadier general, then in the Pentagon to major general at forty-two, the youngest in the U.S. Army. At forty-six he became superintendent of West Point, his shrine and the inspiration of his life. Only Generals MacArthur and Maxwell Taylor were younger when they held the same post.

On the ring Westmoreland wears is engraved the West Point motto that has governed his life: "Duty, Honor, Country." In recent years at the academy, those three words and the honor code ("I will not lie, cheat or steal, nor tolerate those who do") have been found inadequate in teaching cadets to deal with the moral complexities of modern life and military command. "We don't live in a world in which there exists a single definition of honor any more," says a former West Point instructor, "and it's a fool that hangs on to the traditional standards and hopes that the world will come around to him."

Not to Westmoreland. To him the West Point motto and its honor code are holy writ. "Old fashioned virtues may go out of style in a permissive society," he frowns, "but no army can long survive without them." To know Westmoreland is to know that he really means it.

The news media have a hard time dealing with such simplicities—some critics have said, uncharitably, "such simplemindedness." Their mottoes tend to be "All the News That's Fit to Print," "The Voice of Freedom" or a hand-lettered sign on the wall of a cubicle at a television station: "Let's Get the Fucking Story on the Air."

Today at West Point, the Army War College and the Harvard Business School—all places where Westmoreland took courses—the curricula include lectures and seminars on what are called "Media Relations." Not in Westmoreland's day. His earliest lesson in that morass came at the end of the war in Europe from General George Patton, who told him, "Don't forget when you return to the States, be careful what you say. No matter what, they'll put it in the newspapers." Television was yet to be born, so Patton had no words of wisdom on that subject.

Westmoreland had to learn about the press on the run in Vietnam. By the time he took command in May of 1964, there was already open warfare between the press and the U.S. command. Westmoreland had inherited an intractable press problem that was escalating much as the war itself was. Print correspondents, especially, had been the most critical of the inflated U.S. assessment of the Ngo ruling family and the fighting will of their troops. Cumbersome television coverage was still new and spotty. The public, a Pacific Ocean away, was getting its first taste of late, full-color moving pictures of Americans at war. But the television camera's clout was still unrevealed.

The U.S. commander, General Paul Harkins ("I am an optimist and I'm not going to allow my staff to be pessimistic"), was dismayed that journalists "on our side" would not report at face value what he and his briefing officers told them. At civilian headquarters, U.S. Ambassador Frederick Nolting, a southern gentleman of an old school accustomed to having his own way, imperiously decided not to deal with reporters he didn't like.

Nolting told me that he "wouldn't even talk to David Halberstam of the New York *Times* because of the lies he writes." I mentioned to Nolting that Halberstam, who later won a Pulitzer Prize for his coverage, was read at breakfast every morning by the president of the United States, long before the ambassador's cables were digested by the State Department. Perhaps he should try to placate rather than punish Halberstam. It was too late for that, he said.

Relations between American reporters and Vietnamese officials were even worse. The press had simply stopped interviewing government officials, going instead to their wide network of unofficial sources. On one of my visits, I insisted to our bureau chief, Charles Mohr—although he said it would be worthless—that my presence be used as an excuse to get an interview with President Ngo Dinh Diem.

We got it but Mohr was righter than even he had expected. For six hours

Diem droned on unstoppable. He said not one word that was useful or illuminating. An exclusive interview with a leading world political figure of the moment and both Mohr and I were in danger of dozing off. Although our bladders were full from endless cups of tea, our notebooks were empty. His monologue was a combination of a lesson in Oriental ancient history and a *Mobil Travel Guide* of Vietnam's forty-four provinces, complete with road maps. My six-word cable to New York said: "NGO STORY IN SCHEDULED DIEM INTERVIEW." Even the old *U.S. News & World Report* could not have found a single line worthy of the interminable, unread texts it then routinely printed.

For Westmoreland, the task of dealing with the news media had become even thornier than it had been for his predecessors.

Distrust had deepened on both sides. It "reached a level of bitterness," wrote John Mecklin, a former foreign correspondent and a U.S. mission information officer, "I had never encountered in 20 years of foreign duty." Senior U.S. government officials in Saigon viewed a journalist "as a natural adversary who was deliberately trying to sabotage the national interest, or as a child who would not understand and should not be asking about grown-up affairs."

But officers in the field—civilian and military—were more conscious of the reality they faced in the country than the official policy they were supposed to espouse to the media. Reporters lived with those experienced field officers, their troops and lower echelon civilians, sought them out, protecting their anonymity and sending back reports of the war's discouraging and ugly progress in sharp conflict with official headquarters optimism. In the words of a beleaguered "grunt" (i.e. foot soldier) in the brutal movie *Platoon:* "There's the way it ought to be and the way it is."

Compounding the misery was the Washington strategy of escalation. We would crank up one notch and the enemy would be beaten down one. It was to be slow-kill rather than overkill. But as we escalated, so did two other very different players: the Soviet-backed North Vietnamese and the American press. As more American troops arrived so did more American journalists.

Westmoreland had a passionate retrospective view of what went wrong: "It was the first war ever covered by television, and this was a unique experience for those of us on the battlefield and it was a unique experience to the media." At times, Westmoreland had more than 500 reporters accredited to his headquarters: "They were not organized as a group," he later said. "Every individual was on his own. There was great competition for lead stories. Most of the stories were very good and accurate but there were a number that weren't, that were distorted, and it took an inordinate amount of my time and that of my staff to answer queries from Washington on reports that had been made on television or written articles or news items or editorials that were published or aired in the United States. Sure, we were sensitive to press reaction. We would have to be dumb-oxes if we weren't.''

Dumb they were not. But as sophisticated as they were in conventional war, most were innocents in news media engagements during their first unconventional war. Three brief examples:

- Westmoreland's personal daily diary, which his secretary faithfully transcribed, records that he was happy to be able to clear the AP's correspondent, Peter Arnett, of the charge made by one of Westmoreland's officers that Arnett was a communist. Arnett, born in New Zealand, one of the gutsiest combat correspondents in the world, was a Pulitzer Prize winner for his Vietnam reporting. An officer in Westmoreland's headquarters had confused him with Australian-born Wilfred Burchett, who was pro-communist and had covered the war from the North Vietnamese side of the border. The only things the two had in common were that both originally came from down under and both had four-syllable, rhyming names.

- Westmoreland was told that a free-lance writer, Jonathan Schell, was about to publish in the *New Yorker* what turned out to be a memorable article on the devastation U.S. bombing had wrought in two South Vietnamese provinces. As printed, the story was as realistic and vivid for its time as John Hersey's account of Hiroshima was in 1946, on a larger scale and in the same magazine. Westmoreland, who managed to get hold of a draft of Schell's piece, expressed alarm in his diary: "The article is highly exaggerated and will create major problems if published. I immediately proceeded to get more information on Schell. I felt it could get involved in the war crimes arena if taken at face value. I urged that Ambassador Bunker immediately send a message to Washington which would hopefully bring about pressure to withhold publication until the matter could be given further study."

- Rockets about press coverage from Washington kept landing on Westmoreland's desk. At one point, he received a cable from the chairman of the Joint Chiefs asking him to explain a critical story that apparently came from within Westmoreland's own command. Westmoreland promptly replied with the clear implication that some journalistic sin had been committed. The offending correspondent, the New York *Times'* R. W. ("Johnny") Apple Jr., had the impudence to get "information he should not have had and used it. Apple does not research his material with the MACV military staff. He works mostly with personal contacts. He is pessimistic and suspicious and still convinced that we are not honest. He is probably bucking for a Pulitzer Prize. Best regards.''

In later years President Johnson regretted that he had not imposed military censorship, despite the problems it would have created. But military censorship would have made little difference in the way the public viewed the war. Few security violations were even claimed by the military during the entire war. Censorship—unless it had been political, which no one has ever suggested—would not have changed the word or picture reporting the military and the government found so offensive.

Reflecting on it all in 1975 from the solitude of his Charleston study, Westmoreland wrote his own explanation:

> When the President and his Administration failed to level with the American people about the extent and nature of the sacrifice that had to be made, they contributed to a credibility gap that grew into an unbridgeable chasm. The President allowed public opinion to become a leaden liability. Unlike Kennedy, Johnson did not have the background or style to carry public opinion with him, and he became a prisoner of it.

> The military thus was caught in between, and I myself as the man perhaps most on the spot may have veered too far in the direction of supporting in public the government's policy, an instinct born of devotion to an assigned task even more than to a cause and of a loyalty to the President as Commander in Chief. That is an ingrained tradition in the professional military man.

No one has summarized the argument more succinctly than the colonel in Vietnam during the war, who years later became secretary of state, Alexander Haig: ''I have heard some of my colleagues—I have been tempted to do it myself—suggest that the press lost Vietnam. Policy lost Vietnam. Bad policy.''

Westmoreland, the clean-cut fighter, never battled with the press face-to-face. He seemed personally to like most journalists and they him. The visiting ''big feet''—editors, news executives, syndicated columnists, television anchors and celebrity journalists—all walked on Westy's red carpet, often to the dismay of their staffs, who feared they would be snowed by the amiable ''general's tour.'' Among the visitors in 1967 was CBS's Mike Wallace, who by invitation, showed up at Westmoreland's quarters at 8:00 A.M., flew with him to Danang, Cam Ranh Bay and a scattershot of fire bases, then back to Saigon by evening. Wallace remembers it as a ''fascinating day.''

Later, when Wallace did a touching report on Vietnam casualties evacuated to Fitzsimmons Hospital near Denver, Westmoreland, who by then was back in the States, wrote a "Dear Mike" letter, commending him for the piece. So in May of 1981, when Wallace telephoned Westmoreland in Charleston to ask him to appear on a CBS Reports documentary about the Tet offensive and the intelligence leading up to it, Westy was receptive.

He recalls that Wallace said it was to be a different format, "not a '60 Minutes' type program. Westmoreland said he got the impression that it was to be "fair, educational and objective." Wallace introduced CBS producer George Crile, who would make the arrangements. Crile was a total stranger to Westmoreland.

In television journalism, more than in print, subjects who are hard to get are sometimes initially wooed by the big-name television journalists. (In lining up interview subjects, says Wallace, "one concession at a time has always been my motto.") Then they are turned over to the producer, who does the reporting and supervises the making of the actual program. Once Westmoreland was hooked, Crile immediately followed up. On the second call, Westmoreland expressed some concern about the format of the proposed interview. He said that Crile reassured him. Its centerpiece, Westmoreland thought, was to be the Tet offensive, a subject he approached with confidence.

Too much confidence.

4

The Interview

The documentary of controversy was, is and should continue to be the heart and soul of CBS News.
—Burton Benjamin,
Senior Executive Producer,
CBS News, 1982

Network television documentaries are rarely done in a hurry. They are the books of television journalism, not its bulletins.

Before a documentary is launched, the senior executives of the network's news division—up to its president—must approve. Not that documentaries are so expensive to make; they average $200,000 to $400,000 an hour, compared with $900,000 to $1.5 million for most entertainment programs. But they take a lot of staff and executive time because—with rare exceptions—they are done in-house rather than bought from independent producers. Most important, they do not attract large audiences. Advertisers happily pay much higher rates to fill the same time-slots with blockbuster movies, popular serials or wheels of fortune and family feuds. Although documentaries sometimes win prestige and awards, they lose in dollars and ratings.

Nonetheless, ever since Edward R. Murrow's pioneering days, documentaries have been thought of as broadcast companies' concession to public service. In recent years, commerce has increasingly triumphed over such concessions. The number of full-length, traditional documentaries in prime time has declined. In 1985 the three networks together broadcast only fourteen hours of documentaries. In 1982 CBS alone had put on that amount, much of it "blown away" in low audience viewing hours. (In 1970 all three networks broadcast seventy-nine hours in prime time.) The networks today argue that the equivalent of documentaries, under such different titles as "instant specials" or "long-form programming," has taken up the information slack. When documentaries are undertaken, they have a long lead time, with designated executives and staff assigned to them. They are a risky business—not so much financially but because print critics as frequently pick them apart as praise them and their subjects often complain. Sometimes they even sue.

Of all the trademark documentaries of the past, CBS Reports, first produced in 1959 by Fred W. Friendly and spawned in the Murrow tradition, has both the most distinguished and the most contentious history. The programs are better known for their bite than their poetry.

When George Crile telephoned Westmoreland, his CBS Reports project had already been in the works for about six months. But it had been festering in the mind of one man, whom CBS hired as a consultant, for more than fifteen.

For Sam Adams, an indirect descendant of President John Adams, intelligence on the enemy was as much a passion as military life was for Westmoreland. In the days when the CIA was like an Ivy League training camp for the establishment, Adams had all the genteel credentials. First, the right schools—Buckley in New York, St. Mark's prep, coasting through Harvard, followed by a hitch in the navy of "three years, four months and eleven days." He spent two years at the Harvard Law School, before dropping out in the early 60s. Adams tried banking, still not knowing what he wanted—"a downwardly mobile WASP" who "belongs in the 12th century" is his description. But if you were a well-born, educated "gentleman" in those days, getting a job in the CIA was as easy as collecting unemployment insurance.

Adams quickly discovered the CIA was his calling. He made his mark finding "3,012 guys, a bunch of Cubans, holed up in Angola supplied by 26 countries, from Albania to Zanzibar." Africa was a continent away from Vietnam, but on the fifth floor of the CIA headquarters in Langley, Virginia, where Adams worked, it was just over the next partition. He vaulted easily into the Vietnam section, analyzing enemy documents. "The key to good intelligence," says Adams earnestly, "is good files, knowing what's in them and how to retrieve them."

It is hard to imagine a more meticulous file-keeper than Adams. Occasionally, he compared his abstract numbers with the reality of on-the-ground inspection trips to Vietnam because "there were no VC around Washington." What he saw made him suspect that the Viet Cong were far stronger than was reported in the military estimates. Then one day in Langley he had an epiphany. He recorded the event right down to the minute in what would grow into thousands of hand-written yellow pages of notes, which he called his "chronologies."

On Thursday, August 18, 1966, at 10:30 A.M. Saigon military headquarters Bulletin 689 came in with a translation of a captured enemy document from Binh Dinh province. It showed an enemy force eleven times the official figures. "By 10:32," says Adams, "I realized I was in deep." He went "galloping around the CIA like Paul Revere," saying "Look, if you're going to count these people when they're dead, why can't you count them when they're still alive?" For Adams it was the beginning of his own private twenty-year war.

After the Vietnam War, he devoted himself to trying to make enemy strength figures as heated an issue as it was when the war was raging. At the Pentagon Papers trial of Daniel Ellsberg, Adams testified that the military had falsified intelligence figures and lied about enemy strength. He kept collecting documents and expanding his chronologies. He hid some of his evidence not in a pumpkin, like a similarly driven evangelist, Whittaker Chambers, but buried under the loam of a neighbor's northern Virginia farm in more capacious heavy-duty leaf bags encased in a wooden box.

He tried to have his former boss, CIA Director Richard Helms, investigated for his conduct during the war. He urged that Westmoreland be court martialed for "fabrication of enemy strength figures." He wrote the article for *Harper's* magazine laying out his case and started work expanding it into a book. His *Harper's* editor, George Crile, never forgot him— nor the indicting historical record Adams continued to amass.

Investigative journalism was the rage in 1976. It had helped drive Nixon from the White House and was in hot pursuit of other triumphs.

But television networks and stations were still far behind newspapers and magazines in the race, so they began to recruit new talent. One appealing candidate as an investigative reporter was George Crile, who after Trinity College and Georgetown's Foreign Service School, had worked as a legman for those two widely read exposé specialists, Drew Pearson and Jack Anderson. Crile tried to hone his investigative knife at a small midwestern daily, then returned to Washington again to cover the Pentagon for the Knight-Ridder newspapers. Crile had a confident air about him and began writing and editing stories about the underside of the CIA.

Married to (and later divorced from) the stepdaughter of Washington's well-known columnist, Joseph Alsop, Crile knew his way around the capital's *haut monde*. CBS hired him first as a consultant and later as a reporter on an acclaimed documentary "The CIA's Secret Army," which he co-produced. In quick order, he was both reporter and co-producer— occasionally appearing on-air himself—for a series of CBS programs:

"Battle for Panama," "Three Mile Island," "The Battle for South Africa" (which won both Peabody and Emmy awards), "Gay Power—Gay Politics." The last got him in trouble.

It not only buried CBS in protests from angry San Franciscans but brought a censure from the National News Council, an unofficial group formed to hear complaints about news media performance. One irrefutable charge was that the program had violated CBS News policy. It had inflated one scene with a misplaced burst of applause.

For all his charm, Crile could turn on an abrasive reportorial manner. When he was interviewing for "Gay Power" the mayor then of San Francisco, Dianne Feinstein, Crile asked her, she says, how it felt "to be the mayor of Sodom and Gomorrah?" She promptly showed him to the door, an action she recalls she has never taken with any other reporter.

In the backbiting world of broadcasting, Crile's patrician-like aloofness made him many enemies. He was accused by many of his co-workers of walking over the people under him and kissing the bottoms of those above him. He was also still relatively inexperienced—he had never produced a show alone—and his bosses worried about the shortcuts he might take to make a point, as had been done in the "Gay Power" show.

When Crile proposed to his boss, CBS Executive Producer Howard Stringer, that Sam Adams' charges against the military in Vietnam be followed up for a CBS Report, Stringer and other CBS executives were leery. To convince them, Crile produced a long (sixteen single-spaced pages) program proposal, a "blue sheet," in CBS jargon:

> The primary focus of this proposed documentary is the story of how the U.S. command in Vietnam entered into an elaborate conspiracy to deceive Washington and the American public. This is of course the most serious of accusations, suggesting that a number of very high officials—General Westmoreland included—participated in a conspiracy that robbed this country of the ability to make critical judgments.

The word conspiracy appeared twenty-four times. "That was George trying to sell an extremely reluctant executive producer," recalls Stringer, who thought it unlikely that intelligence officers and others would support the charges on camera. "The length of the blue sheet reflected a massive amount of skepticism on my part," said Stringer.

It is rare in any kind of journalism that major stories—especially investigative efforts—are undertaken without a memo outlining the mostly unchecked suspicions and areas of inquiry that the reporter making the suggestion wants to explore. As many such initiatives are rejected as accepted by editors and broadcast executives.

Editorial decision makers always face a dilemma when an investigative reporter asks for the time and resources to pursue a will-o'-the-wisp lead. For only one example, when I was editorial director of the Long Island daily *Newsday*, the paper's top investigative reporter wanted to hire bulldozers to dig up a small potato field in Suffolk County. He had been tipped that it was a gangland burial ground. I asked for more information than his source originally offered. And when I got a little more from him? I suggested starting out with shovels. No bodies were ever found—and the reporter, *Newsday's* Robert Greene, went on to become one of the leading investigative journalists in America. (His title is "Assistant Managing Editor—Investigations," and he headed *Newsday's* teams that won two Pulitzer Prizes.)[1]

CBS was not convinced that Crile could dig up former CIA and military officials who would be willing to testify on camera. So he was given a go-ahead for only the first phase to see if he could do just that. With the amber light came a small initial budget and permission to hire Sam Adams as the program's consultant for what became $25,000 plus expenses. To be allowed to continue, Crile would have to report regularly on his progress and show actual interviews in which the allegations against Westmoreland were made.

Major-league journalism, unlike virtuoso art, is more often a collaboration than the work of a single person. Everybody knows that about television. Fewer know it about print.

If newspapers and magazines unrolled credits the way television does, the list of names and titles would often be almost as long. It would be a mistake, though, to gloss over the real differences in their operations. Television and news magazine journalism are characterized by their group production. So are newspapers. But in newspaper reporting, a correspondent on the scene is connected more directly to the printing press at home. Desk editors may change the copy or challenge the reporting; other editors may kill the story, order a rewrite, or run sidebars (instead of combining the elements into one story). But the byline story that appears in print is supposed to represent the reporting of the correspondent on the scene, not a rewritten or refocused view by home-based editors. Once in print, just as in television or news magazines, the newspaper story has the backing and endorsement of the news organization that put it out.

It is a rare big story in print or on the screen that is the product of a single unaided hand. The bigger the story, the more the hands.

1. After one of his multipart exposés of drug traffic from Turkey to France to New York, Greene told a Washington *Journalism Review* reporter: "I lied. I cheated. I damn near stole. The result obviously was good. I'd do it again. Our fine sense of ethics diminishes in proportion to the importance of the story."

The titles, functions and raw materials are different. But the early stages of television documentaries are not very different from their print equivalent—the blockbuster, cover story, series or major exposé. Reporters or a reporting team (called producers or units in television) get a lead—or are told to develop one—on what may be a good, important, perhaps just an interesting story. Initially, to have the time and resources to pursue it, they need permission from their editors (called executive producers or some such titles in television). If the project is big or sensitive enough, more senior editorial executives are cut in. Along the way, the reporters or producers have to prove to their bosses that they are not wasting time or money and that the quest is likely to produce a publishable story or something that can be broadcast.

Despite the number of people often involved in a big effort, credit or blame can usually be attributed to one person more than to others. Without question, George Crile was the most important single hand in the production of the CBS Report "The Uncounted Enemy: A Vietnam Deception." In the program's on-screen credits he was billed as "producer," "writer" and "director."

His biggest resource was the obsessed, Calvinistic Sam Adams, with his encyclopedic documents and annotated lists of more than eighty sources. Crile's task was to translate the words into television. He doggedly made progress.

Crile is a suave prototype of that special, driven species, the investigative reporter, once described as people who dig up the dead and ring up the living. Like many members of the breed, he wheedled and cajoled, threatened and flattered, finally convincing a dozen key witnesses to be interviewed on camera. On the surface the investigative techniques of television seem similar to the print process. One good fact, document or interview made it easier to smoke out or whipsaw others.

Getting usable material for the kind of television story Crile was working on is much harder than it is in print. Print reporters need only authenticated words, often from sources they need not identify. Most television sources have to agree to appear *before the camera* not just to be quoted or speak for background. Without visual footage there is no program.

By the time Crile called Westmoreland, CBS executives were impressed. They had seen pieces of rough cuts from some of his interviews with former military and CIA men who said the enemy strength figures were rigged. At that point Crile's bosses knew of no shortcuts he had taken or any imbalance in his interviewing. They began to overcome some of their early misgivings and had already agreed to have their best known interviewer, Mike Wallace, as the narrator and key interviewer of the report if

Crile could bring it off. Wallace was not eager. He had never even read the blue sheet and was already stretched by the twenty-five or more pieces he does every year for "60 Minutes," the most financially successful program ever produced for a network's news and public affairs division.

Wallace, who was sixty-three at the time, had spent more than forty years in broadcasting. He started out in radio, reading newscasts and peanut-butter commercials. Then onto the ground floor of television entertainment, initially doing barroom (where the first television sets were placed) beauty contests. In 1956–57 he got his first national attention from a late-night program originally called "Night Beat" (and later "The Mike Wallace Interview"), the first tough, head-on television interview program. On it, recalls Wallace, "we used searching, tight close-ups to record the tentative glances, nervous tics, beads of perspiration." After many downs and ups, he became one of the best known personalities in all of television, the trademark presence of "60 Minutes."

If in the history of television news, Murrow symbolized standards; Cronkite, hometown credibility; Charles Collingwood, sophisticated foreign reporting; Ted Koppel, preeminent moderating; Robert MacNeil and Jim Lehrer, thoughtful analysis; Bill Moyers, social commentary; John Chancellor, lucid explanation of complex subjects; Barbara Walters, Main Street curiosity; Wallace's place in the television news hall of fame was earned for creating the hard-hitting interview.

Wallace was not easy to get for the Vietnam program. When he agreed to do it, he was busy—too busy, "up to my ass." He darted in and out when he was needed or when he wanted to see how it was going. In the more than nine months when others actually worked on the program, Wallace spent no more than three weeks.

The Westmoreland interview was his biggest challenge. It was also the core of the program that Crile was reporting, writing, editing and in which he was appearing as a secondary on-air interviewer. Crile knew better than anyone how important the interview would be. He had already amassed a collection of damaging interviews from others. In a note to Wallace Crile made no effort to hide his intent. "Now all you have to do," he wrote, "is break General Westmoreland and we have the whole thing aced."

In Charleston, Westmoreland didn't seem a bit worried. He sought no professional advice. Crile had read to him on the telephone a draft letter outlining the areas of questions he might be asked. Westmoreland did no more than peruse a few historical records at Washington's Center of Military History and glance at his own autobiography. Naively, he felt ready for his trip to New York. But if Westmoreland was unconcerned, Crile's anxiety was rising.

On Monday of the week of the interview Crile wrote Wallace another memo:

> We're on for Westmoreland Saturday morning. I read him the letter yesterday, and he didn't complain about any of our proposed areas of interest. He puzzles me—seems not at all bright. We've certainly covered our asses, technically at least. But I am a bit worried that he doesn't understand that we are going to be talking to him about American military intelligence during the Vietnam War. I just don't want to have him sit down and refuse to answer questions on the grounds that he can't remember. So I think I will give him another call later in the week and try to bring him a little further along, without hitting him over the head with a sledgehammer.[2]

When Westmoreland arrived in New York late Friday for the Saturday morning interview, Crile's letter was waiting at the Plaza Hotel suite that CBS reserved for him. The letter was unspecific but accurate, saying that the program would use "the Tet offensive as a jumping-off point to explore the role of American intelligence in the Vietnam War: how well did we identify and report the intentions and capabilities of the enemy we were facing?"

The letter listed five general questions they would be exploring. The fourth was the barely concealed weapon: "What about the controversy between CIA and the military over enemy strength estimates?" Guilt-free and self-assured, Westmoreland still saw no problem. He was proud of his record and would be talking about the subject he knew best. There was, after all, friendly "Mike," with whom he had spent the day in Vietnam.

Does it sound as if Westmoreland was walking into a trap? Of course he was.

But consider it from the press's and, even more important, the public's standpoint. In this case—as in many others, including the Iran-contra affair and hundreds of other deceptions—CBS had become convinced that Americans were misled and lied to by high government officials on a matter of catastrophic importance. CBS had done a vast amount of work questioning and exploring that premise. Few print or broadcast journalists could claim to have been more thorough or to have spent more time and resources in amassing evidence than CBS.

In retrospect, Crile and Adams had certainly done more proving of their theory than doubting it. But that is what advocates of a point of view do

---

2. Westmoreland says: "When I retired, I made a carefully considered decision to talk to any group about Vietnam. I do not recall turning down a single invitation. I thought our intelligence was very good—it proved so at Tet. Sam Adams' thesis was unknown to me. I never heard of Adams until he published a specious article which I did not read but heard about."

in any endeavor. It would turn out after the broadcast that there were other problems in Crile's work on the Westmoreland program. By CBS's own admission, after all that homework, Crile couldn't pass the network's own final exam—the "CBS News Standards."[3]

In journalism, unlike law, subjects are not read their rights before they are questioned. It has always been against the canons of journalistic ethical behavior to show or tell the subject of an interview what questions will be asked. The CBS News Standards, as well as other broadcast and news organization guidelines, are clear and uncomplicated on the point:

> Interviews which are not spontaneous and unrehearsed are prohibited. An interview is not spontaneous or unrehearsed if
>
> • the questions are submitted to the interviewee in advance (but the interview will be considered spontaneous and unrehearsed if the advance submission consists merely of an outline of the general areas from which specific questions will be drawn) or
>
> • there is an agreement not to use a particular general area as a basis for specific questions; or
>
> • there is an agreement not to ask specific questions; or
>
> • the film, tape or transcript of the interview is submitted to the interviewee for approval or for participation in the editing process.

So far, for the Westmoreland interview, Crile had gone by the book. What he had not done was reveal to Westmoreland what accusations had been made against him by CBS sources, who his accusers were, or even that he stood accused. Again, until they are in a position to confront their subjects, investigative journalists rarely issue such warnings beforehand. They are more likely to try to get interviews by telling the subject they are doing a "profile" or some such generality, when what they really are after is an exposé.

They know from experience that if they reveal their real intent, the target most often refuses to be interviewed at all, calls a lawyer or public relations person, or at least resists a taped or televised interview until there is more time to prepare a defense against the press accusers.

In a court of law, the accused has a right to know in advance what the accusations are and to face the accusers.

American justice and fairness are based on that. Innocent until found

---

3. CBS General Counsel George Vradenburg III says: "A rather harsh, indeed, overly harsh characterization in relatively minor, non-substantive matters."

guilty by a judge or jury. A procedural misstep by police or prosecutors can wipe out even a clearcut case. Neglecting to read the accused their rights, illegally obtaining evidence, conducting searches without warrants, or any other shortcuts, immediately bring into play the "exclusionary rule," which throws out evidence and often prevents successful prosecution. But not in investigations or judgments by the news media. There are no formal exclusionary rules for journalism.

In the news media, the accused often have neither warning that they are a target nor detailed information about what they are charged with. When they are actually confronted, it is not directly by their accusers, whose names they may not even be told, because the sources could be confidential. They are thrust into the witness box by a journalist. If they answer, their spoken testimony is then edited by media judges before being presented in the court of public opinion. The jury is the television audience or a publication's readers. And the accused's right to appeal, after a trial by media, is severely limited. In the whole process, the only power the press lacks is the power to enforce punishment.[4]

Does that sound unfair to the "defendant"—in fact awful? It does. But historically that is called freedom of the press, a constitutionally and court enshrined process at the center of democratic government. Journalists argue that their uninhibited ways have kept many public officials and others honest more than they have unfairly inflicted damage. But now with the impact, speed and reach of the modern news media, prosecution by press has become a deeply resented problem, not satisfied by the hoary old rationalizations of journalists ("If you want a watchdog to warn you against intruders, you have to put up with a certain amount of mistaken barking"). The public cheers trial by press only when obvious rascals are trapped.

Westmoreland is many things but he is no rascal. Unknowingly, he walked right into the trap. It was a match of unequals. His greatest foe was not his record. It was his naiveté in such matters and the camera—especially the camera.

Like any hi-tech operation, television has its own jargon and shorthand: sound bites, kyrons, outtakes, slopreels, shirttails, dailies, supers, trims, stand-uppers, selects, two-shots, remotes, teases, bumpers, reverses.

For one-on-one interviews in documentaries, a single camera is most often used. Peering over the shoulder of the interviewer, it is trained on

4. CBS's Vradenburg again argues that the accused "has the right to respond, and, if a public figure like Westmoreland, the response will be aired by competitive journalists."

the subject. Infrequently, the camera is placed between subject and interviewer—swinging back and forth like the eyes of a center-court spectator at a tennis match. Even in the rare cases in which the camera is in the middle, it points mostly at the receiver, not the server.

With the standard single camera, the interviewer is recorded on the sound track but infrequently seen. At the end of the interview, the camera crew does a "reverse" or "reaction" shot. The interviewer alone is then filmed or videotaped again. Often questions that have already been answered are reasked for the camera, for the sake of clarity or to improve the interviewer's performance on the air (a practice now forbidden at CBS in hard news coverage). The "reverse" also enables the camera to get facial reactions from the interviewer that the one camera missed while it was trained on the interviewee as the questions were actually being answered. While the one camera reverse process saves money in crew and camera equipment, it is a dubious journalistic device. It obviously gives the interviewers a second-round advantage to brush up their appearance. The interviewees have no such opportunity. CBS guidelines provide some minimum protection against abuse:

> Reaction shots and reverse shots made out of natural time sequence in connection with an interview must either be made in the presence of the interviewee (or his representative) or, if neither wishes to wait for this to be done, only after what is about to be done is explained to and approved by the interviewee; reverse questions must conform to the original questions in tone, character and content.

When Westmoreland arrived early on Saturday morning, May 16, 1981, he was in no immediate hazard from reverses. He was in for a more searing experience. There were two cameras, not one, in the apartment-hotel room near the Plaza that CBS rented for the shoot. For this crucial interview, one camera would *always* be trained on Westmoreland, the other on Wallace. The splicing would be done later. So would Wallace's narration and his argumentative characterization of some of the questions and answers ("What Westmoreland failed to tell . . .") Not that there was any secrecy or deception about it. Westmoreland was just unfamiliar with television techniques and oblivious to the fact that one camera was always on him, whether he was answering or just being asked a question.

Wallace, Westmoreland and the television crew were not the only ones present. Crile and several of his staff stayed out of range while the camera and sound crew did their work. They were using film rather than videotape—a more expensive process but one that produced more nuanced pictures and better sound to a trained viewer.

Absent was Westmoreland's most persistent accuser and inquisitor, Sam

Adams. It was clearly not a lack of interest or because he was a consultant rather than a CBS staffer. He stayed away because his role as a consultant and, in effect, the prime stimulus and chief researcher for the program had never been mentioned to Westmoreland. His presence could have been an alarming tip-off. Present or not, Adams had been a resource when Crile framed close to a hundred questions and follow-ups for Wallace to consider. Then Wallace and Crile had gone over them, rewriting, adding and discarding.

Does that make Wallace, or some of television news's best-known names, "puppets" or readers rather than the journalists they consider themselves and are assumed to be by the public?

Most television interviewers get such help from producers. Some print journalists are scornful of that division of labor in television. To a lesser degree print reporters often get similar help from researchers, editors and others with whom they work on a difficult story. But the public misunderstands the television process as much as many print journalists deplore it.

In television news, the bigger the on-camera stars, the less of their own reporting they do. The producers (and some field correspondents) most often do the digging that reporters do for print. The best television on-screen journalists are well informed generally and have done reporting themselves. But as they climb the ladder of success, they become more and more the presenters of other people's information and spadework. They are less the originators, or in most cases even the writers, of their spoken words (at times, that was true even of deified Murrow). The best known people in television journalism, no matter how deep or shallow their past experience, are admired more for the way they show up on the air than for what they themselves dig up on assignment.

Print journalists often caricature their television counterparts as blow-dried presenters and readers of other people's work, "microphone stands." Too many of them are. But in network news that put-down is more a difference in the requirements of the medium than an invidious comparison between professional skills. A Mike Wallace, a network anchor of the evening news, a commentator like John Chancellor or Bill Moyers, or many a television correspondent, has plenty of help, to be sure. But a Dan Rather, Peter Jennings, Tom Brokaw, Judy Woodruff, Diane Sawyer, Ted Koppel, Morley Safer, Lesley Stahl, Roger Mudd, Robert MacNeil, Jim Lehrer and many others, are every bit as good and as prepared in their kind of journalism as their print counterparts are in theirs.

Around the world in the past, television correspondents were among the very best informed, with a frustratingly limited outlet for what they knew.

Today, too many are "parachuted" in to cover breaking stories rather than being steeped in an area or a subject as a result of their long assignment to it. When they rise to stardom, the best of them have the ability and working experience to do their own reporting and know what they are talking about. But because of the way television works, they have less and less time to do it. Is that an excuse for the superficiality of too much of television? No, it is the reality of a medium very different from print.

Local television news, if it specializes in happy-talk between tweed-ledum and twinkydee, local crime and fires, is another matter.[5] So are some network executives who think and even say, realistically if outra-geously, "We like stories that have wiggle. Sexy stories. Iran has wiggle. Defectors from the Bolshoi have wiggle. Stories about government agen-cies have no wiggle."

In the equipment-filled hotel room, Westmoreland noticed at first that Wallace "was rather cool, which was contrary to the way he had acted in Vietnam." But things heated up quickly and not just from the blinding television lights. When the film started to roll, a Hollywood-style clapstick thwacked in front of the lens ("Take One"), Wallace ordered coffee cups out of sight, and the interview was under way.

It was gentle at first—it usually is. ("I 'choreograph' my questions," says Barbara Walters, "starting with the ones that will be the easiest for the subjects to answer—often about their childhood.)" But gradually, Wallace homed in with sniper shots of facts, information and accusations. As the questions got tougher, the surprised, unprepared Westmoreland grimaced and even twitched. The merciless camera, trained on him, zoomed in for damaging closeups so tight that his reacting face often overflowed the screen. The film unceasingly recorded the beleaguered, nervous general flicking his tongue over his tightened, dry lips, framed by his jutting jaw and unblinking eyes. Westmoreland repeatedly said: "I can't remember figures like that. You've done some research. I haven't done any. I'm just reflecting on my memory." It "seemed a clear case," one reporter later wrote, "of guilt by demeanor."

Westmoreland got mixed up on the Tet battle casualty rate, tripping over his own past public statements. He hesitated and squirmed. The higher enemy figures, which included what he calls the "village defenders," were not sent on "because the people in Washington were not sophisticated enough to understand and evaluate this thing and neither was the media."

5. One local co-anchor in Chicago is reported to have written into his contract a clause that says he is not required to do any reporting. All he has to do is read.

He tried to explain that because LBJ had three television sets in his office and one in his bathroom, "TV had a greater impact on Mr. Johnson than my official reports." He argued that the president "saw sensational reporting which did not portray an accurate estimate of the situation." No, he didn't give LBJ only rosy reports, he gave him the truth, although LBJ, like all leaders, obviously preferred to hear good rather than bad news.

Once when Westmoreland glanced over his shoulder, he was surprised to see Crile "sitting to my right rear" holding up a large note to prompt Wallace. Westmoreland was incredulous, shocked when Wallace repeated claims from officers that they had been forced to rig and suppress intelligence figures. Westmoreland said he never got personally involved in the actions they described. "I didn't do that. I didn't do that," Westmoreland said heatedly. He was being accused of lying, cheating and deceiving his own commander in chief, traitorous acts to Westmoreland. He struggled to fend off the surprise attack. But it was hopeless.

At one point as Wallace pursued his prey, Westmoreland shot back: "See, I happened to be in Vietnam. I don't know where in the heck you were but I was in Vietnam." It was his only successful counterpunch, and it was not used in the broadcast. But he never really got off the ropes. His answers were vague, his efforts to seem cooperative and unruffled ("Well, Mike . . .") didn't help. He called one of the most damaging charges—that he distorted vital intelligence information—a "non-issue." Then a part of the film not used showed him exasperated, saying angrily, "Well, that is absolutely fallacious. I'm absolutely amazed that you would come out with a statement like that." Westmoreland finally exploded, and it was used on the program: "I made the decision," not to pass on the higher figures. "I don't regret making it. Now let's stop it."

When the camera was off, Westmoreland hissed through clenched teeth: "You rattlesnaked me."

As he realized what was happening, why didn't he just leave what he later called "an ambush," a "star chamber," "an inquisition"? He thought of that, he said, because he was "very angry, very disillusioned and my first instinct was to walk out." But he didn't "because I had seen so many times on '60 Minutes' where an individual" looked guilty just by fleeing or refusing to answer.

Westmoreland's ordeal lasted more than two hours. When it was over, he rose stiffly from his chair, exchanged a few perfunctory words with those around him and marched from the room, stunned but in silent dignity.

Crile, of course, had exactly the opposite reaction. He was so pleased that he sent Wallace another memo: "The interview was a classic. It keeps growing in my mind. I don't think you could have possibly done a better job. It was wonderful having you as our champion.''

When Adams viewed the film, he saw it as a vindication of his crusade. He felt it was crucial for the world to know the truth. ''The fact we ambushed him a little bit doesn't bother me.''[6]

Television edits interviews just as print does. In either medium, the actual interview may last half an hour, an hour, or more, with only a short selection of the quotes ending up on the air or in print. Readers of print understand that convention. Television viewers do not. Skilled editing technology makes contractions, interruptions and deletions invisible unless they are made explicit. Only when it is live—a rarity—is the interview on the air more than a tiny fraction of what the camera actually recorded, not unlike using in print a single photograph from a batch of hundreds of shots by a still photographer.

Before the television age, the *Life* photo-journalist Carl Mydans, who took the historic picture of General MacArthur wading ashore in the Philippines, was once asked by one of his subjects why he was taking so many pictures when *Life* could only run a few. Mydans explained:

> What I'm doing is not exceptional. You've been followed by a lot of reporters, too, and they've been scribbling notes all day. They can't use all the things they've written down. By the time they get back to their offices they will have decided on a story line, and they'll shuffle through their notebooks, flipping over page after page to find scenes and color and quotes that will make their story. And somewhere along the way, I'll see a story line too. I shall find pictures that best tell the story. And the editors will make a choice for the story that will appear next week.

The widespread public perception of television tends to be different.

Guests on interview programs often request that they be run in full or not at all. No one ever makes that demand of a newspaper or news magazine reporter. The possibility of distortion or incompleteness is even greater on television than in print. The graphic reality of television interviews (''I saw it with my own eyes''), creates the illusion of authenticity and completeness. In print there is no such illusion. Yet the editing process is alike in both mediums. The person interviewed is ultimately in the hands

---

6. ''Ambushed'' was being used very loosely by Adams, as it later was by Westmoreland. In television, an ambush interview is surprising unsuspecting subjects who did not know they were to be interviewed and gave no permission. ''Mike Wallace jumping out from behind the potted palm,'' says Wallace himself, adding, it is only used as a last resort. Today, he says, ''First we write letters, we phone, we do everything.''

of the journalists, dependent on their judgment of what to use and what to cut—whether it is television or print.

The Wallace-Westmoreland interview produced almost two *hours* of footage. Five *minutes* and thirty-eight seconds were used on the program. They were enough.[7]

"Now for the reaction," Crile said after the interview. "I can't imagine Westy taking this lying down."

7. Westmoreland says: "By the cutting and pasting process, a film could have been produced that reflected the opposite of what was fed the public."

5

The Counterattack

You people always cite the First Amendment and you are correct to do so. What do we cite? Only that we are there to defend the United States against all enemies. Perhaps some day we could put this to a national referendum. Like a small bet on the winner?
—Retired U.S. Army general

When they sense they are about to be in trouble after an interview, people react in different ways.

If they are new to the experience, they may try to stop the story with threats (worse than useless). They may try to go over the head of the journalist they suspect is about to hurt them (even less effective). They may seek advice from lawyers, public relations people or journalist friends (can't hurt—if it is informed). They may try calling or seeing the reporter again to put a better foot forward, if they have one (no reason not to). Or they may do nothing, just go away angry and apprehensive.

Surprisingly, in view of the unexpected hammering he knew he had taken at the Wallace interview, Westmoreland merely returned to Charleston and three weeks later wrote a polite, low-key "Dear Mike and George" letter.

The brief, four-paragraph note said that he found the interview "interesting, but I must frankly say it turned out to be more of an inquisition than a rational interview." He explained that after fourteen years he had been "unable to speak with precision on the details of items presented to you by your researchers." He attached a seventy-two-page sheaf of documents and official reports from his files "that might be helpful to you," adding that your "researchers perceive intelligence as a much more precise matter than it is in fact." Among the enclosed lengthy attachments, he included a note explaining why the official statistics were different from those he had used in the filmed interview.

Finally, in the covering letter, he suggested some others to interview "if it is your purpose to be fair and objective during your quest, which I must assume you intend to be." He never once used the word "correction," either in his letter or its enclosures. He later explained that "I did not and intentionally didn't because I thought I was dealing with honest people. I thought it would be gratuitous. If I had realized this was designed as a contrived hatchet job, I think I would have been a little more legalistic. I wrote this letter thinking I could be very helpful."

It is remarkable to me how few people know how to express themselves clearly and effectively in letters of objection to the press. They tend to make two characteristic mistakes. Either way they wildly overstate their case with turnoff generalizations ("Dear Cur: You call yourself a responsible journalist yet . . .") or, as Westmoreland did, they bury their real beef in a catalogue of information and fail to make explicit what remedy they are seeking.[1]

It was obvious that although Westmoreland may have known everything about attacking an enemy in wartime, he knew little about effectively defending his reputation in peacetime. His letter had the tone of a blindfolded man facing a firing squad, saying quietly to his executioners just before they pull their triggers, "My friends, are you sure this is right?"

Wallace passed the letter on to Crile, without reading the thick attachments, with their numbers, charts and dates. After examining the whole file, Crile sent Wallace back a note: "As far as I can make out, Westmoreland doesn't bring anything to our attention that is particularly relevant. Certainly nothing that causes concern and requires a new look at anything we have been asserting." They both felt Westmoreland was simply sending them some official figures rather than the truer ones he repeatedly used in the interview. Crile believed that Westmoreland remembered the real facts during the interview, forgetting the official cover story.

Crile wrote Westmoreland a short, routine thank-you for his "suggestions and documents." Out of the seven people Westmoreland suggested be interviewed, only Lt. General Daniel Graham appeared on the program. Two of the others on Westmoreland's list were questioned but not in front of a camera.

For the next seven months Westmoreland neither heard about the program nor thought much about it.

---

1. A former Boston *Globe* reporter who often faced critics of the press found that "when people had specific complaints, they were almost always right. When they argued abstractedly about sins of omission or general bias, I could always come up with stories that ran counter to their theories."

Crile's prediction that he could not "imagine Westy taking this lying down" was wrong, or so it seemed at the time. Westmoreland seemed to have forgotten the trauma of the interview. But early on a Thursday morning, January 21, 1982, it came back to him with the suddenness of a terrifying pain.

He was alone having his usual breakfast cereal, idly watching the 7:00 A.M. CBS "Morning News." He abruptly stopped eating "and just about dropped off my chair" when he heard Diane Sawyer say, "On Saturday night CBS Reports will show that the American government in Washington was deceived about the enemy in Vietnam. The broadcast is called 'The Uncounted Enemy: A Vietnam Deception,' reported by Mike Wallace and producer-reporter George Crile, who found at the heart of the deception not the hand of the enemy but the American military command."

The film clips from the program in the promotional piece left no doubt about who led the deception. A hesitating, flustered Westmoreland was shown at his worst. For the first time—spliced between his own weak answers—he actually saw and heard his officers. Both Wallace and Crile appeared in the promo, emphasizing the malignity of what they had uncovered. "What Westmoreland was saying, in effect," Wallace announced, "was the war was too important to let civilians really in on what was going on."

Westmoreland was stunned. He reached for the phone to sound his alarm to David Henderson, a Washington public relations man and lobbyist he knew. But Henderson had not seen the CBS promo. Westmoreland proposed writing an article as a reply. Henderson said that would be "too little, too late." They both agreed that after the program "as quickly as possible" Henderson would arrange a press conference for Westmoreland and others to answer the program's charges.

At home Westmoreland read daily only the local paper and the *Wall Street Journal.* So he didn't see CBS's full-page ads in the next day's New York *Times* and Washington *Post,* and in Saturday's Los Angeles *Times.* If he had, he would have been even more agitated. The ad displayed an overhead view of eight officers huddled around a dark conference table. Emblazoned across it, in inch-high white letters, was one word: "CONSPIRACY." The brief text was even more accusatory: "Who lied to us? Why did they do it? What did they hope to gain? How did they succeed so long? And what were the tragic consequences of their deception? Tomorrow the incredible answer to these questions. At last."

Westmoreland does not change his own marching orders easily. As alarmed as he was, he stuck to other plans. He didn't even pause to watch the program. The Saturday afternoon of the evening broadcast, he flew to

Washington to keep a date for the black-tie Alfalfa Club dinner, where he mixed comfortably with press and political luminaries, including Vice President George Bush, Henry Kissinger and Edwin Meese, then White House counselor.

He was hardly the only one who missed the broadcast. Most Americans did. It was blacked out in his own home area for a local basketball game. Like most documentaries, it got the lowest rating of any prime-time program that week, placing seventy-second on the list of seventy-two rated programs.

No matter. It was a *succès d'estime*. The New York *Times* viewed a cassette of the program in advance and ran an admiring Sunday editorial under the headline "War, Intelligence, and Truth," saying CBS "showed that Lyndon Johnson was victimized by mendacious intelligence." General Westmoreland, the editorial said, "after so many years, still tries to explain away the falsification of intelligence, even to the commander-in-chief." Wire services and papers across the country reported CBS's findings. Conservative syndicated columnist William F. Buckley, Jr., an automatic dissenter from herd opinion, was impressed. He agreed that it "absolutely establishes that General Westmoreland, for political reasons, withheld from the president information about the enemy."

Apart from messages Westmoreland received supporting him and denouncing CBS, other reactions were even more punishing. The Harlingen (Tex.) *Valley Morning Star* printed a cartoon showing Westmoreland cradling an automatic rifle, standing over the dead bodies of three soldiers named "Duty," "Honor" and "Country." A Houston woman wrote him a letter: "You lied to President Johnson and to Congress. You played God with those lives. If anyone ever deserved to be stripped of their so-called honors, it's you. After seeing that show on television I hope the American people never give you another moment's peace."

On Sunday in Washington, Westmoreland had very little peace. He and Henderson canceled their date to shoot geese, went to Henderson's office and mobilized a small strike force of allies. They dissected Wallace's portentous opening "tease," interspersed with the program's dramatic theme music, and a backdrop of gunfire and battle scenes: "The only war America ever lost. Tonight we're going to present evidence of what we have come to believe was a conscious effort—indeed, a conspiracy at the highest levels of military intelligence—to suppress and alter critical intelligence on the enemy in the year leading up to the Tet offensive."

They winced at the witnesses buttressing the program's charge that Westmoreland "chose not to inform the Congress, the President, not even the Joint Chiefs of Staff, of the evidence collected by his intelligence chief, evidence which indicated a far larger enemy."

The documentary pinpointed three accusations against Westmoreland: the worst—that he had suppressed and kept from his superiors intelligence information on the size of the enemy, reporting no more than the arbitrary 300,000 ceiling he had supposedly set; that officers in his command officially reported an enemy rate of infiltration from the north one fifth its actual size; and that after Tet, to cover up, they doctored the computers to look as if they had reported accurately in the past.

CBS's presentation made it clear who had been the leader of the "conspiracy." Though that damaging word was used only once, at the beginning of the entire ninety-minute program, Westmoreland's face appeared throughout.

Hastily, Henderson set in motion the machinery for a counterattack. He and Westmoreland called on former officers from the CIA and the MACV command, asking them to rally around Westmoreland when he faced down the news media at a Washington press conference scheduled for two days later.

On Tuesday, in a crowded conference room of Washington's Army-Navy Club, an angry Westmoreland, who had stayed awake until three in the morning drafting some of his hottest words, stepped up before a battery of microphones and television cameras. Flanking him stood a phalanx of retired military, CIA and civilian officials who had served with him in Vietnam. To Ellsworth Bunker, an eighty-seven-year-old former U.S. ambassador to Vietnam, it was "just like the old days."

This time Westmoreland's guns fired full blast. He had never spoken more bitterly or sharply in public. He recounted that the week before he and his wife had gone to see *Absence of Malice,* their first movie in five years. In the picture, he saw "an innocent man whose life and many others were ruined by the unscruplous use of the media." Little did he know, he said, that within a week "a real life notorious reporter, Mike Wallace, would try to prosecute me in a star-chamber procedure with distorted, false and specious information, plain lies, derived by sinister deception—an attempt to execute me on the guillotine of public opinion."

He called the program a "vicious, scurrilous and premeditated attack," mounted with "arrogance, the color, the drama, the contrived plot, the close shots—everything but the truth." He said he had never known, until he was actually before the cameras, that Sam Adams was once again his accuser (and a CBS consultant to boot). He mentioned that he had sent a letter to "correct my imprecisions" to Wallace and Crile and "received not even the courtesy of an acknowledgement."[2] He explained that he had

2. Here his memory had slipped. Westmoreland had forgotten the thank-you note he had received from Crile. When he was reminded of it, Westmoreland, ever polite despite his rage, apologized for the mistake in a letter to Crile.

done no research and brought no papers to the interview. "If I appeared excited on the film, you can see why, because I was ambushed."

In New York, CBS was interested enough in what was going on in the Army-Navy Club to arrange a live feed of the entire press conference to monitors in its Manhattan West 57th Street Broadcast Center. Burton ("Bud") Benjamin, the CBS senior executive producer who would later play a central role in the Westmoreland controversy, had seen the program when it was aired and said to himself, "Good program. It tells me something I didn't know."

After watching the Westmoreland press conference on the closed circuit, Benjamin walked next door to an office where other CBS executives had gathered. "I'd give a lot of thought," he said to the group, "to running that press conference tonight at 11:30." His suggestion was greeted with disdain.

CBS's only notice of Westmoreland's *cri de coeur* came toward the end of that night's evening news. CBS Anchorman Dan Rather gave it short shrift:

> The commander of U.S. forces in Vietnam during the height of American involvement there, General William Westmoreland, held a news conference in Washington today to challenge charges made against him in a CBS News broadcast. CBS News in a statement today said it stands by both the accuracy and fairness of the CBS Reports broadcast. But the statement added that because of the issues involved, CBS News—quote—"will give further study to the specific allegations made at the news conference."

Without giving Westmoreland the benefit of reporting any of the words of his complaint, CBS had reacted with what most galling, arrogant and empty news media kiss-off, which offers nothing to the complainer: We stand by our story.

Standing by the story has always been the knee-jerk public reaction of journalists when they are attacked. But it is not their real response.

Newspapers, news magazines, television networks and stations get hundreds of complaints, formal and informal, all the time. If the criticism is serious enough—or if it comes with enough weight or skill—their invisible response is to reexamine the material and assure themselves that they were right. Whatever initial doubts they may have had before the story was developed, their conviction inevitably hardens as it gets closer to being printed or broadcast, just as CBS's did. Usually they ask the reporter or producer of the story to respond internally to any serious criticism. After the story has appeared, their presumption is in favor of their staff. After all, they back up their people, and the checking process was supposed to have taken place before the story came out—not afterward.

Most important, by the time a complaint comes in, more than one individual journalist is committed to the story's accuracy; so are his superiors and the whole news operation. Admitting error, retracting, apologizing, even opening the door to doubt—especialy on major stories—has traditionally been considered an admission of weakness rather than of fairness.

So there was nothing unusual in CBS's asking Crile—in effect, now the accused—to answer the charges that Westmoreland made. Crile drafted an eleven-page reply, admitting no error but opening the door an inch to the biggest error of all: "What remains unclear, however, is exactly what the President was told—by whom and in what manner. I don't think we're likely to get to the bottom of that one. Perhaps we should have made some reference to this puzzlement, but beyond this failing I do not at this point have any areas of concern."

"Some reference to this puzzlement"? The program's most serious charge was that Westmoreland had deceived the president, his commander in chief, and his other military superiors. Had he or hadn't he? Was Westmoreland really the villain he was made out to be? Or was it President Johnson and his entire administration who had misled the American public? That point was the centerpiece of CBS's accusation. But it didn't shout from Crile's memo, which his bosses received, read without comment and buried in the company's files. The network was working on other projects. The program remained a feather in its cap, acclaimed as a potential prize winner. The critics had subsided—for the moment.

No matter that Wallace himself later said in a pre-trial examination: "It is my opinion that General Westmoreland participated in a conspiracy. Whether he led the conspiracy or not or whether there was someone above him, I wish I knew." That qualifying doubt was not evident on the program.

One of the most frequent—and most valid—criticisms of the news media is that they almost never report on themselves, and only sparingly on one another. That habit is made worse by the undeniable fact that they have become one of the most powerful institutions in the United States. Government, business and politics regularly make page one in newspapers or lead stories on the networks. News or criticism of the big news media seldom do.

News magazines and special-interest journals have always reported on and criticized both print and television, only avoiding when they can real news about themselves. One such specialty magazine is *TV Guide,* distinguished from other one-subject periodicals by being the largest weekly in the country, with a circulation of more than 17 million. For years it thrived as the only complete and handy national source of program listings. The articles it printed were mostly puffery about television celebrities and programs. The weekly listings sold it.

But when competition to its near-monopoly began to seem possible in the late 70s, *TV Guide* started to run easily readable criticism and reports about television, often by well known writers. Its mostly absentee proprietor, Walter Annenberg, who had enjoyed life in London as the U.S. ambassador to the Court of St. James's, approved of the change without getting deeply involved in its execution, except to insist that the magazine maintain a patriotic, upbeat tone. He had read at least one article and was "delighted." He thought it "a fine piece of journalism," although he had had nothing to do with initiating it.

That eleven-page piece, the longest article in the pocket-sized magazine's history, ran in the May 29–June 4, 1982 issue. On the cover was a blaring headline: "Anatomy of a Smear: How CBS Broke the Rules and 'Got' Gen. Westmoreland." Below were head-shots of Westmoreland, Wallace and Crile.

The word smear never appeared in the article, just in the headline. The word conspiracy had never appeared in Adam's *Harper's* article either, just in its title. Headlines and titles, which as often cause grief as the stories they describe, are rarely written by writers for magazines and almost never by the writers of newspaper stories. Nor do many program producers or news people get involved in ads, promos and press releases. Journalists often wince at the hype promoting their work, though the promoters are confident that such hype helps to sell. The CBS ad for the Vietnam program had gone through several versions without any of the show's direct participants paying much attention to it.[3]

News organizations are notoriously leaky from the bottom even though they tend to be tightly caulked at the top.

When I covered the press for *Time,* news executives headed any list of sources who would duck when reporters asked for information. They are slightly more open now, and their staffs have never had such inhibitions. *TV Guide* had the benefit of a big collection of documents, internal CBS memos and transcripts from disgruntled unidentified CBS sources. The story, by two of the magazine's reporters, Don Kowet and Sally Bedell,[4] lived up to the promise of its billing.

3. Similarly, *Time's* editors did not see the press release that highlighted the trouble they later had with Ariel Sharon.
4. Bedell shortly after left and went to the New York *Times,* covering television. She is now completing a biography of CBS founder William S. Paley.

It made some twenty charges against CBS in its making of the West-moreland program. It expressed no judgment on the overall truth or falsity of the documentary. It quarreled only with CBS's methods. The article described at least four instances in which Crile breached CBS guidelines. It charged bias, unfairness, failure to interview key witnesses and questionable editing. Some sources were later as blindsided by Kowet as Westmoreland had been by CBS. Howard Stringer, the original executive producer of the program, agreed to be interviewed on the phone without knowing that Kowet was secretly taping some of his off-the-record remarks for a book on the controversy.[5]

On the face of it, the article was devastating, its timing perfect. A shipment of magazines was dropped on the newsstand of San Francisco's Fairmont Hotel, where the top command of the network and its leading celebrity news personalities were assembled for a meeting of the more than two hundred CBS-television affiliates. Attending his first affiliates' gathering as the new president of CBS News, Van Gordon Sauter was pummeled with questions. The network had all but ignored the Westmoreland press conference but there was no way to shrug off *TV Guide's* charges. After conferring with other executives, Sauter announced that CBS would examine the *TV Guide* accusations with "the same vigor and objectivity we bring to our own reporting."

He called CBS producer Bud Benjamin in New York and asked him to conduct a thorough, confidential internal investigation of the *TV Guide* claims. Benjamin, who had been Walter Cronkite's major producer for close to thirty years, was widely respected and personally liked at CBS. Rare, if not unheard of in television, he had few detractors—few, that is, until he took on this assignment.

Before the *TV Guide* article and the Sauter announcement, Westmoreland had felt stymied.

After his press conference, he had consulted his cousin, a South Carolina lawyer, about a libel suit. He got no encouragement. Frustrated, he moved to higher ground for a reconnaissance of the leading legal and political lights in Washington. Among others, he called on the noted trial lawyer, Edward Bennett Williams; Clark Clifford, Johnson's former secretary of defense and the dean of the Washington Democratic legal establishment; former army secretary, Stanley Resor; and Senators Strom Thurmond and Barry Goldwater.

Most told him to forget it. No public figure in his position could win a

---

5. Kowet left *TV Guide* and turned his tapes over to Westmoreland's lawyers. He now covers media news for the Washington *Times*.

libel suit of this kind for criticism of his conduct in public office. With neither the savvy nor the money to take on the CBS giant, Westmoreland was about to give up. The *TV Guide* article changed all that.

For years the American legal landscape has been gardened by public interest groups, most with a liberal agenda: the American Civil Liberties Union, Common Cause, the Anti-Defamation League, the National Association for the Advancement of Colored People, Nader's Raiders. But in the past two decades, their conservative counterparts have been blossoming in Washington.

Two leading funders of such conservative groups are the Richard Mellon Scaife Foundation, backed by the banking and oil inheritance of its founder; and the Smith Richardson Foundation, founded by Texas oil titans. One of the long-simmering complaints of many of these groups was against the news media. "We felt," said one of their lawyers, that the courts and the government had "nationalized the right of the press to take away your reputation."

After seeing the *TV Guide* article, Henderson, with the backing and advice of the Scaife interests and others, got in touch with Dan M. Burt, an international tax lawyer who had made a handsome living representing for the most part Arab clients. Burt says he had amassed a "few million" and decided to move from Massachusetts to Washington. There he became president of the not-for-profit Capital Legal Foundation, created to promote a "free market" in ideas and in business. It was supported by contributions from a small group of conservative foundations, a few corporations (Fluor, Olin, Exxon, General Electric, Chase Manhattan) and by individual patrons.

At first Burt was as skeptical as the other Washington lawyers about Westmoreland's chances. But after viewing the tapes of the program, Westmoreland's press conference, and especially after reading the *TV Guide* article, his interest grew. "There never would have been a lawsuit without the *TV Guide* article because nobody wanted to touch it," Burt said. "The piece showed there might be major problems with the broadcast and that was the turning point." The real issue, he felt, was not Westmoreland but "Will the press police themselves?" He met with Westmoreland and made the general an offer he could not refuse. If he took the case, Burt said, it would cost Westmoreland nothing. Capital Legal would foot the bill with the backing of foundation grants and private contributions. Westmoreland needed no further inducement.

What finally decided Burt was not Westmoreland's willingness but a press release from New York.

On July 15, Van Gordon Sauter released to the press his staff memo on the Benjamin Report. It began with the routine "CBS News stands by the broadcast." But from there on it was openly self-critical. "It would have been a better broadcast," said the Sauter memorandum, "If: it had not used the word 'conspiracy'; it had sought out and interviewed more persons who disagreed with the broadcast premise; and there had been strict compliance with CBS News Standards."

He listed specific violations of the standards: Repeating an interview with a friendly witness to elicit stronger answers; showing the same witness tapes of what others had said to get him to talk more; editing the combined answers and footage of one event to illustrate another; using the answer to one question in response to a different one.

Sauter said there was honest disagreement within CBS about the program "but ours is a collaborative business, and such debates are natural and of great value." Finally he announced that CBS would take further steps "to insure that our organization is fully conversant with CBS News Standards and their importance to the credibility of our journalism." He said the network was creating a new post, "vice president, news practices" and "we are also planning a future broadcast on the issues treated in the original broadcast."

Wallace, who was not mentioned in the Sauter memo, had fought far into the night to have Sauter's wording give stronger support to the program. Amidst angry argument, the statement was drafted and redrafted before finally being released. Crile, not named either, hated the statement. In his agitation, even before the Sauter memo, Crile felt let down by his executive producer. He limply shifted the blame when he wrote in another personal note to Wallace, "the person who was primarily responsible for overseeing the show and making sure it was both fair and accurate was Stringer."

At the time and in retrospect, Wallace was bitter. His autobiography (written with Gary Paul Gates), complained that "by making 'a big deal in public' about the internal investigation, Sauter transformed a minor irritation—the *TV Guide* article—into a major *cause célèbre* which, in turn, helped provoke the acrimonious suit that followed."

Newspapers across the country applauded CBS's public candor. The Los Angeles *Times:* "The lesson here is not only for CBS but for all in journalism." The New York *Times:* "CBS was right to take seriously General Westmoreland's complaints." The *Wall Street Journal:* "The CBS investigation of its own documentary on Gen. William Westmoreland and the Tet offensive will go down as a historic milestone in broadcast journalism." The Washington *Post:* "We think it's journalism that is self-confident enough to be self-critical. That is the only credible kind."

For entirely different reasons, no one applauded louder than Dan Burt, who most assuredly was now Westmoreland's lawyer. Burt thought the

Benjamin Report provided the crowbar he needed to try to pry an apology and a settlement out of CBS—or to sue for libel.

Under mounting criticism from all sides—including his own internal Benjamin Report—Sauter proposed a form of redress.

He offered Westmoreland fifteen minutes of unedited time, followed by forty-five minutes for a panel discussion, half the members to be chosen by CBS, half by the general. The panel would be allowed to deal only with the substance of the program's charges, not with the Benjamin Report or the methods used in producing the program.

Westmoreland and his lawyer had other ideas. Dan Burt, who was by then completely in charge, made his authority unmistakable clear. "In this trial," Burt later said, "Westmoreland is a soldier and I am the commander." He rejected CBS's offer, demanding nothing short of unconditional surrender. He countered with a letter, bearing Westmoreland's signature, asking for a full retraction of not less than forty-five minutes, including an admission of deceptive practices; similar apologies to be printed in the same amount of space in the same newspapers as well as on the same airtime that had advertised and promoted the program; damages for the harm done—which were not specified but assumed to be in the multimillion-dollar range, plus legal expenses. Lest there be any question of who would keep the upper hand, all of these apologies, retractions, films and texts would be subject to approval and editing in advance by Burt and Westmoreland—or else.

Even as a negotiating posture, with the threat of a libel suit in the background, CBS was offering too little and Burt demanding far too much. As columnist Mary McGrory wrote, "In keeping with the history of war itself, negotiations failed."

When CBS turned down the lawyer's demands, the network announced it was going ahead anyway with its panel program titled, "Counting the Enemy in Vietnam." It set aside one hour of prime time on Wednesday, September 15, and again asked Westmoreland to participate. By then Westmoreland's team had other plans. Early in the week scheduled for taping, Westmoreland and the members of the panel he had picked pulled out. CBS "temporarily postponed" the program.

Two days before CBS's scheduled air date, Westmoreland ran his own show, another jammed press conference, again at Washington's Army-Navy Club. Once more an attentive CBS staff stared at their live-feed monitors in New York. They watched as Westmoreland announced that he was filing a $120 million libel suit against CBS, Sauter, Wallace, Crile and

Adams.[6] The money he was asking for, he said, would be donated to charity.

Many of the CBS accusations against Westmoreland had been made before.

In 1976 the report of the Pike Committee had used almost the same language as Wallace:[7] "The numbers game prevented the intelligence community, perhaps the president, and certainly members of Congress, from judging the real changes in Vietnam over time." Newspapers, magazines, book writers and public speakers had used far harsher words. Why, then, did Westmoreland decide to sue this time? It was television, with its powerful impact and visual credibility that made the difference, as it does in much of American life.

Westmoreland himself explained, "I went into a profession that puts a great emphasis on integrity and honor." He also said, "When I returned from Vietnam, I was belittled, I was burned in effigy. I could accept that. I knew I had done the job in Vietnam the president had asked me to do. But now Mike Wallace has gone on national television and accused me of being a liar—worse, a traitor. How can my children live with that? CBS was saying that I have the blood of American soldiers on my hands."

At his press conference, Westmoreland's statement, written with Burt's help, emphasized why he decided to sue. "I made one final attempt to obtain redress," he said, but "they remained adamant. The question is whether in our land a television network can rob an honorable man of his reputation."

No doubt Westmoreland meant just what he said in the most personally

6. The suit was originally filed in Greenville, S.C., more than two hundred miles from Westmoreland's home in Charleston but still his home territory. The remoteness of the federal court would make it harder for CBS. Even under those circumstances, if CBS refused to settle Burt expected a more sympathetic hearing for Westmoreland, one of the state's leading celebrities. In Greenville Federal Judge G. Ross Anderson, Jr. agreed with CBS that South Carolina was where Westmoreland lived, not where he might have been most damaged nor the main battleground of the issues. In a major early defeat for Westmoreland's side, the judge ordered the case moved to the Southern District of New York in Manhattan, a few miles south of CBS's Broadcast Center, where the program was put together.
7. Irony of ironies: At the time, CBS correspondent Daniel Schorr got a copy of the secret Pike Committee report and broadcast excerpts from it. After the House voted to suppress the report, Schorr asked CBS to publish the text through one of the publishing outlets it owned. When CBS refused, Schorr gave it to the *Village Voice*. CBS fired Schorr for making public the report whose contents CBS later used as one of the main justifications for its program.

afflicted way. Just as there was little doubt that his backers and lawyer had a far larger agenda. It was especially CBS, they said openly, with its "liberal bias," and all of the big American news media, that needed to be taught a lesson.

The Westmoreland libel suit was to be that lesson.

6

A Very Different General

Time has learned . . . .
—*Time* magazine cover story

Change reels, as they had to during the CBS Westmoreland interview. Switch to a very different general and another war.

Since Israel became a nation in 1948, it has fought five wars. "The only war it ever lost," as Wallace said the U.S. had—off the battlefields—was the fifth, Israel's invasion of Lebanon. Like Vietnam, the Israeli war in Lebanon was ultimately fought against entrenched regular forces and guerillas. But they were not hidden in the forests of a foreign country thousands of miles away. Israel's toughest enemy was holed up, amidst battered civilians, in densely populated Beirut, less than a hundred miles north of its border. Yet like Vietnam, this was also Israel's first war on live, worldwide television, and Israelis, like many Americans more than a decade earlier, bitterly complained about negative news coverage, abroad and at home.

Other deadly similarities were apparent. The battles—and eventual withdrawal—split Israel into screaming, protesting camps of dissent. The war itself created a higher rate of casualties for tiny Israel—close to seven hundred dead out of a population of 4 million—than the Vietnam War had for the United States. And in the aftermath of the war in Lebanon, Israel was wracked by economic, social and political upheaval. There the parallel stopped.

Nobody ever accused Westmoreland—not CBS or anyone else—of starting the war in Vietnam or even of expanding it on his own, as MacArthur had tried to do in Korea and then was fired for his temerity by President Truman. In contrast, Israeli defense minister, General Ariel Sharon, was universally considered, even by his admirers and by his government, as the architect of the expanded war in Lebanon. He had dragged his own prime minister along into the quagmire of northern Lebanon and Beirut.

Not only were the two generals' physical contours decidedly different— one portly (5 ft. 6 in., 235 lbs) the other trim (6 ft., 185 lbs.)—so were their personalities, their motives and their complaints against the press. Westmoreland's would be directed against what he said added up to the malicious unfairness of an entire ninety-minute television program. Sharon would come into court disputing the facts in one paragraph—a few words— in a full-length *Time* cover story.

Like Westmoreland, Sharon had had his Tet. But his reeked of slaughter and evil, not surprise and unpreparedness. It would forevermore be known as Sabra and Shatila.

While the battle of Beirut raged, an effort was made to form a government in fractured Lebanon. Bashir Gemayel, the president-elect, was assassinated before he could take office.

Next day, in the chaotic aftermath, Sharon sent his own troops into West Beirut. At the same time he paid a condolence call on the murdered president-elect's brother, Amin, and his father, Pierre. Sharon also approved the order of his chief of staff for the Lebanese Christian Phalangists to enter the two Palestinian refugee village camps, Sabra and Shatila, in search of armed guerrilla enemies responsible for the assassination. Instead, the Phalangists randomly massacred hundreds of villagers. When it was over, the whole world saw the results of the slaughter on television and read about it in gory detail. Such massacres had taken place in the Arab world for years, though never under an Israeli cabinet minister's *laissez passer*.

No one was more indignant over the bloodiness of Sabra and Shatila than the Israelis themselves. Close to half a million of them demonstrated in the streets of Tel Aviv, carrying such signs and banners as "Sharon is Minister of Death," "Sharon Murderer," "Stop the Monster." The outcry and pressure were so great that Prime Minister Menachem Begin was forced to appoint a special investigating commission headed by Yitzhak Kahan, chief justice of the Israeli Supreme Court.

After extensive secret investigation and testimony, the respected Kahan Commission issued a report charging Sharon formally only with "indirect responsibility" for the massacre. But the rest of the report was hardly exculpatory. The commission's words did not fudge. "It is impossible to justify the minister of defense's disregard of the danger of a massacre," it said. "No prophetic powers were required to know that concrete danger of acts of slaughter existed when the Phalangists were moved into the camps" without Israeli supervision. The report concluded: Sharon "made a grave mistake when he ignored the danger of acts of revenge and bloodshed by the Phalangists against the population in the refugee camps.'' The cabinet vote to accept the Kahan report was sixteen to one. Sharon cast the only dissenting vote. In disgrace, he was forced to resign his post in the cabinet as minister of defense. His political career was in shambles. Prime Minister Begin, under personal and public stress, went into seclusion and a deep depression, finally leaving his office never to recover from the painful aftermath of the war. But Sharon, a bellicose fighter from childhood and a fierce warrior all his life, did not give up so easily.

The week the report of the Kahan Commission came out, it dominated the news of the world. It became the *Time* cover story, entitled "Verdict on the Massacre: 'It should have been foreseen.' " Pictured below were Sharon and Begin, and inside was a story headed: "The Verdict is Guilty: An Israeli commission apportions the blame for the Beirut massacre."

The story described the events leading up to and following the massacre. The commission report, which was the main source for the story, needed no embellishment. It was damning enough. But in the twenty-second paragraph of the *Time* story, the magazine went a step further. It said:

> One section of the report, known as Appendix B, was not published at all, mainly for security reasons. That section contains the names of several intelligence agents referred to elsewhere in the report. *Time* has learned that it also contains further details about Sharon's visit to the Gemayel family on the day after Bashir Gemayel's assassination. Sharon reportedly told the Gemayels that the Israeli army would be moving into West Beirut and that he expected the Christian forces to go into the Palestinian refugee camps. Sharon also reportedly discussed with the Gemayels the need for the Phalangists to take revenge for the assassination of Bashir, but the details of the conversation are not known.

Time's circulation worldwide is 5.9 million; in Israel it is 20,000. Right after the issue appeared, Sharon—without asking for a correction or an apology—signed a libel complaint in Israel against *Time,* asking for 10 million shekels (then about $270,00) in damages; and then a more important suit in the United States for $50 million. Much more than his feelings were at stake, although he passionately felt personally wounded. At fifty-six he wanted to be elected head of his ruling party and Israel's prime minister. Needing vindication on the world scene, he sought it in a U.S. court so as to flaunt it in Israel, where a state tribunal had plunged him into a political decline that seemed irreversible.

Sharon acknowledged that he had met with the Gemayels. But he indignantly denied that he had ever "discussed the need for revenge" and said that the secret Appendix B contained no such information. Begin immediately told the Israeli Knesset the offending *Time* paragraph was "a lie." Sharon denounced it as a "blood libel," which in the history of anti-Semitism is the slander from the Middle Ages that Jews were said to use the blood of murdered Christians to make matzoh on Passover. The charges, he said, had "put the mark of Cain" on him, the sign of brother murdering brother. He accused *Time* of blatant anti-Semitism and grandiosely declared he was seeking exoneration not only for himself but for his nation and the Jewish people.

Sharon's suit was against no individual defendants by name. His action was brought against a group—Time Inc.—the originator of group journalism.

The public knows something—not much but something—about how television news programs are put together. There is even more general knowledge about newspapers. But most people know almost nothing about the very different process of producing a weekly news magazine.

The news magazine Henry R. Luce invented more than sixty years ago was called *Time, The Weekly Newsmagazine,* the last word a sobriquet that has been the magazine's trademark ever since. Upstart *Time* began as a saucy weekly news digest, rewriting items from newspapers and reference books. The magazine's premise was that the news should be divided into logical departments to help readers find their way. Rather than simply record facts, stories should explain and often exhort. They should be written in distinctive language that would leap off the printed page and into readers' heads. It was the first group journalism of its kind, staffed by editors (all male), writers (all male) and researchers (all female).

Its smart-alecky and highly stylized prose was irreverently applied to everything from national and world news to personalities, books, art, education and religion. The new magazine was a quirky attention-getter and an instant success. As it grew and expanded over the years, many of its idiosyncrasies were left behind. What had become well known as "*Time* style" quietly disappeared more than thirty years ago.

Gone were its perversely inverted sentences in Homeric cadence ("Forth from the White House followed by innumerable attendants, the president set out . . ."); many of its double-adjective physical characterizations ("Hen-shaped, balding Mayor Fiorello LaGuardia"); its invented words and titles ("tycoon," "pundit," "gossipist"); its oracular tone ("Death came last week to . . ."); its standard one-line introduction to the People section (" 'Names make news.' Last week these names made this news:").

The magazine's original punch was so strong and distinctive (as well as subject to parody, e.g. "ambitious, gimlet-eyed, Baby Tycoon Henry

Robinson Luce," "Backward ran sentences until reeled the mind") that it took years for the public to realize these quirks had been replaced by more conventional prose. Even its sexist division of labor changed with the times. Most important, *Time* stopped merely rewriting other reporters and hired its own. When I became chief of the renamed and combined domestic and foreign Time-Life News Service, it had more correspondents than any publications or broadcast network in the world (ninety-eight foreign and domestic correspondents in thirty-two bureaus around the world). It still does.

Believing that "objectivity" was impossible, Luce said we might as well admit it and instead just try to be "fair." He was right about objectivity but wrong about "fairness," a much too facile and even more elusive standard. In good journalism, *striving* for objectivity or balance in reporting is a necessity, even though it is an unattainable goal to perfect. Fairness is the essential companion of efforts toward objectivity, not its replacement.

Time, while Luce was alive and editor-in-chief (he gave up the title in 1964, died in 1967), was a news magazine that made no effort to differentiate news stories from editorials. From his missionary heritage, Luce devoutly believed that readers were best served—as was Truth—if they were led to conclusions by skillful use of facts.[1] In social policy the magazine was humane and democratic (small "d"), Republican in its politics (capital "R"). It took head-on all kinds of demagogues (like Joe McCarthy and Father Coughlin), and suffered fools and pomposity not at all.

Both *Time* and *Newsweek* have always been primarily editors' and writers' magazines rather than reporters'. Writers and editors produce the magazine, with correspondents, reporters and researchers providing the information. The stories *Time* prints are no longer entirely anonymous as they once were. At the end of some stories, the principal writer, researchers or correspondents get bylines. *Newsweek* started doing it first. Both print signed columns, essays and reviews. Now both magazines' style and views on foreign and domestic affairs have become as eclectic as, and no more predictable than, those of any of the other news media.

1. His son, Henry ("Hank") Luce III, recalls his father's describing to whom he felt accountable for his magazines: "In some detail, he explained it could not be any of the obvious constituencies: not stockholders who cared only for profit rather than journalistic quality and purpose; not advertisers with their self-evident conflicts of interest; not readers, who could not know what they wanted or needed to read until they read it; not the Board of Directors, a small group of well meaning but not necessarily wise gentlemen. No, he said, 'I decided that my ultimate accountability had to be to my Creator.' "

But they still owe their journalistic as well as their financial success to the way they present and order information, not to how much they add factually to the news of the week. Along with everybody else, they have caught the investigative fever and they try hard for "exclusives." They compete relentlessly with each other and with the rest of the news media. But their exclusives are stimulants and add-ons to their success, not the source of it.

American magazines that cover the world's news are essentially written in New York. They require a special system, created around the comparative luxury of a weekly deadline, not afforded to daily newspapers or the evening television news. Consider *Time's* system (*Newsweek's* is virtually a carbon copy).

Every week its correspondents around the United States and the world send into the magazine's New York headquarters "files," which are wired reports transmitted electronically on telex or telephone lines. Although the published magazine itself contains no more than 50,000 words weekly, more than ten times that number of words are filed by correspondents.

At the beginning of the weekly cycle, there are story suggestions from correspondents, plus confidential Washington, Worldwide and National memos for background. Reams of reporting follow in response to cabled queries from New York. A single story can be reported from dozens of correspondents in as many different locations. The main report may come from Paris, Tel Aviv, Washington or Hong Kong but related files can come from Boston, Chicago, Tokyo or Los Angeles. The premise of this expansive and valuable system is that no matter how good a report from its wellspring, additional perspective, information and reaction from a variety of sources, all combined, can improve and give wider scope to the final story. Above all, especially on big news, the system gives readers one coherent account instead of forcing them to jump around to a number of scattered stories, as they must in more hastily put together newspapers.

New York-based reporter-researchers add to the correspondents' files. They compile information from the morgue (once more grandly renamed the Editorial Reference Department). Writers and researchers draw on books, past stories and correspondents' files, newspaper and magazine clippings, reports from telephone and local interviews or library research and printouts from computer information banks.

The writers and editors have all this material, plus their own experience and knowledge of the subject from travel, reporting themselves and talking to news sources in New York, often at background meetings and editorial lunches. Rarely do the correspondents' words from the scene appear in the magazine. When they do, they are now often identified as such. More typically, the writers, specialists at presentation, compose their own stories based on information gathered by others. After the writer first drafts the story, it goes up a step in the hierarchy to a senior editor, who edits and often revises it. He or (now) she may ask the writer for a new version or may rewrite the story or whole sections of it. When the story passes the senior editor, it goes to the managing editor or to one of his deputies for a "top edit," where it is edited again or may be returned for rewriting or clarifications. Unlike a newspaper or many other publications, the most senior editor in charge of a news magazine sees and has an opportunity to edit every story in the weekly. A new top editor can thus leave a distinctive stamp on the magazine from the first week on the job.

In its final version, the story is sent back to the researcher and writer. The researcher checks every word in the story, at *Time* actually putting a dot over each one—once, a red dot over proper names—signifying the word has been double-checked for accuracy. Contradictions and conflicting facts from multiple sources are resolved. The corrections produce still more revisions. Correspondents are requeried on specific points that are in doubt. They are responsible for the accuracy of their own reports if no other sources can be cross-checked. The entire edited story is sent in a "playback" to the principal correspondents who contributed to it. They can weigh in with more fixes, quarrel with interpretations or suggest reformulations. The magazine is then put together and sent to the printing plants around the world connected by satellite. For an important late-breaking story in *Time* or *Newsweek,* the lapsed time between going to press and arriving on newsstands can be less than twelve hours.

In the sixty-five-year history of *Time*, it is remarkable that the playback to correspondents is only a fifteen-year-old innovation. Before then, correspondents were not supposed to see the story until it appeared in the magazine. If proof were needed of how much an editors' magazine *Time* has been, for ten years I unsuccessfully urged the then managing editor, Otto Fuerbringer, to have us send the whole final story out to the correspondents for checking and review. But he and other editors insisted that it would interfere with the editors' prerogatives and that the extra step would clog up the system with prepublication squawks from the field. More important, they believed that reporters, just like other sources, should not be allowed to quarrel with the editors', writers' and researchers' final judgments. The correspondents had their say in their files. The editors didn't want to haggle with them over how they were finally used and interpreted in print.

This was a massive imperfection in the system. For years *Time* was pockmarked with inadvertent errors and conclusions contrary to reports from the scene. The distortions could be maddeningly small or significantly large. In one case, the magazine described a foreign cabinet minister as "silver-tongued" on the basis of the texts of some eloquent speeches he had made. "For Chrissakes," the correspondent wailed to me on the overseas phone after the story was printed, "the guy has a speech impediment from a cleft palate at birth. Everybody here thinks we're making fun of him." Or even more seriously, before the playback was started, correspondents were too often confronted with stories in print that bore little resemblance to what they had reported. Their reporting was essential but they were left out of how it was used and interpreted.

When Sharon sued *Time*, every step of this system was minutely held up to scrutiny. If *Time* still had no playbacks, its embarrassment would have been intolerably greater over that gaping hole in the editorial process.

In the Sharon case, strange to say, the system had worked perfectly. It was not the system but people, rigid attitudes and a failure in reporting that were to blame. It all began as a tantalizing tidbit rather than a thundering exposé.

The *Time* weekly Worldwide memo (which I confess, with no apologies, I created), is a useful collection of random items sent in by the magazine's foreign correspondents, and given limited internal distribution. It is mostly tentative, unchecked background, sometimes speculative or behind-the-scenes reporting intended more for atmospherics than for publication. The memo's purpose is to give the editors, writers and researchers the flavor and feel of foreign places, and an awareness of what people are talking about, what's in the wind. It is a collection of insights and a recounting of experiences, often not yet fully reported. The memo is marked "confidential." By hard-and-fast rule, *nothing* in it may be printed without prior clearance and checking with the correspondent who filed it (the same rule applies to its domestic counterparts, the Washington and National memos).

In the early days of the Kahan Commission's secret investigation, an item appeared in the Worldwide memo from the Jerusalem bureau on the progress of the inquiry. Titled "Green Light for Revenge?" it said, "The most crucial findings" of the Kahan Commission would not be published for security reasons, but "according to a highly reliable source," these "newly discovered notes" or "minutes" give evidence that Sharon "gave them the feeling, after the Gemayels' questioning, that he understood their need to take revenge for the assassination of Bashir and assured them the Israeli army would neither hinder them nor try to stop them."

The correspondent who filed and signed the item was David ("Dudu") Halevy, an Israeli-born journalist who had been hired initially as a part-time bureau stringer when I was chief of correspondents. At the time I had never met him, which was true of many locally hired stringers.[2]

Halevy, like most Israelis, had served on active duty and in the reserves of the Israeli army.

He had fought in three wars as a paratrooper, intelligence officer and tank commander. Three years after the 1973 Yom Kippur War, my immediate successor, Murray J. Gart, considered his work valuable enough to make him a staff correspondent—a promotion often sought by stringers and not easy to get, especially by foreign nationals working for an American publication. Halevy was said to have excellent sources in the Israeli government and military, specifically within its highly regarded intelligence service. He was well liked and admired by those with whom he worked and had received public accolades in the magazine's "Publisher's Letter." But he had also hit some rough spots.

Chief of correspondents Richard L. Duncan, who said, "It wasn't easy to put Mr. Halevy into a gray-flannel suit," had admonished him in the late 70s for having worked on the side as an adviser to Begin's political opponents. Duncan reminded Halevy that "American standards of journalism require that a journalist take a step or two further back from politics than may be required in many other countries."

Even more seriously, long before the war in Lebanon, Halevy reported and *Time* printed that Prime Minister Begin had been secretly seen by three foreign neurologists and told he was not well enough to work more than three hours a day. When the Israeli government protested, another *Time* reporter was assigned to reinvestigate Halevy's exclusive story. "The balance of the evidence," Duncan's internal report concluded, "is that our story is wrong." In one of its rare printed retractions, the magazine said it "was apparently misled as to the meeting and regrets the error."

Duncan put Halevy on "probationary status" for a year and sternly warned him to be more careful about his sources. He wrote Halevy that he wanted more "printable, reliable information, reflecting not just informed speculation, but the most likely true situation [Duncan's underlining]." He severely rapped Halevy: "I would like to see on your part more effort to evaluate the reliability of various sources, and the likelihood that they in fact *know* what they are saying."

2. "Stringers" get their name from the old newspaper practice of paying them by the column-inch length of their contribution, measured in folklore by a piece of string. In addition to staff correspondents, *Time* has more than two hundred stringers at home and abroad, some full-time, many on retainers, even more paid at a piecework rate—none measured by string.

Duncan had never before put a correspondent on formal probation and his written warning to Halevy was uniquely stiff. So it certainly explains why Duncan—although he had never done this before either—upon seeing the memo item on Sharon, phoned Halevy's bureau chief in Jerusalem, Harry Kelly, to ask how reliable Halevy's sources were this time. Kelly, who felt he had some partial but also unprovable confirmation himself, rechecked with Halevy and was convinced the sources would hold up even though they had to remain anonymous. The memo item was cleared for use but was not included in that week's Middle Eastern coverage. Nothing unusual about that. Many, in fact most, of *Time's* memo items are not used in the magazine.

For no particular reason, nothing was done with Halevy's item until two months later when the Kahan Commission delivered its dramatic report and *Time* scheduled its cover story. In the voluminous reporting from eight different bureaus, the Jerusalem bureau file was the centerpiece. Kelly, in the ninth "take" (i.e. section) reminded the writer in New York about the old memo item, "for which we gave clearance," adding some inconclusive backing of his own. In preparing the take, he asked Halevy to recheck, after which Halevy gave Kelly a wordless "thumbs up" sign.

In New York, William E. Smith, who had been a correspondent before becoming a World section senior writer, retrieved the memo about Sharon and used it far down in the cover story he was writing. His words were slightly different from Halevy's—also not a bit unusual in the news magazine system. "*Time* has learned," wrote Smith, that "Sharon also reportedly discussed with the Gemayels the need to take revenge." With writer's license he had interpreted and changed Halevy's words that Sharon "gave them the feeling after the Gemayels' questioning" to "reportedly discussed." Some evidence of this, the printed paragraph said, following Halevy's and Kelly's information, could be found in Appendix B, which "contains the names of several intelligence agents referred to elsewhere in the report."

To Smith, the change from "gave the feeling" to "reportedly discussed" seemed less damning than Halevy's original words.[3] But anyway, the Jerusalem bureau would get the playback. No objection was raised by the bureau to Smith's slightly different wording.

There are a number of code words, familiar to the public, in print and on television.

Two of them stood out in *Time's* single paragraph. One of them,

---

3. In retropect, Smith says he would have written the entire paragraph differently with many more qualifications.

"reportedly," means either that we hear and find this credible but can't prove it or that we have been told and believe it but can't tell you by whom. The other, *Time* "has learned," means stand up and take notice, you are about to get some hot stuff that no one else is telling you. Both terms are widely used in journalism. (And the paragraph, although buried in the story, was used as the lead in the weekend press release *Time* puts out highlighting the *news* in each week's issue.)

The most familiar and abused of the two terms is the claim of exclusivity. To say that *Time* or CBS or ABC or whoever "has learned" serves no purpose other than bragging or calling attention to yourself. What it really says is that you won't find this anyplace else and we are better than our competition. This kind of self-promotion should be banished from the lexicon of serious journalists. The word "learned" also carries the strong implication of being true, unlike the weaker but usually more accurate "has been told." If the information or the interview is so important, it can be made to stand out and be given significance in other ways. Attaching medals to it or tying it up in display ribbons is hubris, with little benefit to readers or viewers.

"Reportedly" is harder to avoid. But when "We"—whoever the we is— have "learned" is followed by "reportedly," there is a potential for big trouble. The libel suit of Sharon v. Time Inc. was precisely about the question of *Time's* having "learned" what Sharon had "reportedly" discussed with the Gemayels.

For almost two years, *Time* tried in every way to get the case dismissed.

At first very few, inside or outside *Time*, took it seriously. Imagine a *foreign* minister suing an American publication over his official conduct. No high U.S. government official had ever succeeded in such a libel suit. How could a Sharon—or for that matter a Castro, Qadaffi or the Soviet officers responsible for the shooting down of Korean Airlines flight 007— sue for libel in a U.S. court? But there is no clear statute or indisputable court ruling prohibiting it, despite its ludicrous possibilities (a suit by such murderers as Hitler, Stalin, Mao, Pol Pot, Idi Amin?).

Time's lawyers, the same Cravath firm that represented CBS, used every possible argument. They buried the pretrial discovery process in so many requests for documents and depositions from the Israelis, the CIA, the National Security Agency, the State and Defense departments, that they were chastised in Washington federal courts for "clearly inappropriate" delaying tactics, "unprofessional" and "sweeping unfocused" demands. *Time's* lawyers argued that they could not get the "due process" required for a fair trial because they said the Israeli government had put up "a wall of silence." They said they were denied access not only to key documents but to essential witnesses, on ill-defined grounds of national security. (Israelis who reveal what are called, with extravagant vagueness, "military secrets" are subject to criminal prosecution and long prison terms.)

Time tried to invoke the Act of State doctrine, which prohibits U.S. courts from sitting in judgment on acts of foreign governments. It even charged that Sharon was "libel proof" because he was already known to be a "bloodthirsty, insubordinate militarist." "Libel proof" is an old and, to me, offensive term used by journalists and lawyers meaning that some people have such a terrible reputation that anything can be said about them whether true or not. In its final pretrial motion for dismissing the case, *Time* relied most heavily on the constitutional and judicial immunities allowed the press when reporting on public figures. All to no avail.

Time lost pretrial motion after pretrial motion. Now it would have to face a jury.

7

Briefly Brilliant

The First Amendment protects expressions of opinion however unreasonable or vituperative since they cannot be subjected to the test of truth or falsity. It is when the criticism takes the form of criminal or unethical conduct or derogation of professional integrity in terms subject to factual verification that the borderline between fact and opinion has been crossed.
—Federal Judge Edward Weinfeld

The term libel acquired much of its harsh meaning from the French *libelles,* the little books French revolutionaries wrote attacking the aristocracy. But like another French import, fine wine, words that were once full-bodied and clear sometimes turn as they age. The laws of libel in the United States have matured into just such a murky brew. These days, neither the public nor the press is happy with the taste.

In earlier times the laws were clear enough. Even though libel was defined for years by the legislature and courts of each state, two federal traditions provided some underlying consistency.

First there was the precedent, rooted in colonial America by the case of John Peter Zenger, a printer who was jailed for publishing criticism of the British governor of New York. The jury's verdict freeing Zenger in 1735 later established the rule that truth was not libelous no matter whom it might damage. "Seditious libel"—attacking in print or making accusations against the government or its officials for conduct in office—needed to be protected, not punished. To reinforce that freedom, Congress, in effect, revoked the Sedition Act it had hastily passed, and ordered refunded all fines paid during the brief time the Sedition Act was in force.

The young nation had fought a revolution to rid itself of tyranny by government and its rulers. It was not about to allow that again in the new democracy by silencing free speech or the free press, no matter how raucous. "The censorial power," Madison had written, "is in the people over the government, and not in the government over the people," adding that in the case of the press "it is better to leave a few of its noxious branches to their luxuriant growth, than, by pruning them away, to injure the vigor of those yielding the proper fruits."

The other cornerstone of a libel tradition that favored the press against its critics came later. After the Civil War, the force of the Constitution's First Amendment was expanded by the ratification of the Fourteenth (the so-called "incorporation" or "equal protection of the laws") Amendment. By 1925 those two amendments were interpreted by the courts to mean not only that "*Congress* shall make no law" limiting freedom of speech or the press but that neither could any other government body—federal, state or local. Thus sheltered, the printing presses of the country clanked out their political diatribes—sloppy and prejudiced more often than they were accurate or thoughtful—with little fear of retribution.

But while upholding the immunity of the press from government control, the federal courts still left to state laws libel actions against the press. In almost every state, all a journalist had to prove to win in court was either that his story was true or that it was a "fair comment," as harsh as it may have been. High public officials were so intimidated by the obstacles to winning that they rarely tried to fight back by dragging publishers into court. Once, riled at charges of presidential corruption involving the Panama Canal, published in Joseph Pulitzer's New York *World,* President Theodore Roosevelt instructed his attorney general to try to sue for libel. A district court judge ruled that the federal courts had no business hearing such a case:

> If there exists in Washington the shadow of a suspicion that a federal libel suit can be created; if there still remains the likelihood that another Roosevelt will prostitute his powers in order to persecute newspapers that have offended him; if there is a ghost of belief that the federal government has coordinate powers with state governments in the prosecution of an alleged libel and that every American newspaper is at the mercy of the president, then the sooner there is a final decision of the Supreme Court of the United States the better.

Even the indomitable Bull Mooser was defeated. It took sixty years for the Supreme Court to federalize libel law, as the judge had recommended.

In the majestic language of the U.S. high courts, there are events called "landmark decisions and their progeny." In plain lingo these are Supreme Court cases and rulings in their wake that change not only law but the way we must live and behave.

For the press, there are several such landmarks in the past quarter century, none more prominent than the two following cases:

The first came in 1964 when the Supreme Court hewed from its legal granite the well known landmark called New York Times v. Sullivan. This now familiar case reflected the incendiary racial tensions of the 60s. A group of civil rights activists had taken out an ad in the New York *Times*, protesting the "wave of terror" created by Southern officials opposed to Martin Luther King, Jr., and other civil rights leaders. The ad—whose contents the press is liable for as it is its own stories—had several minor errors of fact. L. B. Sullivan, a city commissioner who oversaw the activities of the Montgomery, Alabama, police department, sued the *Times* for libel, although he was not mentioned by name in the ad. An Alabama jury decided in Sullivan's favor and awarded him $500,000 in damages.

When the Supreme Court unanimously reversed the Alabama verdict, it created a federal—rather than state-by-state—rule for libel. The new national rules allowed the press to publish or broadcast almost anything about "government and public officials" (and later "public figures"[1]) so long as the journalists were not guilty of a brand-new piece of jargon that the Court called "actual malice." In Times v. Sullivan, the justices were at pains to point out that *their* kind of constitutional malice had nothing to do with what everyone thought the words had meant before: ill-will, spite, bias, bad motives, a wanton desire to injure, unfairness, or what the dictionary said it meant, "a desire to harm others or see others suffer." Forget all that, said the Court. The new definition was to mean only that the journalists *knew* the words they printed or broadcast were untrue. Or if they didn't know the words were a lie, they recklessly made not the slightest effort to find out.

With that ruling, it no longer mattered in law even if the press could be proved to be unfair or wrong, in cases involving public personalities. Journalists had to prove only that they believed what they were saying; or that they had even the slimmest reason to believe they were right and had not with "reckless disregard" published something without any effort to find out whether it was true or false.

Try to explain to anyone other than lawyers, judges or media addicts that "unfairness" or even false statements by the press about public officials and public figures are perfectly legal. Explainable or not, that was and is the law.

1. Including a mishmash, never precisely defined, of people in the public eye, from football coaches, entertainers and celebrities, to many businessmen, school-teachers, clerics and others who cannot demonstrate a life-style that has no public consequence.

A typical reaction to the malice rule was expressed by the president of Mobil Oil, William P. Tavoulareas, after he lost the first round in his libel suit against the Washington *Post* (see page 102): "What difference does it make that a reporter knew or did not know that a story was false? No one who read it knew any better. They read it for what it was and assumed it was the truth and the harm was done."

But the courts plainly thought more important democratic values were involved than individual pain. Democracy, they said, in decision after decision, *required* "uninhibited, robust and wide open" debate, the "competition" of opinion and ideas. *One* reliable source alone was enough to prove an absence of malice. If that was unfair to public figures, so be it. Fairness and truth in public matters were less important than freedom of expression.

The new definition was so hard to prove against the press that the highest public official ever to prevail in court under the malice doctrine was Senator Barry Goldwater (awarded $1 in actual damages; $75,000 in punitive damages). In 1964 he sued the now defunct *Fact* magazine for printing that he was, among other things, mentally ill, paranoid, sadistic, anti-Semitic and had infantile fantasies and doubts about his masculinity. The putative basis of this abuse was said to be a survey conducted by two untrained researchers, who were repeatedly told by everyone they consulted that theirs was no survey, they didn't know what they were doing and there was no basis for their conclusions about his character. The publisher not only accepted their "research," he hyped it even more, adding material of his own invention. If that wasn't actual malice, the Court seemed to say, nothing was.

In practice, the Supreme Court's definition of "actual malice" might just as well have been written in Urdu.

It contradicted ordinary, common-sense English usage. It was hardly surprising that during the next fifteen years the new meaning didn't work very well. In the years before Sullivan, less than 20 percent of libel suits were reversed by higher courts, as is the average in other kinds of cases. In the years following Sullivan, juries were so confused by the new definition or so reluctant to follow it that more than 70 percent of the federal jury decisions in actual malice cases against the media were overturned. So Sullivan was propped up by another landmark, carrying the usual compound name and obligatory middle initial, Herbert v. Lando. (This case, coincidentally, also involved CBS, Mike Wallace, a "60 Minutes" producer, Barry Lando, and an article he wrote of the *Atlantic Monthly*.)

In this chip off the old granite, the Supreme Court in 1979 spelled out what was only implied in its Sullivan decision. The court ruled that to decipher the malice rule, lawyers could dig into journalists' notes, drafts, conversations with their bosses and materials they never printed or broadcast to discover their state of mind when they put their stories together. If you could not find out what the journalist was thinking, how could you tell whether the journalist knew the story was false or not? "How do you probe," asked Chief Justice Burger, "for the presence or absence of malice if you can't ask what was the state of mind at the time this or that was done?" It was logical enough. But it opened the floodgates further to a pretrial process of searching for possible evidence, known as "discovery," which could drown the contestants in a tidal wave of paper before they ever swam into court.

As loudly as journalists cheered the Sullivan decision for the even greater freedom it gave them, they wailed in pain at the Lando setback, which seemed to invite lawyers into their newsrooms to pursue evidence of actual malice in libel suits. Lawyers could "discover" what motivated the accused journalists and how they went about doing their stories. Efforts to read the minds of journalists, by means of the discovery process, tangled things even more. "Malice in Wonderland" it was called. Former CBS News President Fred Friendly added that "discovery is like a ball game where there is no first quarter, second quarter—no final whistle."

Few of the libel suits pending against the press today in the United States will ever be clearly resolved. The libel action against CBS in the Herbert-Lando case worked its way up and down the federal court system for twelve years, including two trips to the Supreme Court, before finally being dismissed in 1986 (maintaining the record of "60 Minutes" for never having lost in the forty libel suits filed against the program). But the ratification and enhancement of a right to discover journalists' motives and methods, established by the Supreme Court in the Herbert case, remained as a sharp cutting edge in libel suits brought by public figures. Many bitterly called it the "back of the blade" of the Sullivan decision.

In one of the most important pieces of research ever done on the press and the law at work, three professors at the University of Iowa[2] conducted not a poll but an actual study of the plaintiffs and media defendants in seven hundred libel suits decided over the ten years from 1974 to 1984. More than two-thirds of the cases were against newspapers, about 20 percent against broadcasters. Of those who sued, 60 percent were public officials or public figures. Of the cases that went the full course, an astonishing 90 percent were won by the media. Does that make the media sound virtuous? Not so fast.

2. Randall P. Bezanson, Gilbert Cranberg and John Soloski. For more of the results of their study see page 288.

In almost all of the cases, the central issue in determining the final outcome was the media's constitutional privilege, not truth or falsity. "As a practical matter," concluded the study, in law "the truth or falsity of the challenged statement is no longer pertinent," though it certainly is in the minds of the jurors. In other words, what finally decides the case is not good journalism but the protection of the media by the law. That makes the press happy but it confounds the public, not to say the person suing.

At the time of the Westmoreland and Sharon trials, courts all over the country were busy trying press defendants, not just CBS and *Time*. They involved a rainbow of claims seeking retribution and pots of gold in all sizes. Some were more colorful than others:

• The high-flying Manhattan real estate developer, Donald Trump, launched a $500 million libel suit against the Chicago *Tribune* for a cartoon and commentary ridiculing one of his proposed new projects. (Dismissed before trial on the ground that "in the realm of architecture, as in all esthetic matters, what is appealing to one viewer may be appalling to another.")

• The Reverend Jerry Falwell sued *Hustler* for $45 million after the magazine had published a fake liquor ad "quoting" Falwell as saying he drank booze and had sex with his mother in an outhouse. The jurors found the ad such an outrageous, tasteless parody that they felt no one would take it seriously. They decided that Falwell was not libeled but should collect $200,000 nonetheless for "emotional distress." The award, with its alarming and vague category of damages, was resoundingly overturned by the Supreme Court in 1988 (see page 292).

• The Santo Domingo Pueblo Indian tribe in New Mexico sued Gannett's Santa Fe *Daily News* for $3.6 million when the paper ran an aerial picture of its ritual dances, which it said "ridiculed" the tribe and were forbidden by tribal law. (The paper apologized twice and the suit was withdrawn.)

• The whirling dervish political extremist, Lyndon LaRouche, unsuccessfully tried to nip NBC for $150 million. NBC countersued and got a $3 million judgment against LaRouche (later reduced to $200,000) for maliciously interfering with the network's business.

• The proprietor of Mr. Chow, a Manhattan Chinese restaurant, won $20,000 in damages after a critic had choked in print over what he saw were the unappetizing sweet and sour pork, cold green peppers, oily fried rice and thick pancakes. (A higher court reversed the decision saying that "expressions of opinion are constitutionally protected. Reviews, although they may be unkind, are not normally a breeding ground for successful libel judgments.'')

- A California exporter of medical equipment sued the Soviet daily *Izvestia* after that government newspaper accused him of shoddy business practices and, of course, spying. (The Soviets ignored the suit, which was tried in a Los Angeles federal court, and lost by default. The businessman is still trying to collect the $413,000 he was awarded in damages.)

- In Las Vegas, entertainer Wayne Newton, a local hero, sued NBC for linking him with organized crime. After a lengthy trial, the jury decided that NBC knew the charges were false but with actual malice was out to get Newton anyway. In late 1986 the jury awarded him a staggering $19.2 million, plus an added $3.5 million, the largest jury award against the media ever as a result of a news report. (The judge reduced it to $5.3 million, which Newton rejected, and NBC continued to appeal.)

- Even the very young caught the fever. A sixteen-year-old high school editor was threatened with a suit for $10,000 by the school cafeteria cook when the lad commented that her hamburgers tasted like dogmeat.

In the past, public figures were the least likely to sue for libel because of the "heavy burden" of proof imposed on them by the courts. Never mind, for the moment, Westmoreland and Sharon. Now dozens of lesser public lights tried to increase their wattage by suing the media. Some clearly hoped only to intimidate, to squelch criticism or to establish their indignation for public consumption ("If the story isn't true, why aren't you suing for libel?"). Others said they felt genuinely maligned—public figure or not:

- In Philadelphia alone, dubbed the "libel capital of America," where corruption in the city courts is a hot issue, fifteen public officials sued or were suing for libel in nineteen separate cases, including judges, two former mayors, three state legislators, one member of Congress and a city councilman.

- The prize for truly absurd damage claims went to a Maryland county commissioner who sued two local weeklies whose criticism of him caused him such "pain and suffering" that he wanted $8 billion—that's *b*illion—to restore his good health.

- More earnestly, Paul Laxalt, who left the Senate and briefly became a Republican presidential candidate, went after $250 million from the McClatchy Newspapers, owner of the Sacramento *Bee*, for articles about what the papers said were reports of illegal skimming from a hotel and casino he and his family had owned in Nevada, where Laxalt had been governor (see page 183). He also warned ABC and CBS against making similar charges (they held off).

It was such a banner year for litigation against the news media that the Mobil Oil Corporation created a new $10 million insurance policy for its top one hundred executives. The policy would cover their costs should any of them find a reason to sue for libel. If the media carried libel insurance, Mobil reasoned, why shouldn't those who felt they had been defamed have the same backing?

Mobil became the leader in this aggressive policy after a bruising experience suffered by the company's president, William Tavoulareas.

He had sued the Washington *Post* for $100 million after the paper ran, and refused to retract or correct, a page-one exposé headed "Mobil Chief Sets Up Son in Venture." The headline, which jurors found more offensive than the story,[3] charged Tavoulareas with setting up his twenty-four-year-old son in a multimillion dollar oil shipping business, which profited mightily from its special relationship with Mobil. Once filed, the suit bounced back and forth from one court to another like a ping-pong ball.

First a federal jury in a Washington, D.C. ruled that the *Post* had gone too far. It awarded Tavoulareas $2 million in damages. But the presiding judge found the jurors' verdict against the *Post* so contrary to the law that he overruled them and dismissed the case (see page 165). Tavoulareas appealed and the trial judge in turn was reversed by a three-judge panel of the U.S. Court of Appeals for the District of Columbia. Two judges delivered—right after the Westmoreland and Sharon trials ended—an opinion that, on such a high a judicial level, was the severest against the press in memory. One of the two judges was Antonin Scalia, who a year later was appointed by President Reagan to the U.S. Supreme Court.

The appellate court's opinion said that newspapers like the *Post,* engaged in "sophisticated muckraking," presumably like its landmark Watergate triumph, were especially vulnerable. "From testimony it was proper to infer that the *Post* put some pressure on its reporters to come up with 'holy shit' stories, exposé pieces that shock and startle readers." The paper's reputation for "hard-hitting, investigative stories, could, together with other evidence, support an inference that it was inclined to publish reckless falsehoods."

3. Carl Lindstrom, the longtime executive editor of the Hartford *Times* and historian of newspaper journalism, once warned about headline-writing: "It makes correct quotation almost an impossibility; it accounts for most of the misconstructions and distortions; it offends intelligence and rips the envelope of context; it is a constant libel risk."

But the rallying wasn't over. The *Post* wanted the case heard by the *full* appellate court (meeting *en banc,* meaning altogether, instead of as a small panel). *En banc* the court took two years before just as severely reversing its own judges' opinion (see page 292)—deciding in favor of the *Post.* (The U.S. Supreme Court late in 1987 refused to take an appeal of the decision (with Justice Scalia not participating).

Along the way, one of the appellate court judges favoring the *Post* faulted his opposing brethren for appearing "to criticize what it takes to be the general climate in journalism today."

The "climate." That was the trouble.

Many of the lawsuits seemed to reflect that shouted lament from the movie *Network:* "I'm mad as hell and I'm not going to take it any more."

The pressure got so great that some lawyers and their media clients settled out of court rather than expose themselves to the expense and hazard of a lawsuit even if they felt they were right (those who did were known as "Pilgrims," i.e. early settlers). Even big news organizations that could afford the cost were being more careful. They paid tripling libel insurance bills and were screening their stories not just through the ranks of editors but before the unblinking eyes of legal sharpshooters. At times it seemed as if there were almost as many lawyers as journalists involved. To be more careful was undoubtedly a public benefit. To become timid was a different matter.

Ultimately, most of the suits were thrown out either before trial or by higher courts. In every case, judges drastically reduced megabuck awards. They had a lot of reducing to do. Until 1980 only three plaintiffs had ever been awarded $1 million or more by a jury in a libel suit. Since then more than thirty jury awards have been for over $1 million. The *average* trial jury judgment against the media is $2.2 million. Although jury awards are reaching new highs, over the years very few ultimately paid exceeded the award, after fourteen years of litigation and appeals of $481,809 in 1983 to a prominent Chicago lawyer, Elmer Gertz. He won and collected from Robert Welch, the publisher of the fanatic Birch Society magazine. (But ominously in April 1988, the Supreme Court refused to rehear an award of $3 million to Brown & Williamson Tobacco against CBS-owned Chicago WBBM-TV, by far the largest standing libel award in history.) Winning by the media isn't everything. The cost alone to the media of litigation exceeds—by more than 80 percent—any damages they ultimately had to pay.

At times it was obvious that learned judges were wincing in chambers over press performance while upholding essential constitutional principles in court. "Juries," said the St. Petersburg *Times'* Eugene Patterson, "are the American people. They seem to want to punish us."

When Westmoreland filed his case against CBS, he had an obstacle course of libel case histories against him. No one disputed that as a former commanding general, he was a public figure. Westmoreland would have to prove that the program was about him and not just his command (it certainly was—Westmoreland's name was mentioned fifty-eight times in the broadcast); that it damaged his reputation more than he had been damaged already (because of the reach of network television, it surely did); the program was substantially wrong (a tangle of fact and opinion about motives); and CBS and its staff knew their charges were untrue but broadcast them anyway ("actual malice"—hardest of all to prove).

To begin with, the chances that Westmoreland's case would ever reach trial looked slim. Going strictly by the law books, General William C. Westmoreland v. CBS Inc., *et al.*, could easily be dismissed before it came before a jury. If Westmoreland did get his day in court, he faced the precedent that no one in his position had ever won such a case over conduct in public office. He had at least one powerful force working for him—the rising tide of public hostility toward the power of the news media. That force could possibly overcome all the other obstacles.

How can we really be sure that there was more public anxiety over the news media's performance than there had been in years past? We can sense it, cite examples and sniff it in the air. But that's not proof. Of course, dozens of opinion polls are taken on the subject and more spew out all the time. Most show a decline—or at best, a split decision—in the respect the public accords journalists and their work. But the polls are so contradictory, so often abstract and unreliable, that they will not be invoked here. The right poll or statistical survey can confirm almost any point of view or bias. However, there is one big undeniable piece of evidence.

The public, as represented by juries all over the United States has become much harder on the press than the law allows.

In the past, juries handed down far fewer verdicts against the press. Even today, judges dismiss at least three out of four libel suits before they ever reach a jury. But more significant, if they do go to trial, juries now find against the news media 75 percent of the time—only to have judges reverse or revise them in most cases. Unlike polls, these percentages have no sampling margin of error or fuzziness. If the public speaks through its juries, then we are hearing a voice that wants to chastise the press.

Avoid juries if you can, say the media lawyers. Juries are more likely to vote against the press than to embrace complex constitutional principles that favor the press. The media's lawyers have their best chance of winning for their clients by having the case dismissed before a trial by judges who understand the law. Hostile juries are a far greater hazard. Instead of adhering to the fine points of First Amendment law, they often speak emotionally from their own resentment of what they consider press unfairness.

By the mid-80s, not just the public but judges, all the way up to the Supreme Court, were fed up with the libel quagmire and the uninhibited, at times bullying, ways of the news media. The judges were reconsidering their old rulings and decisions. On and off the bench, in *obiter dicta,* speeches and interviews, they spoke of the need to bring the modern news media into greater harmony with society's demands for a more accountable press. The media had become so powerful, so arrogant and difficult to challenge, so self-righteous in protecting their First Amendment "rights," that change was in the air.

The law is an evolving, not a static, master. Judges respond to public sentiment and that sentiment was undoubtedly shouting for the news media to use their unique freedom more carefully. Westmoreland and his lawyers were counting on that to beat the long odds against them.

Most encouraging to Westmoreland was the Benjamin Report, which CBS—other than the parts it released—considered a private internal document.

Westmoreland's lawyer, Dan Burt, thought he should have all sixty-one pages of the report, plus the unpublished notes of Benjamin's thirty-two confidential interviews. He argued that because CBS released the report's conclusions in a press statement, it could no longer assert that the full document had privileged status. Lawyers have the absolute protection of client-attorney privilege. Journalists do not. Benjamin was not a lawyer. Judge Pierre Leval agreed with Burt, and the full text of the damaging report, along with the unguarded and unpublished notes, became public.

The full Benjamin Report went far beyond the Sauter press release. It repeated that "a 'conspiracy,' given the accepted definition of the word, was not proved." The report listed nine "principal flaws" and violations of the CBS News guidelines, including "imbalance" (nine witnesses on the air against Westmoreland, only two for him, including Westmoreland himself), the "coddling of sympathetic witnesses" and questionable editing practices.

Even more damning were the notes from the private interviews Benjamin conducted in his office and on the telephone. Howard Stringer had expressed candid doubts about producer George Crile's abilities: "I thought I could catch him if he did anything wrong." Sam Adams told Benjamin: "I thought early on that 'conspiracy' was too strong a word." Crile himself admitted that "now that I look at it," the charges the program had made against Westmoreland were too broad. Wallace, who had been a friend and classmate of Benjamin's at the University of Michigan, admitted he should have spent more time and been more involved in the program, which he had originally described as a "mystery story" rather than proof of a conspiracy.

The Benjamin Report, an admirable piece of internal self-examination and criticism, was converted into a powerful weapon to use against the network in a libel suit.

CBS's lawyers, to avoid a jury trial, and Westmoreland's to make sure they got one, both unleashed their most powerful, heavyweight arguments in pretrial briefs. In libel cases briefs before trial do not merely set out the philosophical and factual basis for the opposing arguments. Historically, judges' rulings on pretrial briefs have often resulted in even more significant media law than trials themselves.

CBS weighed in with 379 pages in its brief for dismissal. Westmoreland responded two months later with 365 pages. As evenly paired as they were in volume, so they were in logic, exposition and clarity of their arguments—a more remarkable accomplishment for the tiny, understaffed, six-lawyer Capital Legal Foundation group representing Westmoreland than it was for Wall Street's Cravath, Swaine & Moore, whose 225-lawyer firm spoke for CBS.

Half of each pre-trial brief was devoted to arguing whether or not the charges in the program were true. Each side unleashed an avalanche of statistics, affidavits, documents and opinions. CBS said that its charges were true and, on that ground alone, there was no reason for a trial. Westmoreland argued the reverse. The brief for him said there was no conspiracy, no dishonesty, no cover-up, just an open argument over intelligence estimates, described by Westmoreland as an "imprecise science." In fact, he said, it was about as inexact as journalism. "It is not like counting beans," he said, "it's more like trying to estimate roaches in your kitchen."

Capital Legal's brief for Westmoreland argued that if there was any doubt about whose facts were right, the issue was questionable enough to require a trial. Juries are meant to decide on truth, judges on law. CBS countered by saying that the "truth" of what happened in a war as controversial as Vietnam was for the verdict of "history—not for a judge or jury."

For the press, there was a more troublesome question. The answer could radically change the relationship between the news media and government: Could a public figure of the stature of Westmoreland challenge the press in court for criticism of his official acts? Relying for half its brief on the legal precedents against such suits, CBS said that whether the story was right or wrong, Westmoreland, on constitutional grounds, had no case. No legal malice had ever been proved against defendants who checked a story with a single source, believed to be reliable, much less almost a hundred. CBS's brief concluded:

> Every broadcast has flaws and this broadcast was no exception. Nevertheless, after 20 months of exhaustive discovery, plaintiff has found no more flaws than CBS acknowledged months before this lawsuit began; none of those flaws implicates either the truth of what the broadcast said, or CBS's belief in it. Not since the Sedition Act of 1798 has an attempt been made to penalize criticism of government. These are things about which the press and public must have the right to inquire and debate without the threat of libel litigation—politically motivated or otherwise. Such a suit represents a frontal assault on "the very center of the constitutionally protected area of free expression."

To counter CBS's powerful, classic argument Westmoreland's lawyers had a freshly woven tapestry of answers.

Its warp and woof was an ingenious new conception of what now, in the modern media environment, should be considered malicious *unfairness,* although the brief used different words to avoid a frontal assault on past decisions. Never mind, the brief said, that fairness about public figures had never been required of the news media. This egregious unfairness was a different matter. Acting on the popular premise that the Sullivan landmark decision created a "real license for irresponsible people to do things wrong," the Westmoreland lawyers listed twenty-seven "indicia of actual malice." Taken together, the brief said, they made a fulsome collection of CBS bias, ambush interviewing and self-serving duplicity, aimed at proving a theory based on prejudice. Westmoreland's case rested heavily on the Benjamin Report and its notes, which the brief took to be CBS's own admission of doubt, bias and unethical editing practices.

What was unusual about the Westmoreland brief was that it was the strongest argument ever advanced that mistakes in *method*—that is, failure to give weight to conflicting opinions, and failure to interview people who had something to contribute—could add up to a new definition of actual malice. The brief played to all the public frustrations with the news media, weaving them into a pioneering legal argument for new standards for judging the work of journalists. It maintained that no court had ever held that because people "assume a risk" in entering public life, they are libel proof, concluding:

> Although they expose themselves to the risk of criticism through their own voluntary conduct, they often have a greater interest in their good name, honor and reputation. No entity, such as CBS, should be given unfettered power to

destroy the reputations of citizens who choose to take an active role in public affairs.

CBS and the entire press were worried. If Westmoreland could sue, why could Nixon not have sued over some of the media missteps in the Watergate exposure?[4] Or how about Herbert Hoover for "criminally" ordering federal troops to shoot at the veteran bonus marchers during the Great Depression? Or Roosevelt, over the savage articles in the isolationist press charging that he "lied" us into World War II? Or Ronald Reagan for "killing" the poor? And what about all the lesser public figures, generals and politicians? *If* the theory of the Westmoreland brief prevailed, journalists and their lawyers said, it could convert robust debate about public issues into cowering press timidity.

When they sniff any ill wind blowing in their direction, the media always post hurricane warnings. But this time they had good reason to worry. Few libel cases have ever had a greater potential for changing the rules of the game against the press. It came down not to one case but to one thought: If a victory for Westmoreland were ultimately sustained by the highest courts, it could be as big a blow against the press as the Sullivan decision had been for it.

It is rare in the heated combat of the courtroom for both sides to agree— not just in advance but especially after a trial—that they could not have had a fairer, better and less ideologically predictable judge. His Honor Pierre Nelson Leval of the United States District Court for the Southern District of New York (Manhattan, the Bronx and six counties to the north), was, by unanimous agreement, just such a judge.[5]

His informality and an unstuffy ability to instruct the uninitiated in the mysteries of the law made him, at forty-eight, one of the most highly regarded younger judges on the federal bench. Leval's sense of humor and quiet wit rarely seemed to desert him. Once at a New York dinner party

4. One member of his staff suggested just that to Nixon, who replied, "Well, it's God-damned near impossible for a public figure to win a libel case anymore. What's the name of that—I don't remember—but it was a horrible decision— Sullivan."
5. Not so in the Sharon case. Although they never asserted it publicly, many on the *Time* side said to one another that they felt Judge Abraham D. Sofaer should not have heard the case because, they said, he was active in American-Israeli charitable affairs, regularly visited Israel and had taken an interest off the bench in the politics of the Middle East. Sofaer's conduct of the case during the trial seemed to me and other court observers energetic, evenhanded and fair. Judge Sofaer adds: "I would not accept the proposition that an American Jewish judge should abstain from cases involving Israel."

someone asked him about the progress of the Westmoreland case. Without blinking, he replied, "I'm just the groundskeeper of the stadium. I make sure the grass is clipped." In court he was not beyond using "ain't" for emphasis or admitting a mistake with the confession, "Is my face red." When he kept the jury waiting, he apologized: "I was delayed in getting back to the courtroom because I was presented with an urgent application to suppress counterfeit Cabbage Patch Kids." Or, "Sorry for the delay. It was not because anyone was off playing pinochle or something. I have ruled on 22 different disputed issues in the time that you were waiting."

In the Washington *Post,* I wrote a piece commenting on the Westmoreland case in which I had said, in passing, that "nobody enjoys libel suits." After the trial, Judge Leval sent me a cheerful letter pointing out one "inaccuracy" in my article. "I enjoyed every minute," he wrote.

With curly, sandy hair and glasses that he often removed to read, Leval stood an erect 6 ft. 1 in., despite a chronically bad back. Given to wearing pastel-colored, button-down shirts accented by colorful bow ties under his black judicial robes, Leval had the unpretentious grace and assurance of his well-born upbringing. He was the son of a prosperous grain merchant family, whose father had come to the United States from the French-speaking part of Switzerland, with a name one letter "a" different but an alphabet of political distance from the French quisling, Pierre Laval. Leval went to Exeter and Harvard, and then, after six months as an enlisted man in the army, to Harvard Law School where he made *Law Review* and finished near the top of his class.

His college roommate was the scion of a famous American family, later to become a governor and United States senator, Jay Rockefeller. On the wall of their shabby Harvard digs, Leval, who as an undergraduate majored in art history, had a small Utrillo painting borrowed from his mother. He clerked for the Court of Appeals Judge Henry J. Friendly, worked as a federal prosecutor in New York under U.S. Attorney Robert Morgenthau. By 1977 at age forty-one, Leval was appointed for life to the federal bench by President Jimmy Carter.

In the summer of 1984, before the trial started, he had stepped on a sharp open clamshell on the beach and got a badly infected foot that put him in the hospital for two weeks. It healed, requiring him temporarily to carry a cane and to wear comfortable blue tennis sneakers, which peeked out beneath his courtroom robes. Leval had a great interest in innovative jury management. It would play a critical role in the case on his docket.

Leval was an imperturbable, fatherly intervener in the sibling rivalry of the two clashing brethren at his bench, Cravath's David Boies, forty-three, CBS chief counsel in the case, and Capital Legal's Dan Burt, forty-two, the commander in chief for Westmoreland and his forces. Superficially the two had much in common: both had outstanding records at Yale Law School, both had been married three times, and both had marched in the streets demonstrating against the war in Vietnam. Other than their quickness of mind and depth of knowledge of the case, everything else about them was different.

Boies had gone from Yale to Cravath, a Wall Street establishment law firm. Burt, who had been a day student at Philadelphia's LaSalle College, won a scholarship to England's Cambridge, where he earned the high academic distinction of a "first" (i.e. highest honors). Unlike Boies, he had been turned down by a stiff Cravath recruiter, who neither liked his runty (5 ft. 6 in.) looks nor his bombastic mouth ("those snobbish bastards," Burt bitterly recalled). Boies left Cravath briefly to be counsel to Senator Edward Kennedy, when Kennedy was chairman of the Judiciary Committee. On returning to Cravath, he became, in his thirties, one of the firm's top litigators, earning plaudits for his victory in one of IBM's biggest antitrust cases (and much later, after the Westmoreland case, for his work on corporate takeovers and the final round of the CBS-Herbert libel suit).

Burt had done well in a different arena. Spurned by the "better" law firms even though he had graduated near the top of his Yale law class, he went to work at the Treasury Department in Washington, then set up his own shop in Marblehead, Massachusetts, specializing in international tax law. Surprisingly, for someone who constantly talks as if anti-Semites ruled his own and everybody else's world, his biggest clients were rich Saudi Arabians before he decided to join Capital Legal in Washington.

Boies is unflappable in the courtroom ("medium cool," a television producer video-rated him). He is a master at litigating techniques and relentlessly demanding of his associates, yet despite his massive support system, he is a loner. Boies affects Sears, Roebuck suits and loafers, shirts from L.L. Bean. He masks his piercing intelligence with a quick, diffident smile. Reporters at the trial began quietly humming the theme music from *Jaws* when Boies started his cross-examinations. For recreation, to ease the high tension of his professional life, he often runs off to the gambling tables of Atlantic City. At work, he is pure lawyer. When asked if he would have taken Westmoreland as his client instead of CBS, he answered that he found nothing "philosophically" difficult with such a somersault.

Burt, a pussycat in the courtroom, was a prowling, snarling tiger outside.

Dressed for court in custom-made suits from his Washington Italian tailor, he spit out expletives that would make a pornographer blush. Delete the expletives—as most journalists must—and you cannot begin to describe the real Dan Burt—whoever he may be. When he was not engaged in berating the rest of the world for anti-Semitism, he described himself as a "short, foul-mouthed Jew." His devotion to Judaism was invisible to me—being a Jew myself—but he certainly worked at proving the "foul-mouthed" part of his characterization.

In one of a hundred exchanges I heard, he described himself as a "libertarian," a member of the American Civil Liberties Union, and if the Washington *Post*'s media reporter, Eleanor Randolph, ever called him a "conservative" he would punch her or anyone else "in the fucking mouth." He denied he ever said "We are about to see the dismantling of a major news network," a quote that first appeared in *USA Today*. When that paper's meticulous young trial reporter, Bruce Frankel, approached him with a question on another subject, Burt's only answer, before turning his back, was "Fuck off."

In my very first encounter with him—total strangers to each other—he said to me on the telephone: "You wouldn't believe how those CBS motherfuckers and those other shitheads lie. I'm just a little Jew but if they'll do it to Westmoreland, you can imagine who they'll do it to next. Has it ever occurred to you that CBS could be taken over by anyone, and imagine what could happen to minorities like me and others? I feel more comfortable in Saudi Arabia than I do in this country. Have you ever been to the Middle East?" The answer was yes, many times, but there was no chance to get even a word into his stream of meanderings. Changing the subject, he proudly described the elaborate house he was building overlooking Bar Harbor, Maine, and boasted of the architectural recognition his house in Washington had received.

Although there are eminent and experienced media lawyers who specialize in libel, Boies had never tried a libel suit. In high-stakes libel suits before juries, however, experienced general trial lawyers are increasingly sought rather than libel specialists. Burt had never tried a case of any kind before a jury. But in their pretrial jousts, differences in personal style and trial experience didn't seem to matter. Under their command, both sides filed brilliant pretrial briefs.

Burt volunteered that before the Westmoreland case he did not watch television, did not own a set and didn't even know what time the evening news went on. He had no trouble filling that gap. In his many effective television appearances and press conferences to argue Westmoreland's case before the public, Dan Burt cleaned up his act and looked like an innocent, school-boy David up against a bemused Wall Street Goliath.

By the summer of 1984, things were not going especially well for CBS. Burt was making a powerful case in public and winning on most of his motions.

In a trial about television practices, it was appropriate that the last pretrial argument be about television coverage of the trial itself.

Despite the fact that more than forty states allow live television coverage of some trials, no federal court ever has allowed it. CNN, the national cable news network, applied to broadcast the Westmoreland trial. Leval said he favored such coverage because television equipment was no longer "cumbersome and noisy. It appears that filming can be done without the slightest obstruction of dignified, orderly court procedure."

But long-standing rules against television in federal courtrooms prevented him from allowing television coverage. Contrary to Leval's more permissive view, the Judicial Conference of the United States thought that "the alleged public benefits are outweighed by the risks to the administration of justice." There would be no television at this trial of television.

Burt and his team were disappointed. They wanted to play their imposing looking general against the vulnerable CBS staff to a national jury as well as the twelve jurors (and six alternates) in the courtroom. CBS, which in principle had always argued for full television coverage of court proceedings and thus publicly had to support the CNN petition, heaved a silent sigh of relief when it was denied. More important to Burt, Leval wrote in his television ruling that the trial could be expected to go beyond immediate, narrow questions into "appropriate standards for both military commanders and press commentators, a rare debate and inquiry on issues of highest national importance." It was obvious then—even without his formal ruling five days later—that there would be a trial and not a dismissal.

On September 24, 1984, Leval issued his twenty-two-page denial of CBS's request for summary dismissal of the case.

He wrote that the conflicting evidence on the facts offered by both sides could be dealt with only in court. The heart of the case, he said, was "factual," not a matter of "opinion." If CBS had merely charged Westmoreland with "conspiracy" that could be taken as opinion. But the network had accused him of specific dishonest acts. That was more like a direct charge of rape or committing a crime than critical commentary. Nothing in the Sullivan actual malice doctrine gave the news media absolute immunity if they made such factual charges against public figures.

He found most "forceful" the CBS argument that there was no proof of actual malice. But, nonetheless, for the time being he was willing to concede that Burt's "27 indicia of malice" *could* make journalists liable if they "knowingly or recklessly misstate evidence to make it seem more convincing or condemning than it is." That was a "triable question." Leval had opened the door to the new possibility that the editing process itself may have so bent what the sources of the program said that malice needed a more expansive definition. The press read his opinion and worried even more.

The Westmoreland demand for a trial in open court before a jury had prevailed—hence *Newsweek*'s cover story on "The Libel Trial of the Century."

Westmoreland's lawyers, who up to then had spent close to $2 million preparing for the trial, reveled in Leval's opinion, treating it as if they had already won their case. "We believe," said Burt, "it is a victory for responsible journalism. It is proof that even the largest network in the world, represented by one of the finest law firms, can still be held accountable in an American court of law when they destroy a man's honor."

For its part, CBS clenched its teeth, budgeted a minimum of $250,000 a month beyond the $5 million it had already spent, and got ready for the trial. Jury selection would start in two weeks. It would be a long, hard, cold winter.

Trials in a courtroom are more about justice under law than they are about truth in life. The two need not be the same. What seems reasonably true in journalism or in life is often not true in law.

John De Lorean, the high-living automaker, was adjudged by a jury as "entrapped" into buying cocaine, and therefore not guilty. The verdict kept him out of jail, but the exposure destroyed him in the world of friends and business that mattered to him. "Praise the Lord," De Lorean exclaimed on hearing the verdict. But "praise the law," would have been a more apt incantation. The rogue-about-town, Claus von Bulow, was found not guilty of attempting to murder his wife. But in the eyes of most of the world, he was culpable, at the very least, of not preventing her from becoming terminally comatose. Jean Harris, headmistress of a tony Virginia girls school, was convicted and sent to prison for killing her doctor lover when pride prevented her from pleading, with more likelihood of success, that she was crazed by his abuse and the pills he had prescribed for her.

"Almost all criminal defendants" says defense lawyer and Harvard law professor Alan Dershowitz, "are in fact guilty." Because of legal protections, few are found guilty. In the American system, defendants in both criminal and civil cases are surrounded by protective legal barriers that are *intended* to give them rights making it hard to prove their wrongs.

Libel suits against the press that reach trial are not very different. They are harder to fathom because the cases rarely relate directly to the jurors' own experience. They involve reputation, which is hard to measure, and abstract principles, which are hard to grasp. For juries, libel cases are frequently as complex as public utility rate-making petitions, antitrust suits, or the scientific mumbo jumbo that comes tumbling out in product liability and malpractice claims.

Libel cases are made even more difficult because there is rarely a story—whether in television or print—that does not show up with minor or major errors of fact, or embarrassments of judgment and methods. Placing stories under a microscope for the word-by-word, frame-by-frame, step-by-step dissection allowed by law is often damaging to the press. But being "substantially" true or "believing" it was true is enough to satisfy the law in favor of a news media defendant, if the person suing is a public personality. That legal standard satisfies the democratic requirement of a free, unrestrained press. It does not satisfy the demands of a frustrated public, which has concerns beyond malice as defined by law. Nor does it necessarily create good journalism.

8

A "State of Mind"

The libel suit has given my father a new sense of purpose.

—James "Rip" Westmoreland

"Hear ye, hear ye," the bailiff chanted, "give your attention and you shall be heard." He might better have shouted, "heard and be *seen*." Courtroom 318, where Westmoreland v. CBS was on trial, was as much a television viewing room as it was a hearing chamber.

To be sure it was designed and decorated in old style Judicial Impressive. The Great Seal of the United States overlooked churchlike pews for 150 spectators (80 reserved for the press). Reaching up to the courtroom's twenty-three-foot high ceiling, illuminated by golden chandeliers, were gray-green marble walls, crowned by carved wood pilasters. Armchairs for jury, judge, and plaintiff and defense counsel were comfortably deep.

Because television and still cameras (and tape recorders) are banned in federal courthouses, a Dickensian remnant takes their place. In the first press row were perched close to a dozen chalk-dusted sketch artists, their heads bobbing up and down from pad to principal, making the only visual record for the world to see. In the "family" row, sat fifty-seven-year-old Kitsy Westmoreland ("I've never been in court before—only traffic"), threading her gold and silver needlepoint yarn into a small evening bag. "I'm glad I've got my needlepoint to do," she said, "you see, I'm not a sitter." Nor was she a Madame Defarge but a spirited, attractive general's wife (her youngest brother had been killed in Vietnam) whose generous manner quickly made her the most popular and leavening figure in the court.

When a spectator approached her and said, "If I were you I'd be fighting mad," she replied, "I am." Yet as Mike Wallace walked by, she said, "It's so hard for me to dislike someone." One day, after Wallace mentioned he was coming down with the flu, she fed him orange juice and

115

aspirin and sent him home to bed. Of the judge, she observed "He's so cute"; and "Poor jury, I'm sorry for them, it's so complicated." When her husband had trouble on the stand finding a document, she pointed out that "West [her name for him] isn't used to looking for anything."

Amidst all the classical trappings of law, there was one latter-day intrusion. The subject of the trial was a television program and, for the benefit of the judge, jury and press, no courtroom in the United States has ever been equipped with so many television sets—ten monitors connected to banks of video players. Not that any scenes were broadcast into or out of the courthouse. Barred from coming inside, television cameramen and photographers were forced to wait outside the building like chilled hunters in a duck blind.

When Westmoreland and his wife took their first lunch break, they were pursued across the street in full flight. "You see those TV guys," said one passing spectator, "they're like animals. I'd be more afraid of them than anyone."

Westmoreland's lawyer, Dan Burt, predicted it would be a "Star Wars production," adding, "the print press is a dead duck, don't you know?" Not quite. But from the first cold, drizzly October day when it began to the slushy February morning almost five months and sixty-seven court sessions later, it would have other astral distinctions for the future of news media stars and their public universe as well as for the laws that governed them. It would also drive three of its leading players to hospital beds: Westmoreland (for painful back tension), his wife (for migraine) and Wallace (for emotional exhaustion).

Right at the outset the judge made a unique decision. On the central issue he ordered the trial conducted in English rather than judicialese.

Leval confronted head-on the confusion over the misunderstood legal meaning of the words malice and actual malice. Even though they were the language of the Supreme Court and hence the law of the land, he banned their use in his courtroom. In his chambers, the judge got agreement from both sides that the technical meaning of the words was both "misleading and prejudicial." So in his courtroom the words malice and actual malice were never to be used. They were to be replaced by "state of mind." Leval added that "I have no doubt that someone will slip up at some point and will say it, but let me make that mistake, not anybody else." (There was only one slip during the entire trial—when the jury was not present—but Burt immediately corrected himself for using the word malice: "Excuse me, your honor. I misspoke. State of mind.")

The clearer phrase state of mind became as much a punctuation mark in the litany of the trial as "Ladies and gentlemen of the jury" or a lawyer's interrogatory opening to a witness, "Did there come a time . . .?"

There were other innovations.

Because of the interlocking web of issues, Leval allowed the lawyers an aggregate total of two hours each for "minisummations" to address the jury directly whenever they wanted to underscore or clarify points, not just in their opening and final statements. Having given them that license, he then got agreement to restrict each side to 150 hours for presenting its case. He also encouraged the jurors to take notes—which is usually prohibited—and refused to sequester them. He realistically acknowledged that he could not prevent them from reading newspapers or watching television. Instead, he just urged them to try not to be influenced by anything other than what they saw and heard in court.

In a last-minute move, Burt cleverly reduced and sharpened Westmoreland's complaint. He confined it to the CBS charge in the program that the general had deceived only his military bosses and the president. "Everybody accused everybody of lying to the press and public back then," said Burt, "and we don't want to retry the entire Vietnam War." He knew that the more focused he could make his claim of damaging malicious untruths in the broadcast and the more villainous CBS's charge against Westmoreland could be made to sound (lying to *the* president, his commander in chief), the better his chances of winning sympathy from the jury.

Leval warned the lawyers: "I'm not going to allow this trial to be broadened into some kind of historical inquiry into how we fared in Vietnam" or they would be there "until the end of time." The question had been narrowed before trial: "The issue is not whether President Johnson or anyone else in high military command correctly understood what the true figures on enemy strength were. We are not going to get into whether Tet was a surprise or not. We are not going to get into whether the Joint Chiefs understood or not. The issue is whether Westmoreland undertook to and instructed his officers to distort those figures."

At its best good journalism is about reality. Libel trials, on the other hand, are a game. The bigger the game, the more the players are coached. In the Westmoreland World Series the players were coached to the point of nervous exhaustion.

Journalism's objective is to inform and illuminate or just interest and amuse with facts rather than fiction. In libel the object is to win, or short of winning in law, at least get a chance to answer back. Under strict rules of the game, libel trials are one way for an individual to gain an audience to answer the press. For both an aggrieved public and the embattled news media, there should be easier and better ways. There are—but more of that later.

At the start of the trial, expectations and coverage were high. An all-star cast: a most prominent retired general and the most prestigious broadcast network in the United States, both equally unsure and nervous over the outcome; lead lawyers who were very different but apparently well matched; and a judge willing to consider important new issues affecting the news media and its public.

Burt's opening statement laid out his case. He described the CBS program as a "powerful work of fiction that creates the illusion of a wrong that did terrible damage to a sixty-eight-year-old man who has served his country in three wars, ambushed, frustrated, forced back to a fourteen-year-old memory." All this was deviously contrived, he said, taking advantage of television's ability to "cut, splice and put together images that make the appearance of a reality that never occurred." He said he would persuade the jury not "to accept as reality the images seen on the television screen."

Avoiding a direct attack on Wallace, Burt instead went after Crile as the villain who knowingly "fabricated" because "he had never produced a show on his own and needed a big, sensational story" to advance his career. As he talked, he lighted up the court's television sets with snippets of footage from the program, outtakes of interviews never broadcast but that appeared to contradict what appeared on the program. He made a powerful case for his client—as lawyers usually do in opening statements. He kept his voice at monotone level, "trying to out-WASP Cravath," said one reporter. There was none of his pretrial rambunctiousness, only an occasional scurrying around the courtroom, like a sandpiper on the beach, to fine-tune the balky video equipment. But he also displayed one ominous portent of his trial inexperience. Through his octagonally shaped eyeglasses, he read every word of his three-hour opening argument from a script planted on a lectern in front of the jury. A lawyer *reading* his plea to a jury can be almost as much of a no-no in trial practice as a surgeon reading from Gray's *Anatomy* in the middle of an open-heart operation.

David Boies' opening for CBS was no less—nor more—persuasive.

More conventionally, he addressed the jury informally, without a script or even notes in front of him. He ran his own videotapes and used easel-mounted flip-charts to give visual impact to his points. Experienced trial lawyer that he was, never throughout the trial did Boies stick to a prepared scenario in answering Burt. He would typically begin by attacking the last strong impression Burt had made on the jury, before moving on to the rest of his counterattack.

There were only two issues, he said. "One, was the broadcast true? And two, what was CBS's state of mind about that broadcast?" His own television show in court was as often the videotaped depositions he had taken as it was excerpts from the broadcast itself. Both the jury and much of the press were confused—as they would be throughout the trial—as to whether what they saw on the courtroom television screens, including outtakes, had actually been in the broadcast or not.

Boies regaled the jury with similar accusations that had been made against Westmoreland by the Pike Committee and by newspapers, magazines and books. "Sometimes newspapers get it wrong," he said. "Sometimes television stations get it wrong. That's true, too. It's hard to understand exactly how all these people would have been this wrong all at the same time."

He also pointed out that "more than a dozen substantial officers of our government—military and civilian—came forward. Why would these people say these things if they aren't true?" Just as Burt had avoided attacking a celebrity like Wallace directly, so Boies was careful with an impressive General Westmoreland. He explained Westmoreland's actions as "politically motivated" because "pressure began to develop either to show progress, light at the end of the tunnel, or to get out of the war." But he was quick to add, with a moral neutrality not evident in the broadcast, that "one can conceive of somebody doing that in what you might call good faith, believing that that is in the best interests of our country."

The case, he said, was "not about whether we should have been in Vietnam or even whether the deception that took place had a good or bad motive." Then picking up Burt's repeated use of "fabrication," Boies described his strongest evidence in documents, videotapes and depositions, ending each with the refrain: George Crile, Mike Wallace or CBS "didn't fabricate this, didn't make it up." The events portrayed in the broadcast, he said, were not the "good faith debate" over intelligence matters that Burt had portrayed them to be. They were plainly and simply the "deception" CBS had said they were.

Westmoreland sat stoically at the plaintiff's table, at the most punishing moments grimacing and rhythmically stretching his neck muscles. Sitting right behind me, Kitsy Westmoreland left her needlepoint in her lap while she listened to every painful word.

Judge Leval moved out of his soft-leather swivel chair closer to the jury box where he could better see the charts and the opposing lawyers. He pressed his pained back isometrically against the hard marble wall. At the end of the presentations, he complimented the "salesmanship" of both lawyers: "I thought both opening statements," he said from the bench in open court, "were extremely forceful and well delivered."

Game score so far: a 1-1 tie.

Everyone in the press has potential conflicts of interest. Of these, the least obvious can be the most harmful. Journalists—like other humans—have friends, families, careers, ambitions, responsibilities and predispositions that are more complex than any rule book can proscribe. Newsroom policies banning the more obvious conflicts are necessary and welcome. The best additional remedy—even though it is far from perfect—is disclosure. It at least has the virtue of trying to let everyone know where everyone stands so better evaluations are possible.

Journalists can and should be scrupulous in not joining organizations or any fray that could compromise them, not free-loading, not engaging in political activity, certainly not making potentially conflicting investments, and a dozen other exclusions. But they are still citizens with entangling alliances. Joseph Pulitzer's resounding axiom that journalists have no friends sounds good but doesn't work. My own variation has always been that "I have friends but none in print." I find that better, but like most rules, still too simple.[1] For example:

Five months before the trial, I had written letters to both Burt and Boies describing this book and inviting their cooperation. At the end of the three-page letter, I wrote:

> In the interest of full disclosure: before I anticipated writing this book, at the request of CBS's counsel, I entered a short affidavit in the case, making available a widely distributed report ("Vietnam: A Conclusion") I wrote in 1967 on the eve of Tet, after an interview I had with General Westmoreland in Saigon [see page 42]. I offered it, as mentioned, on request as I would have if the plaintiff's counsel has asked me. This and any other relevant disclosures will be made in the book itself.

Reporters rarely testify voluntarily beyond what they have written or broadcast unless they are the subject of a lawsuit themselves, are forced to testify, or have an overriding reason to do so, as they most often are asked to in criminal trials. Traditionally, they confirm in a "neutral" affidavit or testimony what they have already published. Mine was such a neutral affidavit. The full report that I attached happened to be as personally complimentary to Westmoreland—perhaps too much so—as it was critical of the progress of the war.

Two weeks before the trial, my former colleagues at Time Inc., from which I had retired, agreed that because I was covering the case for this book I should also report regularly as "special correspondent" for *Time*. I registered in the court's press office with that affiliation.

1. I have non-professional, personal relationships—some very close—with a number of people mentioned in this book. How to deal with that fairly in journalism is a complex matter. See page 9.

During the week of the opening arguments, Dave Henderson, who was doing some press relations for Westmoreland without a fee, protested to *Time* that my affidavit, entered in the court record by CBS, disqualified me from reporting fairly and made me a potential witness. *Time,* which I had told of the affidavit before accepting the assignment, yielded to the complaint. The magazine was having libel troubles of its own in the Sharon case and wanted no further problems from plaintiffs' lawyers. "We were a little chilled," a *Time* executive said. After the first story, which I had already reported and which *Time* used despite the protest, I agreed to drop the assignment.

Outside the courtroom, Burt apologetically but firmly mentioned to me the successful intervention. I told him he had obviously never read or perhaps seen my full report, else he would not have questioned my role in the case. He said he would look into it.

Because I am now reporting on myself in a controversy involving conflicts of interest, perhaps the least self-serving way to describe what happened next is to reprint my exact notes. They were typed right after the encounter they describe and are reproduced here in full, with no deletions or additions:

DAY FOUR, FRIDAY, OCTOBER 12

BURT AND CLURMAN

Court session is called for 11 A.M. At about 10:20 Burt comes down the hall, where I am standing outside the courtroom, talking to Bill Prochnau of the Washington *Post* [who was on leave to write a book for Random House]. Burt purposefully comes towards us and says, "Mr. Clurman, I need to talk to you please."

We go around the corner to an empty foyer, but that's not private enough for him, so we go a few steps away to a landing in the stairwell at the end of the hall. He says, "I read your letter and the affidavit. I also read your report and I want to apologize to you. But I also want you to know," his voice rising, "that you were sandbagged by Cravath." "How?" I asked. "They never mentioned the report you were confirming," he said, "and didn't include it in the papers I got. They sandbagged you, and you should know that." I allowed as how I didn't wish to argue that point one way or the other with him.

"I'll tell you what," he said earnestly, "you draft a letter for my signature to *Time* apologizing for my complaint to them against you and I'll sign it." I demurred on the grounds that I didn't want to be drafting letters for him. "Well, what do you want me to do? It's wrong," he said. Was he the one who called *Time,* I asked, or was it his PR man, Mr. Henderson? "Anything that happens in this case is done by me," he said not answering the unimportant question.

"But what do you want me to say to *Time?*" I replied that he could just withdraw his objection and remove the ethical cloud I found uniquely unpleasant since it was based on incorrect information. "Don't you want me to say anything else" he asked? I said that I could handle my own conversations and relationships with *Time* and that his withdrawal of his complaint would be sufficient. How did I want it done, he asked? Well, said I, since my understanding was that originally someone had called Ray Cave the managing editor, that seemed the best place to go again. "Okay," said Burt.

At that moment we ascended the stairwell into the hall, where he beckoned to a tall slender man I had never seen before. "Mr. Henderson, this is Mr. Clurman. Call Ray Cave, managing editor of *Time,* that's Ray Cave managing editor of *Time* and tell him that we withdraw our complaint on Mr. Clurman's conflict. It was a mistake. I'll explain the whole thing to you later. But call today."

Burt and I shook hands, said we'd talk some more about other things in the future as he had agreed we would, and he parted for the courtroom to hear the opening statement of CBS lawyer, David Boies.

Episode over—except to add, that Cravath lawyer Randy Mastro, who like the others defending CBS has never been made aware of this matter by me, does assure me that they never had any intention of calling me as a witness and now commit not to do so.

"Apology" or not, I never renewed the *Time* special assignment again. But whatever happened to Burt's splenetic language in these exchanges? He could always turn it on and off (the jury and judge *never* heard it). For some reason Burt, even more complex than most hyperactive people, turned the expletives off from then on when he and I talked alone. In fact, a few weeks later when he claimed to me that he had been misquoted (about "the dismantling of a major news network") in a speech by Time Inc. editor-in-chief, Henry Grunwald, he asked me to call Grunwald and "just tell him what my real character is." I never made the call because, among other reasons, I would not have known what to say on that puzzling point.

The Westmoreland case against CBS had everything to do with how stories are crafted and very little to do with the actual Vietnam War. Its message was about modern journalism.

"Many of us are accustomed," Burt said, "to accepting as reality the images and sounds we see on television screens, particularly younger people who have grown up with television all their lives." Burt said he would show how superficial television truth could be distorted into damaging fiction and used against real people.

Burt's opening case lasted thirteen weeks and filled 6,481 pages of trial transcript. He called eighteen "friendly" witnesses who argued Westmoreland's side, and one "hostile witness," George Crile, whose credibility Burt hoped to destroy before CBS could put him on. His most powerful testimony, and harmful to CBS, came not from the live witnesses, but from the CBS outtakes shown on the television sets mounted all over the courtroom.

In television, outtakes are just like reporters' notebooks, only more vivid. They contain the full interview not just the part selected for broadcast. They are raw stuff. In them are the interviewers' bumbles, side remarks, efforts to persuade or provoke to anger, as well as *all* the subjects' replies, denials, caveats and corrections. In the past ten years, broadcasters have tried unsuccessfully to keep them out of court. Reporters' notes—when the judge determines them relevant—have become only slightly less accessible to exposure. "An outtake," CBS's Don Hewitt reminds print reporters, "is nothing more than the news that isn't fit to print—or to broadcast. Did you ever hear of a newspaper office without a wastebasket?"

The networks and other news organizations have a dilemma. If they destroy rather than save outtakes or notes, they lose valuable material for future use. And as in the case of the Nixon tapes, to destroy them in contemplation of a lawsuit could be an obstruction of justice. Not preserving them, says press critic Thomas Griffith, encourages the press to "operate like a fly-by-night bookie, keeping no records that might later embarrass." Most outtakes are saved on the sensible ground that their value is greater than their hazard.

The CBS outtakes, initially, were a shock to a jury unschooled in the techniques of journalism. CBS could be judged as much for what it didn't put on the air as for what it did.

What better way to attack the methods of television than by using television itself? Burt knew that from the start. Outtakes were his weapon.

The outtakes recorded many of television's methods unedited and uncut in full color on videotape. A half hour on the screen can be more powerful and credible than thousands of words in documents. It also makes it hard to deny—as can be done with spoken words or even documents—that something happened the way it was reported. The outtakes record everything the camera can see and the microphone can pick up. In addition, the people who appeared in many of the CBS outtakes could be—and were—called to testify in court. (Not all of them. In a federal civil case, third-party witnesses cannot be *compelled* to appear if they live more than a hundred miles away.)

Media lawyer Floyd Abrams has said that juries, like all consumers of news, "tend to take visual material very seriously. They watch it; it has an aura of reality which the written word sometimes doesn't carry." Boies argued against showing some of the full outtakes because "what was selected and what was not by the people that edited this program is not at issue." It may, he said, be "relevant to journalistic considerations" but, under law, not to libel. Judge Leval disagreed, ruling that a properly instructed jury should decide what was and what wasn't relevant.

Television interviewers look much better on their edited programs than they do in their outtakes, just as print reporters' stories make more impressive reading than their notes. "When it comes to making cars, aspirin and TV documentaries," the Philadelphia *Inquirer*'s David Zucchino reported, "the process is never as pretty as the finished product."

In Burt's presentation of the outtakes it looked as if journalists led double lives.

They revealed one side to their public in well-packaged programs and stories. The other side was concealed, erratic and dark, replete with favoritism, manipulation, entrapment, *ad hoc* judgments and censorship of views that hurt their thesis. The outtakes were powerful stuff, as troubling to many spectators in the courtroom as the program had been convincing on the air.

Burt played the two sides of journalism—the process and the results— back to back against each other. He alternated between showing what he called "Acts" of the five-part program that had been broadcast (divided by breaks for commercials), and segments of the outtakes that had never been seen before. Together they were intended to evoke two emotions. First, that the CBS interviewers were hostile and tough toward those who denied their point of view, friendly and helpful to those who agreed with it. Second, that what was not used on the program undermined the CBS thesis about Westmoreland's duplicity more strongly than the material that was included supported that thesis.

Judge Leval had tried to insulate the jury from an emotional, sympathetic stampede against the investigative methods of journalism and law. "Getting the truth from a reluctant witness," he warned, "often requires either cajoling and flattery or a rough cross-examination. The use of such tactics is often necessary to arrive at the truth. By itself it does not demonstrate disregard for the truth. Nor is the reporter required to accept denials of wrongdoing as conclusive or to prefer them over apparently creditable accusations."

But the wisdom of his abstract warning was no antidote to the reality on the screen. It showed, in the Westmoreland interview, a relentless, prepared Mike Wallace beating up a confused, surprised Westmoreland. They showed Crile interviewing one supporting witness twice to get better answers (a violation of CBS rules) and urging him on with such phrases as "come to the defense of your old protégé, Sam Adams." The same witness had also been shown films of other interviews (another CBS violation). Even the subject was surprised at the prompting he got. "Is it really kosher to go over this?" he asked Crile. "I'm sorry George, I don't know what you want me to say."

Crile said he was most worried about how he would look in the full interview with a former navy commander, James Meacham, who had worked on enemy estimate figures in Vietnam.

Meacham had willingly given Adams and Crile access to more than three hundred letters that his wife had stored in a shoebox. As a young navy officer in Vietnam, between July 1967 and July 1968, he had written the letters to his wife, Dorothy (who, divorced from Meacham, now lives near the Westmorelands in Charleston). Many of the letters expressed bitterness about the argument in Saigon over intelligence estimates. "I have never in my life assembled such a pack of truly gargantuan falsehoods," he wrote to his wife about his work; they were "outright lies," "dishonest." They were "falsifying" and "doctoring the strength figures" to show that "we continue to win the war."

If there was any doubt about what he meant, at least one letter made it very clear: "I'm not talking about confusion and inefficiency which to a certain extent are products of all wars, but about muddle-headed thinking, cover-your-ass orders, lies and outright foolishness on the very highest levels."[2] He wrote "some day it may come out," and he wanted his letters preserved as a historical record.

In print journalism, such contemporaneous, unvarnished evidence can be persuasive stuff. It requires only authentication, a check on the author's position, credibility and credentials, plus (if they are private letters) permission to use them. For television Crile had to get Meacham to say something like that on camera. By the time Crile interviewed him in London's Brown's Hotel, Meacham had become the military affairs correspondent of the London *Economist,* a grown-up member of the British establishment.

On the outtake, Meacham pooh-poohed his old letters, saying they had been written in the youthful "heat" of the time. Although he had refused

2. However much they knew, some U.S. intelligence officers were obviously as surprised as anyone by the Tet attack. Meacham said that on the night the offensive began, close to two hundred senior intelligence officers were having a Vietnamese New Year's party. It was reminiscent of Pearl Harbor day when startled officers, nursing hangovers, were awakened at dawn by Japanese attack bombers. Earlier, junior civilian staffers at the embassy invited friends to their own American New Year's party with an invitation that said: "The Flower Children of Saigon Invite You/To See the Light at the End of the Tunnel."

to appear in court in person, there he was on the court's television screens telling Crile: "It was certainly not falsification of official records if that's what you're asking. You clearly know what you want me to say but that's not the perception I have. I think we could have lost an argument before an objective jury about this. We certainly weren't faking any intelligence. It's not a question of honesty or dishonesty. I understand perfectly well what you're trying to say. I don't agree with it." When Crile asked him if changing the Saigon computer records, which Meacham confirmed, wasn't the equivalent of burning records, Meacham replied: "No, no, not at all." None of these denials appeared on the program.

Crile's most damaging outtake was his interview with retired Colonel Gains Hawkins, a drawling, self-described "old country boy" who had been a leading MACV expert on the Viet Cong. On the program Hawkins was a prime supporter of CBS's charge—if not the owner of the smoking gun, at least he owned the holster carrying it. He was shown on the program saying, "These figures were crap, they weren't worth anything." Asked by Crile how he could support them if they were such a fraud, Hawkins said he was a loyal staff officer and "defended the command position" even though it was "schizoid, dealing from both sides of the deck."

But in the outtake, pressed by Crile to name the "villain," Hawkins ducked. He said that he would not "point a finger at anybody," adding, "when you get down to it who the hell can prove one figure is better than the other?" Hawkins said he was sure the White House "was acutely aware of every figure that was being presented." The damning "crap" quote was transformed into evidence *against* CBS, when it was shown that for the program Crile had moved it around in the editing process. On the outtake, it was clear Hawkins was actually answering a question about another set of numbers, not the ones at issue in the program. Crile had spliced the two together.

On the program Westmoreland's only supporter used by CBS was General Daniel Graham, who had been chief of Westmoreland's current intelligence division. Confidently, almost unctuously, he knocked down everything Wallace asked him. "You managed to confuse" Westmoreland, "he misspoke himself," Graham told Wallace. He countered every charge made in the program and said that he thought Sam Adams "has a hangup that verges on a mental problem." Only a few of his unruffled denials in the ninety-minute interview were used in the two sound bites totaling twenty-one seconds that Graham appeared on the air.

Burt also played parts of a three-hour interview with LBJ's former national security adviser, Walt Whitman Rostow, in which Rostow said

LBJ always knew exactly what was going on. Rostow warned Wallace, "You've really got to take this seriously because you're going to do great damage to the country and you're going to get it wrong." Not one frame from the Rostow interview was used.

From the outtakes, CBS in the court and journalism in the world looked biased and unfair.

The impression the outtakes made was deeply disturbing to the reporters covering the trial. At every recess break and over lunch they gathered in intense, soul-searching discussion of how they would look under such scrutiny.

"I guarantee you," said one veteran television NBC correspondent, only half jokingly, "by the end of this decade we won't have any outtakes." An ABC producer worried more seriously that he would "hate to see every interview by me paraded in front of a jury. They don't understand that we shoot 40 minutes and end up using 20 seconds. Even if you do your 20 seconds in absolutely good faith, what you *could* have put on is always there to be used against you. Juries are now basing their libel judgments on what was *not* aired, instead of what *was*."

For a brief moment, some of the print reporters shook their heads smugly at how television works, how compromised certainly Crile and even Wallace looked. Crile had plainly used techniques and practices that were unacceptable by any journalistic standards. After some reflection, most of the reporters at the trial agreed that their own equivalent of outtakes—notes, memos, rewrites, recordings of their own interviewing techniques—could also be very embarrassing in controversial stories, especially when they interviewed people they thought were misleading them or withholding information. But Crile—his mind made up before he started—had gone too far in pushing his interviewees to reflect conclusions he had already reached. He was not testing his thesis. He was determined to prove it.

A New York *Times* media reporter, Peter Kaplan, searched for an explanation: "Reporters, including television journalists, typically fling their nets widely and then must pick and choose representative specimens of what they have found. The function of a journalist is not to provide an unevaluated transcript."

True, but not good enough. Some methods journalists use are satisfactory to the public only when the result is both important and conclusive. Very few complained about investigative reporters like Seymour Hersh when he reported the My Lai atrocity, or Woodward and Bernstein when they started the Watergate avalanche that buried Nixon, or a usually placid

French press when it flailed its government for blowing up the Greenpeace antinuclear ship in New Zealand.

Yet no one in journalism believes that righteous ends justify any means. Both means and ends were on trial in the Westmoreland case. *Newsday* columnist Murray Kempton, who consistently provided the most insightful analysis of those issues in the case, wrote:

> If CBS had undertaken a study of the blunders and self-deceptions of our intelligence establishments in Vietnam, it could have serviceably instructed us and gotten a Nielsen rating of six. Instead it set out as a hanging judge. These excesses got it a rating of seven and the jury is now inspecting every pot in its kitchen and leaving us journalists as uncomfortable as any short-order cook has to feel when he sees the health inspector entering the three-star restaurant down the block.

Burt's case for Westmoreland was advanced more by the outtakes than by his parade of supporting witnesses. Senior military and civilian eminences called by Burt and cross-examined by Boies, buried the jurors under crossword puzzles of agencies and an infinity of statistics.

At the trial, the alternative to refighting the war in Vietnam was fighting the war of numbers. The weapons were computer printouts, dense written reports, endless readings of depositions, tables of organization and a jumble of acronyms that a platoon of crytographers would have had trouble unscrambling.

The courtroom was filled to standing room only at the start, but during long stretches there were more empty than occupied seats. A "hot-bed of ennui," said John Scanlon, the head of CBS's trial public relations group. The story that began on the front pages, often moved, during its dog days, to the back or was dropped from the news altogether. "They're making the war sound boring," Westmoreland said to me after one stupefying day of numerical and alphabetical acrobatics. Some examples:

PERINTREP (Preliminary Intelligence Report), CINCPAC (Commander-in-Chief, Pacific), NSA (National Security Agency), OB (Order of Battle), CDEC (Combined Document Exploitation Center, which alone received some 16,000 pages a day of captured enemy papers), SD's (Self-Defense forces), SSD's (Secret Self-Defense forces) SNIE (Special National Intelligence Estimate). At one point, a witness said with a straight face, "The SNIE had run into a snag." One lawyer asked a witness, "Was the CIIB a WIEU?" (Translation: Was the Current Interim Intelligence Briefing a Weekly Intelligence Estimate Update?) Together the jury sent a note to the judge: "Your honor, would you be so kind as to have a list made up of the military initials and their meanings."

The real war in Vietnam disappeared in the procedures of the court, the testimony of the witnesses and the arguments of lawyers. Those of us in the court—reporters, spectators, witnesses, Vietnam veterans of all kinds—all heard about a war we had never seen nor cared much about. It was a battle of bloated headquarters bureaucracies, "American intelligence agencies shelling each other with computer printouts," one reporter said. Not more than 20 percent of U.S. troops sent to Vietnam ever engaged in combat operations. But the bureaucratic numbers battle bore as much relationship to the bloody, cruel and mixed-up war we all experienced as a summer breeze does to a hurricane.

Bob Brewin, who had been a marine in Vietnam and who colorfully covered the trial from the grunt's perspective in a weekly column for the *Village Voice*,[3] wrote: "Five kinds of Viet Cong! All I knew in 1967 was that a bunch of guys in black pajamas had devised various fiendish ways to do in my young marine ass." I asked him whether in Vietnam he had ever heard of the terms SD and SSD—the centerpiece of the trial's number argument—to describe the Viet Cong guerrillas. Neither I nor any of the others who covered the war had. "Hell no," he said, "we called them slants, gooks or indigenous personnel."

How could any jury follow the acronyms and numbers alone, when even Southeast Asia war buffs were dozing off under blankets of soporific jargon? One juror, who was required as the others were to unravel the intricate threads, requested a private audience with the judge after a lunch break. She had an urgent problem that could require a trial recess. "I had a chicken noodle soup," the pleasant nursing home assistant explained, as was faithfully recorded in the transcript. "Oh, I feel so sick. I throw out."

No matter. Juries are supposed to be "peers" of the general public not peers (i.e. equal in rank or ability) of the experts or celebrities involved in the trial. In that mandated role, jurors as often take the measure of witnesses and lawyers by the personal impressions they make as they do by testimony or argument. Very often, jurors trust or distrust, like or dislike, and make up their minds not on courtroom evidence alone but on the evidence of their senses.

Every reporter knows that in exposés, the higher the source, the more likely the request for anonymity.

Whistle-blowers who ultimately are willing to stand up and be identified are more likely to come from below. Burt's complaint against CBS's program was that it used "low-level, friendly" witnesses. So his first live

3. And with his wife, Sydney Shaw, has written *Vietnam on Trial: Westmoreland vs. CBS* (Atheneum, 1987).

witnesses were an array of graying formerlies—Harvard, Yale and West Point graduates, who had once served at the highest levels.

"I used to say everything would be all right," the writer-lawyer Louis Auchincloss reminisced in an interview after the publication of one of his novels, "if only my class at Yale ran the country. Well, they did run the country during the Vietnam War and look what happened." The trial had the same overtones. The articulate, older and educated civilian leaders who had directed their military emissaries, were opposed mostly by a younger generation of doubters and dissenters. As the jurors later reported, the civilian gray eminences on the witness stand were—with a few exceptions—mostly a bust.

Burt scheduled Walt Rostow for three hours—the same amount of time Rostow's unused interview with Wallace had lasted—but yanked him after one. Boies got him to admit that he was not present at critical meetings, that he advised the president only on how to handle the public relations and politics of the war, and that Westmoreland never discussed enemy troop estimates with him or, so far as he knew, with LBJ. "Bizarre," Rostow said over his shoulder to an acquaintance, as he marched out of the courtroom at the end of a grueling day of cross-examination. (Mike Wallace sought respite that evening by discussing the 1984 Reagan campaign for reelection and sipping champagne in the Waldorf Towers with an old friend from Chicago, Nancy Reagan.)

Another high-level witness, Robert ("Blowtorch") Komer, lived up to the nickname he acquired, as pacification chief in Vietnam, for his arrogant, congenital optimism, by seeming to conduct his own trial on the stand. "Just a second," the judge admonished him, "wait for the question." When Komer volubly complained about being deposed so late and not being represented by counsel, a smiling Judge Leval parried, "Where did you get the idea *you* needed a lawyer?" The method of counting the enemy, Komer said, was "Byzantine, it reminded me of the three witches in Macbeth." He testified that everybody, senior civilian and military, knew about the disagreement at the time—"a cable war, ridiculous," but "I was not a participant in the debate over the numbers." It was, he said, "a tempest in an intelligence teapot."

As the weeks passed, Burt argued that witness after witness proved that the debate about enemy strength was more like a "disagreement over which football team is going to win the Super Bowl" or a dispute with your boss or your spouse as to how the same set of facts were to be interpreted. It doesn't mean you were dishonest." Boies' repeated answer: "Of course everybody knew there was a debate. The issue is whether that debate was in good faith or not." One witness said that figuring out the size of the enemy was "like counting roaches in a dark barn with a flashlight.'' Finally, finally, in the numbers wrangle, another intelligence officer in the witness box introduced a brand-new term he said was built into his enemy estimates, the "SWAG factor." What was that? "Scientific Wild-Assed Guess," he replied, as judge, jury and spectators all broke into relieved, appreciative laughter.

The case portrayed in court was a muted, pointillist rendition of an explosively Goyaesque war.

But there was one witness who provided an aching self-portrait of the conflict that had gripped the press, the public and the government all during the war. Before the trial, the jurors, revealing a generational gap or an astonishing lapse in historical memory, indicated that none of them had ever heard of him. His appearance in the witness box moved the stories onto page one. Robert Strange McNamara, secretary of defense to both Kennedy and Johnson, had steadfastly refused ever to discuss Vietnam since he left the government in 1968. The trial forced him by law finally to talk.

At Burt's urging, McNamara had one year earlier innocently agreed to submit a standard character reference for the beleaguered general. Burt drafted it and it was no more weighty than a letter recommending a friend for membership in a country club. When the affidavit became part of the court record, it sucked McNamara into talking about the war in a way he had always resisted: "I want it clear on the record that you are extracting these answers against my wishes." Furthermore, he couldn't believe his old friends at Cravath would let this happen to him and he was outraged that Crile had secretly recorded his telephone interview.

As well spoken and deferential as he was on the stand, he revealed two faces that glared at each other in tortured conflict. He had brought to the Pentagon a new, automated managerial system from the Ford Motor Company, where he had become president and was the whizziest of the "whiz kids." The system produced all the numbers, including the grotesque "body count" he came to deplore. McNamara was a leading public endorser of the war but a most private, anguished naysayer against the policies he created and carried out.

He revealed for the trial that as early as 1967, he had told LBJ the war could only be won by bringing the enemy to the conference table, not by military means alone. Boies produced the top-secret memo to LBJ in which McNamara wrote of "the world's greatest superpower killing or injuring 1,000 non-combatants a week, while trying to pound a tiny, backward nation into submission on an issue whose merits are hotly disputed."

Despite these views, McNamara continued not only to run the war as

LBJ's trusted deputy for military affairs but to defend its effectiveness. He distorted U.S. progress to the Congress, the press and the public. Most charitably, it could be said that he lied for his country and lived with the moral ambiguity of dissenting from within while toeing the line outside. But a publicly unrepentant McNamara refused to give that plausible explanation. He declined even to fall back on the old Churchillian epigram, "In wartime, truth is so precious that she should always be attended by a bodyguard of lies."

His testimony had little do to with the facts of the case, except for such improbable generalizations as "no responsible military officer would ever hold information from a superior that conceivably could bear on the superior's rightful decision-making power." But for a brief moment his appearance shed light on real history and on the complexity of a high public official in deep inner conflict at a critical moment in American life.

As McNamara was going down the courthouse steps, a Vietnam vet ran up to him and shouted: "If you knew we were not winning the war militarily, why did you keep sending my buddies and me over there?" Disconsolately, McNamara replied, "That's really a good question, read my memo," and walked on.

Again, as Murray Kempton wrote:

> McNamara had arrived at a realistic assessment then dutifully, if sometimes hollowly, blown the smoke of official fantasy whenever his forum was a public one. He had been telling the White House that the national security adviser, the joint chiefs of staff and Gen. Westmoreland were wrong in their estimate of the war's progress. It had been lonesome work and cruel to his peace of mind, but he carried on with it and perhaps with the not improper excuse that, if he quit, his place would be taken by someone else who was also wrong and would help make matters worse. There are arguments against that decision but it was by no means a dishonorable one and it would indisputably have a fairer look than the one McNamara put on yesterday with his insistence that he had never said a public word he did not think the unadorned truth. But he would not offer any such excuse. McNamara was certainly saying what he believed false and Westmoreland was probably saying what he thought true. It seems curious that the issue here is Westmoreland's honor and not McNamara's.

Journalism is most valuable—and most chancy—when it attempts to explain the reason why.

Reporters must first establish that something actually happened the way they say it did. A matter of provable facts. But the better and more ambitious the story, the more it attempts to explain why. Facts without whys leave readers and viewers with information but no explanation.

Describing motives is inviting and important because it offers a context. It can also drive a reporter to hazardous mind reading, more the license of novelists than journalists. Too often reporters who pick the most obvious motives are speculating or reporting someone else's guess and are wrong as a matter of fact. Good reporting tries to prove motives with facts rather than assuming them with logic.

CBS's ambitious program had tried to do both. The broadcast said that Westmoreland concealed and suppressed the real enemy figures, a flat factual assertion. It further said that he engaged in that deception—here comes the motive and meaning—not because he thought the figures wrong but because he wanted to keep them from the president, the Joint Chiefs, the Congress and the public. It was a combination of what CBS thought was factual reporting and an explanation of why it happened that way. For viewers of the program, the sum of the two was that CBS had clearly charged Westmoreland with deception at best, with lying at worst. There was no doubt his honor—the spine of his life—was fractured by the broadcast.

There is no more powerful spokesman on the subject of Westmoreland's honor than Westmoreland himself. On the stand, in civvies that could not conceal his military bearing, he looked more like a portrait of himself than a witness at a trial. Well prepared, Westmoreland stood in sharp contrast to the defensive, confused figure who appeared in the Wallace interview and outtakes.

For four days (with a four-hour limitation so as not to tire the aging general), Burt led him to describe a life of all-American rectitude and service to his country. Then through his unexpected confrontation with those trappers from CBS who "deceived" him, people he thought could be trusted to be fair.

Even Westmoreland expressed bafflement over the numbers-and-alphabet war. Like other old Vietnam hands, he said he had never heard the term SD (self-defense) forces or SSD (secret self-defense) forces used in the field. His troops "were not acquainted" with the civilian Viet Cong "in any great detail," he added (much to the consternation of those who estimated possibly as many as 40 percent of all American casualties were inflicted by that "hidden enemy"). He disdained their effectiveness against the air, land and sea power of his forces. He repeatedly described them— the way all his supporters at the trial did—as civilians, not soldiers, "old women, young boys and old men" ("OWYBOM," the press began to call them.).

He was a regular army general, commanding his troops in the field against units of an elusive but known enemy. He exhibited almost as little interest in the layers of his own intelligence bureaucracy as the jury and court spectators had. What had really concerned him was where the enemy was that day or that week, or where and how it was building up its forces, so that he could attack. As to the trial's crucial order of battle reports, he wasn't even sure who prepared them. "That was historical data, it wasn't something useful to me," he said. He "didn't get involved in the nuts and bolts of this. My responsibilities were much broader." He was busy fighting a real war, day by day. "Intelligence officers tend to be myopic," he said disparagingly, "they get brownie points for finding more enemy. I just didn't want to be bothered with it."

He had an "open-door" policy. Westmoreland explained this so earnestly that it almost overcame the emptiness of what he was saying: "If anybody had a grievance or complaint he could seek an appointment with the commander and talk about it" or he "could go to the chaplain." Westmoreland proudly produced a pocket card that he had distributed to all his officers and in which he placed great faith. It contained a fifteen-point code of conduct. First, "Make the welfare of your men your prime concern with special attention to mess, mail and medical care." Second, "Give priority emphasis to matters of intelligence, counterintelligence and timely and accurate reporting."

Westmoreland recreated the crucial session at which he was accused of suppressing the new, higher enemy figures.

As he remembered it, his intelligence chief, Maj. Gen. Joseph Mc-Christian, walked in without an appointment—"quite an irregular" visit—late one day, at about 6:30 or 7:00 P.M., just as Westmoreland returned from the field to his headquarters office.

McChristian gave Westmoreland a draft cable, addressed to higher headquarters in Hawaii and Washington. It reported a significant increase in enemy organization, as a result of new McChristian staff studies that included the "irregulars" as part of the total enemy strength figures. Westmoreland said he was taken aback. "Joe," he recalled saying, "we're not fighting those people. They don't belong in any numerical representation of enemy strength."

He said he told McChristian, that this questionable new report coming out of the blue, could create "a major public relations" misunderstanding. It would confuse the press, the president and the public. So he refused to send the message forward until more work could be done on it. Instead, he said, he put it in his desk and ordered further study and briefings. Burt asked whether McChristian disagreed with him. "I don't see how he could," Westmoreland answered, straight from military training manuals, "after all I was the commander." McChristian, said Westmoreland, "in effect passed the buck to me."

George Carver, Adams' boss and special assistant for Vietnamese affairs to CIA director Richard Helms, supported Westmoreland's casual view of the whole ruckus, despite the heated contrary views of other CIA staffers.[4] He testified that after months of wrangling between the CIA and the military, he went from Washington to Saigon and agreed to settle the dispute with Westmoreland in about twenty minutes, just "long enough for one pleasant, leisurely cup of coffee."

One of Westmoreland's most emotional moments came when he described what he said was the effect of the war reporting on his men in the field: "My troops did a wonderful job. I was proud of them, they were proud of themselves and properly so. They did a difficult job in this time frame. They were doing it magnificently. They never thought—and I got this everywhere I went—they were getting a fair shake from the media. How the war was reported was important to my troops on the field. They got clippings from home and when they didn't get this credit it was detrimental to their morale."

Boies objected to Westmoreland's speech-making on the witness stand, arguing that the media coverage of the war was not a relevant issue in the case. But Leval dismissed the objection. "The issue of the press has been in this case since the very beginning," he said.

Westmoreland again described in detail how Crile and Wallace had "ambushed" him, done a "hatchet job." Flushed with hurt, he recalled his own and his family's reaction to the hate mail and press abuse he suffered after the CBS broadcast. His wife Kitsy wept quietly from downcast eyes.

In cross-examination, with a two-day interruption to relieve the general's ailing back, Boies managed to befuddle Westmoreland again on numbers and on contradictions from his fifty previous hours of testimony in depositions. Boies even got testy at times, but pulled back short of really attacking this personally impressive witness. It never got hotter than Boies asking sarcastically, "You were the commander of MACV, correct, sir?" "Mr. Boies, you know that," Westmoreland shot back. "Yes, what I'm wondering is whether you forget it, sir." The judge stepped in, like a referee in the ring breaking up a clinch that could lead to foul blows.

The weight of Westmoreland's testimony was that he was fighting against an organized, armed and deadly enemy. That enemy, resupplied by troops flowing in from North Vietnam and sanctuaries in Cambodia and Laos, was not a bunch of untrained, ragged civilians who took pot shots or set up crude booby traps. Westmoreland said he thought of those irregulars as "unarmed elements." Who could be surprised at these conflicting perspectives on the war?

4. Westmoreland says he was not even aware of the scope of the argument until Carver briefed him.

That larger argument had raged, with heated variations, in the 60s and early 70s, on and off the battlefields. It was fought out between the CIA and the military in Vietnam and Washington, in the White House and the Congress, in the newsrooms and on the public squares and in the streets of the United States. It came to be known, in the cliché of the times, as the "other war, winning the hearts and minds of the people," in which we rarely seemed to be succeeding. In the military war, we won battles over and over again without ever achieving victory. Westmoreland fought more conventionally in systematic "search-and-destroy" missions. The "other war" was someone else's job, not really a military matter.

Long after the war, I attended a screening of the first realistic film about Vietnam and the atmosphere of the fighting, *Apocalypse Now*. As I left, a woman in our group said, "I didn't understand that movie. I couldn't tell who was the enemy and who were the friendlies." I told her she had understood both the war and the movie very well.

Two floors down, on the very same day that Westmoreland started his testimony, another general, Ariel Sharon, fifty pounds heavier and from a continent away, waddled confidently into the witness box.

Now both cases were twinned on front pages. "This is very bad for the press," the publisher of a major newspaper said to me one night while both cases were on. More surprisingly, from no competitive instinct but sharing a popular sentiment, a senior corporate executive from another network whispered in my ear, "I hope CBS loses. We all do terrible things on the news."

By the time Westmoreland left the stand, the jury members later said, they felt that he might have been wrong in his views but he certainly seemed neither a liar nor the leader of a secret "conspiracy." Most of them also later said that Westmoreland might have been mistaken in what he did, but it could have been more a difference of opinion than a deception. The judge had repeatedly told them that *fairness* was not an issue in a libel case. Legal issue or not, almost all the jurors—even at that point—felt the program had been unfair to Westmoreland.

Now they wanted to hear CBS's side of the story. Oddly, they began to hear it not from CBS's lawyers or witnesses but from Westmoreland's lawyer, Dan Burt.

9

Judgments

Under the libel law, there is no obligation to be
fair or to present both sides of the story.
—Judge Pierre N. Leval

Daily coverage of trials—whether civil or criminal—can be misleading to the public. This is another built-in shortcoming of everyday news media performance that the media have never solved—nor even given much attention.

In a libel trial reporters do not try to protect, or show bias in favor of, news media defendants. On the contrary, because that would be such an obvious conflict of interest, they lean over backward to avoid the charge. Certainly they did so in the Westmoreland and Sharon cases. But they have another difficulty, especially in newspapers, where the reports are longer and more detailed than the occasional "standuppers" outside courthouses so typical of television's coverage.

Trials are played like most games, inning by inning, or quarter by quarter. They are reported, without odds or point spreads, as the game goes along. The biggest early scores are made at bat or by the side on the offense. In court, the plaintiff (in civil cases) or the prosecution (in criminal) goes to bat or gets the ball first. The defense—CBS, in this case—by exceptional fielding, or interceptions and recovering fumbles, can reduce the advantage in cross-examination. But the defense doesn't really get to mount its offensive, other than in cross-examination, until the accuser is finished.

Reporters in court are chained to the shibboleth of objectivity, that impossible and much overvalued standard implying fairness. No matter how guilty or innocent one side may look at the start—especially in hideous criminal cases—the serious press tries to be evenhanded. The distortion in what the public reads about how the trial is going arises from the sequence of the trial itself. For days on end, when one side is at bat, the press reports that side. The fielding skill of the defendant in cross-examination may rise to prominence, but it is the batter who usually scores most heavily.

If the testimony of a witness lasts more than one day or until very late in the day, there may not be a chance to balance the report with the cross-examination. Trial reporters are in another bind. They have few neutral sources they can quote on the reliability or the importance of the day's events. The adversaries—or their press agents—argue the case outside court as well as inside. They are entirely one-sided, so they are of little help in making evaluations. Judge and jurors are obviously mute and may not even be approached until the trial ends.

In the Westmoreland case, some of the coverage suffered badly from this built-in handicap, especially in the most influential paper of all, the New York *Times*.

Its reporter was Myron Farber, the experienced trial hand, who in 1978 spent time in jail himself for criminal contempt of court after he refused to turn over his notes in a murder trial.[1] For the first weeks of the trial, Farber was entirely accurate but maddeningly misleading. He regularly began his story—and the headline was written from his lead—with the assertions of the witnesses. Because he left the courtroom early and rarely updated his story later, he often missed the cross-examination entirely—as well as the judge's rulings—which could be as important as the original testimony.

One example of this sort of early distortion in the Westmoreland trial: After the testimony of a former intelligence officer in Vietnam, the Washington *Post* headline read: "CONFLICTS ARE SEEN IN TRIAL TESTIMONY, WESTMORELAND WITNESSES SEEM TO AID CBS." The New York *Times* headline and story on the same day gave exactly the opposite impression: "COLONEL DISPUTES CBS DOCUMENTARY AT LIBEL TRIAL."

News coverage has another built-in hazard that afflicts all reporting, not

---

1. Farber had written an investigative story in the *Times* that was followed by the indictment for multiple murders of a New Jersey surgeon, referred to in the story only as "Dr. X." He subsequently was identified as Dr. Mario E. Jascalevich and indicted on a charge of killing patients by injecting them with poisonous curare. After what was at the time the longest trial of a single criminal defendant, Jascalevich was acquitted but his state medical license was later revoked and he moved back to Argentina, where he died. New Jersey Governor Brendan Byrne pardoned both Farber and the *Times* ordering returned $101,000 of the almost $300,000 the *Times* had paid. Byrne said that neither Farber's nor the paper's intent was "to insult or frustrate the judicial process, but to stand on a noble, if sometimes imperfect, principle."

just trials. What's important in an event that has no obvious centerpiece of hard news ("there's no lead") is completely a matter of the judgment of the reporter or editor. They just take their best pick from their impressions, notes or outtakes. In long trials, no matter how dramatic the subject or well known the combatants, days often go by without real news or highlights. Newspapers and wire services that are committed to daily, complete coverage must make judgments, as they always do, of what stood out on a peakless day.

On another day, the Philadelphia *Inquirer* story carried the headline "ONCE-SECRET CABLES INTRODUCED TO REBUT CBS." The Washington *Post* chose a completely different angle: "WESTMORE-LAND TOLD NOT TO INFORM MEDIA." *USA Today* had still another view: "ARMY CABLES SCORE POINTS FOR CBS" and *Newsday* played it safe with the dead-head, "LIBEL TRIAL SEES NEW EVIDENCE."

No one is more sensitive than the news media themselves, and no one gets angrier about what they consider skewed coverage, when they are the subject.

CBS was dismayed over the New York *Times* reporting. It tried to figure out strategies to change the *Times*'s coverage. To whom should the CBS people complain? To the reporter, his editor, the executive editor, the publisher or just to friends on the *Times* who might informally pass on their complaints? What should they do? Nothing formally, they decided, other than vent their anger to one another and anyone else who would listen, including reporters at the trial. Complaining directly might hurt them even more. They were every bit as frustrated and as helpless as are people who try to overcome, with as little success, what they may consider CBS unfairness.

Farber had no bias against CBS in favor of Westmoreland, or against Boies and for Burt. Yet his conventional, chronological system of reporting and his missing cross-examination at the beginning of the trial made CBS look especially bad. By the end, all the participants agreed that if anyone saw it all and added it up, the total press and television coverage gave a fair, impartial account. But very few people saw it all. The public's impression of the trial as it went along varied from city to city and paper to paper.

Is there a better way? I believe that at least two reporters at the Westmoreland trial, David Zucchino of the Philadelphia *Inquirer* and Eleanor Randolph of the Washington *Post,* found one, as did a few others from print and broadcasting, especially National Public Radio's Mike Shuster. Without betraying any consistent favoritism toward either side, they tried to cover in the same story both the charge of the witness and the answer to it. They also wrote impressionistic characterizations of witnesses, lawyers and the atmosphere of the courtroom. That is, of course, hazardous in inexperienced or prejudicial hands but less misleading than straight chronological accounts.

One impression that every journalist covering the trial expressed was that the conventions of "straight" daily reporting prevented the public from knowing how reporters in court really thought the case was going. The coverage concealed the daily judgments of the informal and unsworn jury of reporters (rightly, no one confidently speculated on how the real jury was reacting). Reporters covering the trial talked about the case much more informatively than they wrote about it, which is always a very bad sign of how incomplete their stories may be.

A better way, I believe, would be to do more writing and less stenography. Reporters covering such a trial need to be steeped in pretrial depositions and exhibits offered as evidence (Farber and others were). But they also need to reckon with rulings the judge makes in chambers outside the hearing of the jury, and at the sidebar. In the Westmoreland trial, such exchanges were available at the end of the day, giving those covering the trial for newspapers an opportunity to explain and expand on the courtroom testimony rather than simply record it or save their impressions for weekend pieces.

Such evaluative stories demand that reporters be exceptionally open-minded, self-confident and fair, and will always involve dangers, including the possibility of influencing jurors who see press accounts despite judges' admonitions. But the present system is worse. It can be misleading to the public.[2] As for the jurors, they are more influenced by other factors—predispositions, personalities, loose impressions, misunderstandings—than by fairer and deeper press coverage.

Compare, for example, Zucchino's lead in the *Inquirer* with Farber's in the *Times* on the same day. The *Inquirer*: "With homespun humor and rambling recollections, a self-described 'redneck lieutenant colonel from Mississippi' leisurely fended off questioning yesterday by an attorney for Gen. William C. Westmoreland." The *Times*: "Lawyers for Gen. William C. Westmoreland renewed their efforts in Federal District Court in Manhattan yesterday to show that the general had not concealed higher estimates of enemy strength in South Vietnam in 1967." Is there any

2. In Britain, where the press is much more restricted in most matters, once a trial starts only testimony without comment or characterization can be printed. The integrity of the courtroom is thus preserved. But the public's understanding of what is actually happening in court is severely reduced.

choice? The *Times* apparently thought not. It tried to hire Zucchino eight months after the trial ended. (He stayed with the *Inquirer* and got the new assignment he wanted, covering South and East Africa.)

Then there is the Renata Adler way.

Adler is an intense *New Yorker* writer, a searing critic and accomplished novelist, whose work I have admired. After working for the House Watergate committee and later writing about Nixon's downfall, she became so absorbed in the law's intricacies that, although in her late thirties, she enrolled in the Yale Law School and received a degree in 1979.

Adler, always personally quixotic, showed up infrequently at the Westmoreland trial, more often at the Sharon, mostly to soak up atmosphere. In the spring of 1986, she wrote for the *New Yorker* a two-part, scathing— and in her usual fashion, erratically brilliant—indictment of almost everyone involved on the media side in the Westmoreland and Sharon cases. Her broad conclusions about the arrogance of the media and their abuse of constitutional protections were as right as many of the vehement arguments and some of the information she used in condemning them were wrong.

After taking some notes when she infrequently attended the trials, Adler discovered that it was a "waste of my time since I could get it all from the transcripts." At the heart of her reportorial method was the conviction that reading was better than being there:[3]

> One peculiarity of transcripts and trial depositions is that almost nobody ever reads them. A study, to some small depth, of the transcripts of depositions and trial in *Sharon,* and of certain events at the trial in *Westmoreland,* reveals, with a clarity perhaps greater than that of the litigation as it unfolded day to day, just what the personalities and issues were, and what was decided in the end.

> Depositions make most civil trials unsuitable to coverage, on a daily basis, by the press. In most civil trials the record is for the most part already in, and the only persons to whom it unfolds each day are the spectators and, most critically, the jury. The outcome had nothing to do with Westmoreland's reaction to testimony of any kind. He knew, in substance, what the witnesses were going to say. The litigants know in advance almost everything except how opposing counsel will proceed, how the judge will rule on various questions, and what the jury will decide.

"It was not difficult," she wrote, "when all the testimony was in, to reconstruct what must have happened." But examining her reconstructions "to some small depth," as she wrote in the *New Yorker*'s casual

3. A Bloomsbury wit in England is said to be responsible for the insouciant observation: "People say that life is the thing, but I prefer reading."

style, I found that Adler, this time, falls far short of her own exacting standards.

The trial itself, she seems to be saying, is a mere formality to let the jury in on what everybody else already knows. She writes as if she were a court of appeals judge, yet she went beyond even the appellate method, in which the judges examine the trial record but not the pretrial depositions, unless they become part of the actual court testimony. Judge Adler found virtually everybody guilty of a full range of sins, from foolishness to perjury and subornation: lawyers; Supreme Court and trial judges; CBS and *Time* witnesses; the reporters covering both trials; journalism in general; and CBS and *Time* in particular. At the outset, with the back of her delicate hand, she summarily dismissed the most fundamental historic disagreement about the war in Vietnam: the nature of the enemy.

Adler approaches the Westmoreland case with the overall view that "as an intellectual and historical matter, the thesis that underlay 'The Uncounted Enemy: A Vietnam Deception' was, of course, preposterous," "absurd," "obviously implausible."

Why? Because, she says in a yawning truism, all wars are lost by underestimating enemy strength, so what's new? But the program's focus was not that the *United States* underestimated the enemy's strength. It was the charge that *Westmoreland and his staff* conspired to hide it.

She unquestioningly accepts Westmoreland's argument, writing that the "irregular" forces were "non-combatants, the sympathizers, grandmothers and the children," who "in no official capacity, supported enemy troops. To treat noncombatants or civilians as soldiers would be an outright violation of the Geneva conventions and inhumane." Inhumane? Wars certainly are. But the Geneva Conventions, written between 1864 and 1949, have marginal relevance to modern insurgency wars or terrorism, in which the uniformed, identifiable enemy is only part of the problem. The Geneva codes are about as applicable to the fighting in Vietnam, Lebanon, Central America or Northern Ireland as the Boy Scout oath.[4]

Her analysis of the war itself is so abstract and legalistic that she rejects the central issue in advance on essentially semantic grounds alone. Adler says that "if the size and composition of the enemy" were correct in

4. Westmoreland vehemently disagrees: "I was sensitive to the Rules of Grand Warfare (derivative of the Geneva Conventions)—a subject I had taught at the Army Command and General Staff College. I wanted to bring that out in court but Burt feared that such would bring before the jury the tragic My Lai incident which he would rather avoid. I now regret that I did not insist on making known the importance of the Laws of Grand Warfare."

Adams' estimate, "then the war in Vietnam was not a war but an insurrection." So, in part, are all modern insurgency wars, in which outside military powers recruit or impress to their side adherents who fight in and out of uniform. In more general terms the nature of the enemy was the central issue of the Westmoreland trial, which Adler airily rules out-of-bounds before she even analyzes the actual case.

Both Westmoreland and Sharon were *jury* trials. Jurors are instructed to consider only what takes place and is presented in open court. They do not read depositions unless parts of them are introduced or read in court. They are supposed to rely on what they hear afresh, *their* impression of the credibility of witnesses, which can be very much at odds with a legal interpretation gleaned only from reading the record.

Adler describes testimony of key witnesses that the jurors later said had had the greatest impact on them (e.g. McChristian, Hawkins, Adams, Crile) as "unresponsive," "dishonest," "bumbling," "senseless and maundering," "babbling," "patronizing," "nattering," "rambling," "mulish," "technically inadmissible" and "farcical." She is entitled to her impressions from the transcripts, although not only reporters present but, more important, jurors interviewed after the trial had sharply different reactions to what happened in court.

Adler's underlying premise is that the "fair" and "rightly decided" Supreme Court Sullivan decision, which redefined U.S. libel law, was nonetheless "strange" and "not very carefully reasoned." Neither is she intimidated by lower court judges. When she disagrees with Judge Leval, in her otherwise admiring treatment of him, she brushes him off with the dismissal that it was "one of the few moments of the trial when Judge Leval was not entirely alert."

The only lawyer really to escape Adler's wrath, and whose performance gets a ringing endorsement, is David Dorsen, Burt's deputy at the bar. She had encountered him when he was assistant chief counsel to the Senate Watergate committee and she was working for Congressman Peter Rodino on the House Judiciary Committee. Dorsen, she says, cross-examined CBS witnesses "sweetly but inexorably" and with "devastating effect." Dorsen, who examined major CBS witnesses only toward the end of the trial, displayed unquestionable legal skills. But again the jurors and most reporters found Dorsen a welcome relief from Burt, but his manner ineffective and unimpressive in his brief open-court appearances.

As for the press coverage, there is not a shred of evidence for Adler's charge that it was protective of the media. If anything, the reverse was true. Both CBS and *Time* took far more of a beating in the trial coverage and commentary than either Westmoreland or Sharon. In terms of facts, she also seems unaware that the regular reporters at the trial had read the depositions, contrary to her implication that only she had taken the trouble to get behind the courtroom charade. Reporters also *did* have available to them, in time to make their next day's edition, daily trial transcripts, including the judge's bench, in-chambers and robing-room conferences. Although they reported on these matters, she mistakenly writes that "day to day coverage of trials simply does not include bench conferences."

How does someone with Adler's obvious gifts and intellect go so far astray? The question is puzzling, not to say disturbing, for there is nothing unserious or casual about her work. The explanation may lie not only in the intensity of her opinions when she approaches a story but in the even more important fact that she is more a writer-intellectual than a reporter-journalist. Instead of tracking and reporting the events of her "Two Trials" as they really unfolded, she relies on abstract analysis that often wanders away and distorts what actually happened. That which fascinates her, she at times illuminates brilliantly. That which runs afoul of her interests and views, she illuminates not at all.

One of Adler's familiar and most telling points about the press in general—and both CBS and *Time* specifically—was its arrogant refusal to broadcast or print replies to accusations it makes. But on that subject she was even more vulnerable than those she accused.

Adler's formidable polemic drew cries of pain and anger from CBS and *Time*.

Van Gordon Sauter sent the *New Yorker*'s editor, William Shawn (see page 244), a letter charging "plainly false, gross misrepresentations and distortions of the record, pervasive inaccuracy." Sauter attached a forty-nine-page detailed rebuttal. *Time*'s editor-in-chief, Henry Grunwald (and others from the magazine), also wrote at length to Shawn, including a fifteen-page quarrel with Adler's facts and opinions. Grunwald's letter asked Shawn to break the *New Yorker*'s long "tradition" and "allow a reply or replies to be seen by your readers."

CBS and *Time* were both as angry and frustrated as Westmoreland and Sharon had been. And they got just about the same treatment they had originally dished out. The *New Yorker* stonewalled just as CBS and *Time* had when they were first challenged by Westmoreland and Sharon. The *New Yorker* announced: "The editors here have studied the CBS News [and, by implication, *Time*'s] memorandum carefully. As far as they can see, Ms. Adler's facts are solid and her opinions are supported by her facts."

Shawn, who in manners may be the most polite editor who ever lived, wrote CBS and *Time* similar "Private and Confidential" letters. Shawn said he felt "high regard" and had "the friendliest feelings," the "best personal wishes," but their disagreements were all a matter of "impressions and opinions." He repeated: "Even though Miss Adler's tone was at times severe, her facts, as far as I can see, were solid and her judgments were supported by her facts." He regretted that he saw no reason for his magazine to do anything in print about their complaints. Take that! Gloved in velvet, he displayed the very same unyielding arrogance that had been at the heart of Adler's indictment of the rest of the press.

When the articles later appeared in book form (*Reckless Disregard*, Knopf, 1986), Adler accused CBS (and presumably *Time*) of trying to stop publication by "intimidation" with complaints and requests for corrections. But neither threatened—or ever intended—to sue. They were simply asking for the kind of hearing that Adler berated the media for not giving others and that the *New Yorker* itself refused to give them.

In a "Coda" to her book, Adler said proudly that "the CBS-Cravath harassment did not lead to (or require) a single change in the manuscript." It was a point so evasive and disingenuous that it required tweezers and a magnifying glass to understand it. For, in fact, the book contained several corrections of her magazine pieces—at least one to head off a libel suit by a peripheral trial figure. But the changes she did make, which she neglects to acknowledge or identify, were *not* made, she craftily says, as a result of the "CBS-Cravath harassment."

If Adler, in one sense, knew too much, many other reporters know far too little.

There is an old saw in journalism that "a good reporter can cover any story." If it was ever true, it is certainly not true any longer. The more complex the subject, the more knowledge and background the reporter requires to get it right. Whether it is the police beat or the State Department, the New York subway system or a shot into space, an academic convention or a summit meeting, a war in Central America, a stock market crash or a takeover fight on Wall Street, it helps—indeed it's a necessity—to know something before you start scribbling or rolling the camera. Good general assignment reporters—in print or television—are an invaluable asset. But specialists are an imperative.

Facts are the bricks of journalism, understanding and explanation its mortar. Generalized knowledge or the ability to "take the information down right" is essential but today it is insufficient. Even a well-rounded education, while far better than undergraduate trade-school journalism courses, is no longer enough.

Very few big stories are any longer simple. They are intertwined with economics, law, government, new technology, history, sciences. The essential homework on many an assignment can no longer be done by simply reading the clips. (A shocking number of reporters and researchers, before beginning a new assignment, do not bother with that step, even when they have time.) There is the obverse hazard of having reporters so specialized that they identify more with the subject they are reporting than with the readers or viewers to whom they are reporting. But a deeper understanding of the subject, unless it is the simplest event, is a requirement.

True, the media have recognized this by hiring more specialists, people with particular knowledge, experience or background, as well as an ability to report and write. In an earlier time, we rarely did. People were hired— my contemporaries and I certainly were—for reporting and writing talent. It was assumed we could learn the rest on the job. My first assignment on *Time* was to write about business, even though I did not know the difference between a stock and a bond, much less about the reorganization of a railroad empire, which was one of the first stories I reported and then wrote.

Not that an advanced degree or working experience in a complex field is a necessary qualification to be hired as a reporter or editor. It turns out to be harder to teach specialists journalism than to take the time to educate journalists to become specialists. Undergraduate journalism schools are mostly a way to learn the mechanics to qualify for a beginner's job (an estimated 21,000 bachelor's degrees in "mass communications" were awarded in 1986). Graduate courses in journalism (1,600 master's degrees and 65 Ph.D.'s estimated in 1985) are often in communications research, press history or publishing finance, which have nothing to do with improving the working breed.[4]

A newer and fruitful source of education has been a leave of absence to actually work in the field that reporters and editors have covered. Not long ago—and still in some places today—working in government or politics on leave was thought to be an automatic conflict of interest that disqualified journalists from covering the subject when they returned to the news media. I thought so myself. Now, more sensibly, most news executives

4. Columbia University's and Berkeley's University of California Graduate School of Journalism are among the very few exceptions, where communications research, public relations, advertising and other such subjects are *not* taught. Mid-career fellowships, often financed by the news media, at Harvard, Michigan, Chicago, Yale, Duke, Stanford, Maryland, Ohio State and other universities, where journalists go to study specialized subjects, are particularly useful. In addition fellowships for independent study are offered by the Gannett Center for Media Studies at Columbia University, the Knight-Ridder Center for Specialized Journalism, the Alicia Patterson Foundation and others.

regard working the other side of the street as an invaluable enrichment rather than a handicap. Some editors are even thinking of taking the process a step further, by actually encouraging reporters and paying them to take time to work in the complex fields they cover, then return as much better informed journalists.

As important as knowledge and experience are in journalism, so they are in law.

Dan Burt had a masterful understanding of the materials of the Westmoreland case that was every bit as impressive as his opponent's. He was as quick of mind and compelling in his legal logic as anyone in the court or in the judge's chambers. But he had never tried a jury case before. He was no litigator. Taxes were his specialty, not courtroom tactics. And that began to show.

Burt repeatedly missed opportunities to clinch a point. Frequently, the judge had to tell him he did not understand his questions ("I have found this examination very confusing"). With his own witnesses, Burt by mistake opened doors of vulnerability that allowed Boies to walk in and score points against Westmoreland's case. Burt was so repetitive in his questioning ("Send him back to law school," one reporter muttered) and so slow getting to his conclusions that he used up valuable time against the 150-hour allotment for his entire case.[5]

Reporters and neutral spectators in the court were disappointed, not in Burt himself but in the larger consequences of his fumbling. In the pretrial brief, he had sharply raised a popular public issue: Should the law demand a new accountability from the news media because they are so different from and so much more powerful than they were when the older laws were crafted? The ultimate answer to such a question could easily end up in the Supreme Court. It also could bring an opinion—for or against the news media—approaching the importance of the landmark Sullivan decision twenty years earlier. Instead the Westmoreland trial began to become a contest in mismatched courtroom skills.

Nowhere did Burt's inexperience show more than when he began that essential part of his case in which he was required to prove to the jury that CBS knew the program was wrong but ran it anyway. For that he would have to delve deeply into the editing and reporting process, the way the story and the program were put together. He would have to demonstrate how his catalog of complaints against CBS's methods added up to a

5. Anthony S. Murry, one of the lawyers on his staff closest to Burt, says: "An important factor in this was the simple physical fatigue that Dan was suffering by this time."

punishable offense. He needed not only to prove actual malice but to extract a new accountability from the news media. The leading witness he called and hoped to attack on that point was George Crile, who was as responsible for the broadcast's flaws as he was for its strengths.

For Burt, Crile was a vulnerable and wounded prey.

He had been repeatedly and severely criticized in CBS's own internal Benjamin Report for violating the network's rules while producing the program. He had later been suspended by an embarrassed, fed-up CBS when it discovered that Crile had been taping telephone conversations without telling the people he was interviewing; if the network had not been in the middle of a libel suit, it might have fired him. Crile's own lawyers said they worried about the impression he would make on the jury. He had to look confident but not arrogant, substantial but not overbearing, unar-gumentative but not wimpy. For CBS he was potentially the most hazard-ous witness.

But Burt got nowhere with him. Elementary law school text dictates that in a trial a lawyer never asks a hostile witness "why" he did something; that affords the witness too great an opportunity to give explanations instead of answering accusations. Burt repeatedly gave Crile that chance. Crile responded with long, quiet and often impressive an-swers, intelligently explaining how investigative journalists work on a story they consider of high public significance.

Even when Burt attacked him for rearranging the Hawkins interview so it appeared as if Hawkins were describing one set of figures as "crap" when he was actually talking about another, Crile slipped away. He said that Hawkins had used just that word about the figures at issue off camera so it was an "absolutely accurate portrayal of Hawkins' views." Print reporters, Crile pointed out, do just that all the time. But there is real difference between visual reporting on television, which has the appear-ance of actuality, and quoting words in print, which everyone knows is fragmentary.[6] Burt did not pounce on Crile for blurring that distinction. His weapon was sarcasm rather than the devastating disdain of a more experienced lawyer.

6. Crile says: "I have long since given up trying to defend this editing decision but I can't help pointing out that the "crap" quote is given in the midst of a chain of questions about contemporaneous figures. It can be read to refer to both old and new figures. Hawkins, in depositions, stated that I had faithfully portrayed his views. He confirmed that the old and new figures were the same and that both were "crap." I would do it differently were I to have the chance. But I did not consciously do what you say I did. I recognize, however, that this attempt to explain what happened has fallen on deaf ears before and I only comment on it because it is the truth as I understand it."

Crile conceded nothing on coaching witnesses, taking statements out of context or giving friendly spruces an unfair advantage. He justified his secret recording of telephone conversations as a "back up for my note-taking." As to trapping Westmoreland when he was unprepared, Crile said, "You are talking about a four-star general. Eisenhower, Patton or MacArthur wouldn't have to review their records." He saw no reason to give Westmoreland the opportunity "to deny the undeniable." From her seat in the courtroom, while her husband shook his head incredulously, Kitsy Westmoreland muttered, "I've never heard West called a liar to his face before. Jesus!"

During close to thirty hours—longer than the testimony of any other witness—Burt unsuccessfully tried to upset Crile's well prepared testimony. But when Burt attacked him frontally for his choice of people to interview and his editing, Crile curbed his combative instincts and answered with patient aplomb. "The TV medium," Crile explained, "can bring you people who were participants. For a print reporter it is considerably easier because he can pick it up and paraphrase. It is particularly difficult for any reporter to convince a person to come forward and acknowledge with their own name involvement in some kind of official misconduct." It was almost unprecedented, he said, for so many witnesses to confess to conduct that "did not reflect well on their personal involvement."

Under Boies' friendly cross-examination, Crile displayed a thoughtful knowledge of the issues in the war and a mastery of the materials that went into the broadcast. Few reporters, under any circumstances, could demonstrate a deeper immersion in their subject.

If there was any doubt how hard it has been purposely made to win in court against the press, the Westmoreland case repeatedly offered the example. In the middle of Crile's testimony—and unknown to the jury—Westmoreland's side suffered its biggest setback. Judge Leval issued an order that underscored again how steep an uphill climb it is for a public person to win a libel suit against the press.

In his chambers, after having read and heard arguments for months, Leval issued a ruling in favor of CBS. The critical Benjamin Report, on which much of Burt's malice argument rested, could not be used in court. Leval's ruling:

> The Benjamin Report is largely irrelevant to the issues before the jury. The jury would not be permitted to consider whether the publisher had acted fairly or unfairly—only whether he acted in reckless or knowing disregard of the truth. If it is the case that various internal rules of CBS were broken in the making of

the documentary, that fact has no bearing on whether the documentary was made in reckless or intentional disregard of the truth.

From the beginning of the suit, Burt boasted that he couldn't wait to get his hands on the CBS crowd.

But he had made no headway with Crile, his main target. His next witness, thirty-three-year-old Ira Klein, the youngest witness at the trial, was to be his star attraction. A free-lance film editor, Klein had worked for Crile, physically putting the program together. After leaving CBS and refusing to talk to its lawyers, Klein had helped Burt prepare his case. He also was the main inside source for a prosecutorial book attacking CBS, *A Matter of Honor,* by Don Kowet, the co-author of the original *TV Guide* exposé. Burt was expecting Klein to unmask what he considered the program's tricky editing and shoddy ethical practices. On the stand, Klein turned out to be a dud. He displayed so much slanderous personal animus toward Crile and others at CBS, and so little involvement in the substance of the program, that he added nothing to Burt's case. He appeared to be the office crank rather than the conscience of CBS Reports.

Westmoreland's case was stumbling on the witness stand and being trampled by Judge Leval's ruling on the Benjamin Report. Burt had another alarming problem. He was running out of time. Judge Leval warned him that he might not be "well in control of his time budget." So Burt radically changed his game plan.

He decided to rely on cross-examining CBS's witnesses instead of calling them himself. He abruptly canceled his plans to call to the stand everyone from Wallace, Adams and Benjamin, to Stringer and the program's chief researcher, Alex Alben. He even abandoned his dramatic plan to end his case with a curtain-lowering finale of Westmoreland's wife testifying about how much the program had hurt the Westmoreland family. Instead, he suddenly rested his case.

The Westmoreland side would have to try to repair the damage with cross-examination of CBS's witnesses. Though the floundering Burt still remained in charge, most of that cross-examining counterattack would now be mounted by David Dorsen, the former federal prosecutor on the Westmoreland legal team. (Burt belatedly insisted that he had always intended for Dorsen to play that role.)

A chastened Burt rose for a mini-summary of his client's case. It was very mini, five minutes in all: "There was no suppression, no deception. Eighteen men came from all over this country and subjected themselves to cross-examination, took the time, risked their reputations and their dignity so that you could learn first hand what had taken place."

He had succeeded in raising doubts about the accuracy and certainly the fairness of the broadcast, largely by using outtakes and his best witness, Westmoreland. But he was still in the foothills of a legal mountain he had not even begun to climb.

After forty-five days, even with the advantage of presenting his case first, Burt was about even with CBS on the question of whether the program was substantially true. And he was far behind in demonstrating a dishonest "state of mind," i.e. "actual malice," which, though the words were forbidden in Judge Leval's courtroom, remains the hardest and the final test in a libel suit by a public figure.

"We are about to start the defendants' case," Boies told an attentive jury, still refreshed by a two-week Christmas recess, "and I would probably be overly optimistic if I promised you light at the end of the tunnel quite yet." The light was to shine sooner than he predicted. It beamed from three of the trial's most powerful witnesses.

After building a foundation of depositions and testimony from junior officers who described how they rigged the enemy intelligence figures, Boies brought on Sam Adams, who was invited to describe the research on which the program was based. "The so-called numbers," Adams said, "were actually people who were killing American soldiers. The grunts had to fight these people."

As the snow fell hard outside, Adams's tweedy but unpolished earnestness warmed up the courtroom. He sounded more like an appealing moralist than a vengeful vigilante. Westmoreland's witnesses had described him as a fanatic with a mad obsession. There was no doubt he had a passion. But he certainly appeared more like one of St. Francis of Assisi's disciples than Machiavelli's. Myron Farber of the New York *Times,* loosening up from his stilted earlier coverage, evoked the view of most in the courtroom when he wrote that "for a man who will soon be portrayed on cross-examination as both mistaken and 'obsessed,' Mr. Adams appeared guileless."

Why was he so dedicated to the subject? Adams said quietly but with dramatic effect that he had "visited the Vietnam memorial and asked myself, how many of those were killed probably by people not listed in the order of battle, trying to figure the odds, it was probably a third, maybe as much as a half. When intelligence has failed that badly, I think that ought to come to light, so we don't repeat the same mistake."

Dorsen managed to show that Adams' prodigious notes and memory were not as infallible as they may have sounded. And he got Adams to confirm that he had written a letter three days before the broadcast that said, "There's a major problem: the documentary seems to pin the rap on General Westmoreland when it probably belongs higher than that."

Both Adams and Crile had only a limp answer to that major flaw in the broadcast. They said that LBJ's culpability was a different story, which they felt was much harder to document than their charges against Westmoreland and his command. So they homed in on Westmoreland. But that was no more justifiable in journalism than it would be in police work. It was the equivalent of accusing someone of robbery because there was proof he drove the robber's car but no compelling proof of the real thief's guilt; then sending the driver to jail while letting the crook go free. The program had not said Westmoreland was an accessory to a government conspiracy. It plainly accused him of initiating and leading it.

Boies called Crile back on the stand and, as he had done with Adams, showed the jury the entire program. He stopped the tape at every key point, asking Crile to justify what was behind every scene, while the jury watched on the courtroom screens. When the program and Crile's libretto were finished, Boies challenged Burt to ask Crile whether he really believed that the points made about Westmoreland were true or not.

To everyone's surprise, Burt declined the offer to cross-examine Crile further. Instead he said with his biggest, most boyish grin: "I spent a lot of time asking Mr. Crile why he put in that broadcast what he put in. We've all been here a long time and we're not fighting over nothin'."

Burt's new insouciance was neither a tactic nor a personality change. He had already used up 140 of his 150 hours. More important, his case was losing its early momentum and Burt his brassy confidence. There was dissension in his own camp. The Westmorelands were increasingly disappointed and put off by his overbearing and rough off-stage manner. His own legal staff and advisers became sharply critical of his courtroom tactics and his management of the case.

Two other CBS witnesses destroyed him—and left his client hurt and reeling.

The first was Major General Joseph McChristian. For the two-year period in question he was Westmoreland's intelligence chief. He was also the highest-ranking officer on the CBS program to testify to the withholding of reports of higher enemy figures. Just before the broadcast, McChristian made a note summarizing a memorable phone call he had received:

> About 9 P.M. General Westmoreland phoned. He talked about 30 minutes and stated that based on my statement that he would not send my report of higher strengths to Washington because it was not political to do so, was the basis for his integrity being impugned. I replied that I only spoke the truth on what I knew. He is very upset. He said he thought our conversation was private and official between West Pointers. I replied that I spoke the truth. He said that he did not question my integrity but maybe my judgment—that I had been used by

CBS. He repeated several times that he is a public figure and cannot sue anyone. He said that he has stood up and took the brunt of Vietnam for all of us. He as much as accused me of being the one mainly responsible for his integrity being impugned. He said two or three times "Sam Adams has won." He intends to have a press conference Monday and Graham and others have volunteered to be present and support him. I did not volunteer.

On the witness stand McChristian confirmed much of his old boss's account of the crucial meeting of the two in Westmoreland's Saigon office. He added that although Westmoreland had "every right to question the intelligence, this isn't what happened at that meeting. This was the only time he ever exercised any control over my reporting and I was being asked to hold up information based upon a political consideration. It was improper."

He also talked graphically about the casualties inflicted by the uncounted enemy. He held up a homemade hand grenade and described the sticks-and-stones arms industry of the Viet Cong, who cut through unexploded U.S. bombs with hacksaws to get fresh explosives for their own.

McChristian admitted he had complained to Crile after the program that his answer to one hypothetical question made him sound as if he were tarring Westmoreland on the program, which is just what he did in court. McChristian explained: "There's a difference in answering under oath and talking to a journalist on the phone."

As they had entered the court, the two old West Pointers—both with outstanding military careers—accidentally encountered each other and exchanged civilities. McChristian was ill at ease. Westmoreland had not expected him to appear in person in court and enjoyed the encounter even less. Now not only journalists, junior officers and civilians in government had accused Westmoreland. He could painfully take that. But not the assault of a brother in arms, linked forever, he thought, by the West Point code. It appeared, said Westmoreland later, as if McChristian had "shaken the long gray line."

Then came the second military witness everybody was waiting for. He had already appeared in the courtroom on videotape. His outtake was damaging to CBS. Now he was live, testifying in a courtroom as jammed with spectators as it had been on the day the trial began almost four months earlier. Retired Colonel Gains Hawkins, sixty-five, was the seventeenth CBS witness, his face as red and as furrowed as the Mississippi farmland where he had been raised.

During the Vietnam War he headed the order of battle section, under General McChristian. Their operation was the central issue of the CBS program as well as the trial. Retired in 1970, Hawkins now ran a nursing home in West Point, Mississippi. It did not take much imagination to envision the roly-poly retired colonel jawing with his boarders in rocking chairs under the shade of a southern pine.

From the moment he mounted the witness stand, he peered directly at the jury through his heavy, horn-rimmed glasses. His earthy manner and self-deprecating good humor kept judge, jury and courtroom spectators bathed in laughter. "Country Boy Has Judge & Jury In Stitches," said a New York *Daily News* headline. At first he was rambling and nervous but he radiated warm, homespun directness. He described how, under Mc-Christian's orders, he attempted to develop more reliable figures on the enemy than the old Vietnamese numbers the Americans had been using.

When he began to wander off the point in describing how he put together intelligence estimates—"like a journalist, but that's not my business, but integrity—" the judge interrupted him. Hawkins apologized, "I'm sorry, sir. I am wrapped up in the subject. If you would tap me on the shoulder, I will shut up when you say so."

Hawkins said they "skewed and screwed" the figures so as "to attrite the enemy" by analysis rather than by battle. He described Adams, then in the CIA, as so honest "he made me a little ashamed of myself at times." In the outtake Burt had earlier shown, Hawkins said he had never been given any direct instructions to cut the estimates. "I deduced it," he had said on the tape. "I was not given any specific orders. This was the message I perceived."

On the stand he said he told Crile that responsibility for the "intelligence fraud" went right back to Westmoreland himself.

The general, he said, told him at a briefing that the new figures were "politically unacceptable." Hawkins confirmed testimony of other witnesses, who related that Westmoreland had asked, in obvious consternation, what could he "tell the President, the Congress and the press?" Westmoreland, he remembered, had answered his own question by suggesting "we'd better take another look at these figures." Why did Hawkins tell Crile all this and why was he now confirming it in court? "The war was over then," answered Hawkins, "there was need for an after-action report."

"General Westmoreland had established a ceiling," he said. Although he never got the direct order to stay under it from Westmoreland himself, other senior officers had constantly told Hawkins to bring his estimates in line with the ceiling. He recalled that he finally told them, in exasperation: "If you don't like these figures you just make up your own rules and I'll carry out the orders."

In the most carefully prepared exchange, Boies asked him whether he thought the numbers he was ordered to report represented the best available. Hawkins answered, "No sir, they did not. They represented *crap.*" It was as pat as it could be, intended to back up Crile's testimony that although it appeared on the outtake that Hawkins used the word to describe different figures, the reality was that he meant the ones in question as well.

As Hawkins got more accusatory, his bearing became crisply military. He began to spit out answers like a West Point plebe in a choking collar responding to an upperclassman at inspection time. Boies asked him whether he bore any personal ill will toward Westmoreland: "No, sir," Hawkins snapped. "I carried out these orders as a loyal officer in the United States Army, sir," he barked in an even louder voice. Westmoreland sat flushed and stonefaced at the plaintiff's table.

At the end of his direct examination, Boies asked Hawkins whether he knew how serious his charges against Westmoreland were. A choked Hawkins, almost sobbing, quietly answered, "Yes, sir." Was he absolutely certain, Boies repeated for climactic effect? "Yes," he answered looking right at Boies, "I feel certain."

In cross-examination, Dorsen's low-key, studious city manner was no match for Hawkins' disarming old-boy palaver.

When he asked Hawkins whether the enemy lied about its strength, Hawkins drawled that the Viet Cong were "just like Democrats and Republicans in the way they all do some lying now and then and you find some once in a while who will tell you the truth." Dorsen complained that Hawkins had been "prepared to an incredible extent," and that CBS lawyers and Adams had visited him about ten times in Mississippi.

In open court Dorsen made a similar accusation. Hawkins said yes, he had read documents, affidavits and depositions, like every other witness. "Is this evil, sir?" he jauntily asked the solemn lawyer. Dorsen then read him the draft of an unpublished article Hawkins had written describing his intelligence boss General McChristian: "A cold, relentlessly ambitious man. He had a passion to excel. He drove his staff subordinates unmercifully. He drove himself with no more mercy; he was not a likable man." Hawkins was unfazed. "I think General McChristian might be proud of this statement," he said.

But there was nothing funny about the effect of his testimony on the jury.[7] If it was a question of honor, truth and patriotism, Hawkins was

---

7. Westmoreland lawyer Murry says: "In fairness, Hawkins was unable to testify to more than that *he* had done things *he* disagreed with, or even thought were wrong. Judge Leval's discussion and criticism of how CBS conducted the direct examination of Hawkins shows how little he actually could testify to. The press corps may have been livened up by the Hawkins' road show, but the facts were only muddied."

every bit as impressive in his homespun folksiness as Westmoreland had been in his stiff, rocklike formality. Hawkins supported CBS as relentlessly as Crile and Adams—with the added advantage that he had been in Vietnam at the time. He was also the admitted executor of what CBS charged was a conspiracy.

Two floors below, Ariel Sharon faced a different kind of accuser.

10

Winners and Losers

*It is an important vindication of Time's
reputation.*
—Henry Grunwald,
Editor-in-Chief,
Time. Inc.

I came here to prove that Time *magazine lied. We
were able to prove that* Time *did lie. I feel we
have achieved what brought us here.*
—Minister Ariel Sharon

CBS's problem in the Westmoreland case was not its sources. They were identified and most appeared on the program. In the Sharon-*Time* case the sources were invisible.

There is no more troublesome dilemma in journalism than the use of unidentified sources. Readers and viewers want to know: Who said that? How do you know? Who made that charge? What or who is your authority for reporting that? The answers are rarely either easy or satisfactory.

Consumers of news have a right to be suspicious of unnamed "authorities," "observers" (thoughtful, informed and longtime) of one scene or another, "sources close to" the president, the mayor, law enforcement officials and endless other substitutes for naming names. Anonymity, of course, is often abused by sources with motives of their own. Reporters can also hide behind anonymity as a dodge to conceal the fuzziness or shakiness of their information.

There is an easy solution, say many non-journalists. Tell us who or what is behind what you are reporting or don't tell us at all. That way there is no mystery, no cowardly accusation, no hiding behind masks. Such disclosure would also require reporters to work harder to document their stories. Above all, it would be fairer and more honest. The press would then be engaged in forthright disclosure. No evasions.

But there is a price for that remedy. It is so high as to be unacceptable, not only to the press but to the public. Full disclosure would eliminate much of the most valuable information and insights that regularly appear in news stories. Unnamed or unmentioned sources are more than a starting point for exposés. They are also essential to most explanations, assessments and analyses.

Every day unidentified sources are used in dozens of stories, in some of the best reporting in the world, "Political observers," "sources in the industry," "high officials in the government," "foreign ministry officials." Eliminate them and gone would be most of the candor, much of the explanation and the real opinions, personalities and behind-the-scenes events that move the world. Gone also would be a large percentage of the valuable, accurate and important stories that appear in print and on the air. Frequently there are good—not malign—reasons why many valuable sources of information and illumination would rather talk, or would speak much more freely, without being quoted by name, if the reporter lets them. On a not unusual day, the Washington *Post* attributed information to unidentified sources 106 times in the entire paper, the New York *Times* just about as many, and the *Wall Street Journal,* 42 in one story alone.

Even if it were possible to name a source for everything, in many stories identifying each name in the collective group would be no service to readers or viewers. Doing so would clutter up stories with names, titles and origins, which in many cases are unfamiliar and unnecessary. Readers and viewers would never find the story midst the who's who of irrelevancies. Without anonymous sources there would also be far less investigative reporting in the public interest.

But there are times when the use of anonymous sources is indefensible. For example, when a serious factual charge is leveled anonymously, with the victim's having no chance to answer and little awareness of where the charge came from; or where no effort is made either to describe the possible motives of the unidentified sources or to pinpoint what type of sources they were. Some sense of the origin of an accusation can be as newsworthy as the information itself, as for instance, one faction in government trying to undermine another or one person engaging in a vendetta against another for self-serving reasons.

Hairline decisions are often involved. In political campaigns, damaging material often comes on a non-attribution basis from opposing political camps (e.g. the damaging Senator Biden plagiarism tape—see page 16). If the material is factual and can be proved without the anonymous source, some reporters feel no obligation to indicate the source's intentions. Perhaps the information—if it is real information—is much more important than where it came from. But even then every effort should be made at least to characterize its origin, such as a "rival campaign" or a source "hostile to" the person involved. In the Biden-Dukakis story, the Des Moines *Register* did just that, but the New York *Times* gave no hint.

Out of a concern for fairness, more and more news organizations have recently been refusing to repeat unattributed criticisms and charges unless the accuser can be identified or unless there is independent confirmation. The New York *Times* (and an increasing number of other papers) has a policy that mandates "Shun anonymous pejorative quotations. When negative remarks are newsworthy, as they often are, we try to get them on the record. Failing that, we paraphrase them, signal the source's motive as closely as we can, and print responses from the other side." The Associated Press is even more stringent. It rejects favorable or unfavorable opinions if the source cannot be mentioned, only using unattributed sources "on matters of fact, when it is not available from any other source, but we make clear in the story that the person providing this material would do so only on the condition of anonymity." And the Los Angeles *Times* has a rule "when there is no other way to obtain information, we do all we can to describe for the reader where the source is coming from."

It's a trade-off. The simplistic remedy of always identifying sources could never be worth trading for the abuses that come from anonymity.

But what about the abuses? All conscientious journalists strive for sources they can identify. When they cannot identify sources, they must rely on their own—and their editors'—judgment of whether the value of the information, background or opinion is greater than the value of sacrificing it because it cannot be tied to some person.

The strictly numerical rule that at least two or three independent sources are necessary for confirmation is a formula that sounds better than it is. Two or three can be as wrong or as misleading as one.[1] No absolutes can govern the subject of sources. Everything depends on the reliability of the reporter, on the judgment of the editors about the credibility of the sources and on the possibility of independent proof, or some explanation of the motives of those sources who refuse to be named.

One prevailing myth, widely repeated, is completely contrary to my own experience. I have never had a reporter working for me who, after guaranteeing anonymity to a source, would not tell me who the source was

1. Writes historian Robert Lacey: "To anybody else venturing into the field I would suggest inverting a widespread journalistic rule of thumb: if you get information that only one source can confirm, it may possibly be true; if two sources confirm it, tread warily; and the more people repeat it thereafter, the higher you have risen into the clouds of what the world would like to believe true—and probably isn't."

if I asked. Reporters, even good ones, can be misled or blindsided. It never seemed to me a breach of the reporter's confidential relationship to tell at least his boss before the story was printed. Since the romance of Watergate's "Deep Throat" (who, I believe, without knowing, was a created composite, not one person), I am told that some editors no longer want to know the source of a hazardous story they are about to print or put on the air. I find that hard to believe, except as a charade to limit liability in case of trouble.

In the Sharon case, *Time*'s managing editor, Ray Cave, said he did not know the confidential sources of the disputed items in the cover story because for him to know would be "at least a fractional violation of confidentiality." Not to me.

Unnamed sources, or the vaguer attribution "reportedly," cannot be banished entirely. They can only be used more carefully, especially when they are putting out pejorative charges. And they should seldom be used to make a specific and factually damaging assertion against an individual, unless it is so important that the editors are willing to go out on a shaky limb, knowing that if they are wrong they will suffer the consequences.

In the Sharon case, *Time* climbed out on just such a limb. Claiming only sources it did not, perhaps because it could not, disclose, it accused Sharon "reportedly" of an act it had "learned" of. It said the evidence was in a secret Appendix B, which it had not seen but others had. It did not tell Sharon of the charge to get his response in advance and made only routine efforts to reach him. Nor was the accusation a key that unlocked the larger story. It was incidental to the documented main story, which was damaging enough to Sharon, *Time* seemed to be including the paragraph not because it was essential but because it was exclusive and offered the ultimate "proof" of Sharon's character.

As a witness at the trial, Sharon had none of Westmoreland's appeal. Sharon was blustering and long-winded, almost as uncontrollable in the courtroom as he had been on the battlefield.

It was *Time*'s unwillingness to concede any error that helped Sharon's case most. *Time* staffers could offer no hard evidence or proof of their charge. Their unfamiliar editorial system was held up to ridicule for its performance rather than being admired for its checks and balances.

The few words *Time* said it had "learned" took on a far greater importance than the much more significant condemnation Sharon had already suffered from Israel's Kahan Commission, which had bluntly accused him of at least "indirect responsibility" for the massacre because he had ignored the high probability that it would occur.

From researcher to editor-in-chief, a parade of witnesses described the

Time system. Step by step they went through how it was used in the Sharon cover story, all expressing both confidence in reporter Halevy and belief in the story. Halevy on the stand was not required to name his sources, only to suffer whatever consequences there could be for not doing so. They were variously described as sources "1,2,3 and 4" or as sources "A, B and C," or two unnamed Israeli generals, a government official and someone connected to Israel intelligence.

Halevy was forced into two humiliating admissions. First, when he was asked how he knew the evidence was in Appendix B, he replied that he "inferred" it "based on my knowledge of 43 years living in Israel," rather than actually knowing it was there. Then he was challenged to describe what he meant by Sharon's giving the Gemayels "the feeling" he understood their need for revenge. Halevy could only reply weakly that it "could be a body movement, could be silence, could be a non-outspoken rejection of their raising the issue and could also be indifference to the fact." In life, such confirmations are standard fare. In a courtroom, with its rigorous standards of proof, they sounded preposterous. Halevy's admissions were disastrous for *Time*.

Sharon's side had called fourteen witnesses, *Time* none—relying on cross-examination to make its case. In the two years before the trial, many Israelis, enemies as well as advocates of Sharon, had clearance to read the secret appendix. They told everyone, including *Time* staffers, that there was no such evidence in Appendix B. *Time* itself began to believe it was quite likely wrong on what it called that "minor" point. But the editors refused to withdraw it or apologize. They said they had not been allowed to see all the documents and were in the middle of a libel suit, which was not the moment for retractions. Shaken by a growing awareness that Appendix B offered no support for its case, *Time* belatedly announced it would "print a correction or retraction of its story, as appropriate," if there was proof it had been wrong.

Finally, to break the deadlock over what was or wasn't in Appendix B, both sides agreed to have it read by the man who had headed the Israeli commission, Judge Kahan himself. He would answer a questionnaire from Judge Abraham D. Sofaer, the trial judge, in the presence of lawyers for both Sharon and *Time*. The trial was adjourned, while the inspection took place in Jerusalem. There Kahan conclusively said the appendix contained neither the "evidence" nor even the "suggestion" that *Time* had said it did. Even though they had agreed to accept Kahan's inspection of Appendix B and its supporting material, *Time* and its lawyers strenuously objected that they had been denied access to notes not included in the report. But their argument was crumbling. They sounded more like high-handed sore losers than high-minded journalists.

At last, on the very day the jury went out to consider its verdict, *Time* printed the promised retraction, almost two years later than it should have done. The magazine admitted error on Appendix B and expressed regret, but said it was "relatively immaterial" to the case and "*Time* stands by the substance of the paragraph in question."

I spent some twenty gratifying years working in journalism at Time Inc. So I may be forgiven for taking personally both *Time*'s response to the Sharon case and its outcome.

I had hired some of the principal journalists involved, and the Worldwide memo that triggered the whole uproar was my invention. It would be vain, not to say absurd, for me to feel any residual responsibility for that staff or its methods at this late date. I don't. I know them to be accomplished professionals who take their work seriously in a system as careful, by present intent, as any in journalism. Lest there be any confusion on where I stand, I also believe that *Time* itself has become a better magazine in most respects year after year since I left.

But I was a senior contributor to and perpetuator of the climate that is widely called *Time*'s "arrogance." The difference may be that my perspective has changed over the years. So has *Time*'s in major ways—but little or not at all in one way. Not at least until right after the Sharon trial. Why is *Time* (along with other news media) so grudging about admitting mistakes?

Is it really the special "arrogance" of *Time*, or the swaggering of journalists altogether? It is some of both. Once committed in print or on the television screen, news people—more than other humans—hate to admit they were wrong. That feeling is so strong that even in the face of arguable contrary evidence, they tend to convince themselves their story was right and hold their ground. They work hard on stories. They have apparatuses and chains of responsibility that try to get things right and fair. They are committed to what they finally report. Serious journalists tell themselves, at times much too grandly, that they are acting in the public's interest.

They are also surrounded by critics. Many of these are plainly whiners and self-serving axe-grinders, whose narrow purpose is to have stories come out the way they want. The complaints and petitions for corrections are often questionable, matters of opinion or without merit. As a result of torrents of complaints that have little or no validity, journalists develop a reflex of suspicion and defensiveness, which is automatically activated whenever their work is challenged. They would rather fight on a marginal issue to seem right than retract in public and admit they were, or might be, wrong.

At *Time,* as well as elsewhere in the news media, such one-sided stubbornness has been a tradition. I must have said to complainers more than a hundred times, "Write us a letter." Then there was the inevitable question, "Will you print it?" No assurances. Let's see the letter first. Or for years, whenever any aggrieved caller mentioned even the possibility of a libel suit, I would end the discussion. "Libel? Don't talk to me. Call our lawyers."

If the caller chose to write a letter, there were other obstacles besides the uncertainty of having it printed. Was it worth printing? When it was, it was most often severely cut without consulting the writer. If it was answered at all in print, the most frequent reply was an elliptical *"Time* stands by its story." No further explanation or justification. Occasionally, the letter was rebutted in an editor's note, of course giving the magazine the last word. In very rare cases, and always on minor matters, was the letter followed by the two or three reluctant words, *"Time* erred" or *"Time* regrets the error."

Admitting error was subliminally felt to be the opening wedge in undermining the aura of authority *Time* tried to convey. It is also reasonable to question why the victim of a clear mistake should be required to write a letter to have it corrected. But other kinds of corrections were not regularly to be found in *Time.* As a matter of policy, a letter printed and unanswered was considered to be a correction—but only by the editors. *Time* readers were said by the magazine to "understand" that. *(Newsweek* and *U.S. News & World Report* usually adhered to the same policy.) The *New Yorker,* uniquely and even more indefensibly, publishes no letters from readers, a policy that both CBS and *Time* found intolerable when the *New Yorker's* editor applied it to them.

The news media have all kinds of ways of avoiding an open admission that they have made a big error. One of the most memorable mistakes— and famous evasions—was the Chicago *Tribune's* renowned premature banner headline, "Dewey Defeats Truman." When the vote was going just the other way, the *Trib's* final election-day issue "corrected" itself only by replacing the banner with "Early Dewey Lead Narrow."

I know of only once in the past when the phrase *"Time* erred" was inserted in the body of a story. It was on Luce's orders. He wrote it in himself in an effort to tamp down a firefight within the magazine's staff over a story the week before in the Press section. It had savagely and wrongly criticized correspondents in Vietnam for lazy, distorted, pessimistic reporting. Luce told me with some puckish glee, "Well that's a first. At least we admitted we were wrong in the story itself." But he was wrong. His insertion proved such a trauma to the magazine's managing editor,

Otto Fuerbringer, that after Luce and I had left the building, the editor took out the exculpatory two words just as the magazine was going to press. The managing editor knew that Luce would admire his guts in censoring even his super-boss. Our Saigon bureau chief, Charles Mohr, with my support, bitterly complained about the distortion of his reporting on press performance. He quit and was immediately hired by the New York *Times*.

The tradition of self-righteousness lingered on, right through the Sharon case. It is not fake conviction, it is true belief. To this day many of the editors and writers at *Time* believe that the "essence," as they call it, of their Sharon paragraph was right (and it could be), even though they had to say they were wrong about the confirmation being in Appendix B. If you believe you're right, many journalists argue, isn't it even more dishonest to concede you are wrong just because you are honor bound not to reveal publicly the source of your proof? They call that sticking to their principles. The public calls it arrogance or being unwilling to put up or shut up.

Journalists should not expect to be blindly trusted, any more than doctors, judges or mystics. They cannot simply say "Believe us, have confidence in us, we have the public's interest at heart, unlike the self-servers who are attacking us." It is not enough for the press to offer only a plea for faith in its truthfulness without proof of its facts.

Time had another problem. Over the years, lawyers had played second or third fiddle to editors. As a matter of policy, they never advised editors what to print or what not to. They simply pointed out what was actionable in law and what *Time*'s exposure would be. Editors made all the decisions. Beyond that kind of advice, the lawyers did not tell editors what to say or not to say in public, or how to conduct themselves with other members of the press. In the Sharon case, *Time* abdicated its editorial independence and allowed itself to be governed by its lawyers.[2]

News executives under fire often take the position that they say what they have to say in print or on the air, so there's no need for them to go beyond that, a privilege they find intolerable in others. They are only slightly less inaccessible and inept in answering press queries than most

2. As in many another company, Time Inc. has expanded in so many fields (magazines, cable, films, video, records, books, acquisitions, etc.) that in addition to retaining outside counsel—such as Cravath and other firms—for litigation and different matters, Time Inc. now has 57 in-house lawyers. Most work on corporate affairs. Eight work in the magazine group. As late as the early 70s, there were only three full-time Time Inc. staff lawyers, along with outside counsel.

lawyers. Many lawyers—with notable exceptions—make the mistake, if they do respond to reporters, of being as circumspect as they would be in addressing a judge. They would do far better if they talked to journalists as they do to jurors. Lawyers tend to protect and nurture their case in court as if there were no court of public opinion outside. Yet the way major civil suits are covered in the press can be as helpful or as damaging to clients as the outcome in the courtroom.

On the advice of lawyers, *Time* was frozen into the kind of silence it never accepts from others. The magazine's own reporters covering the trial, warned that they could create a further trial record, were required to have their reports vetted by lawyers, before sending them through normal channels. *Time*'s staff was as closemouthed in public as a Mafia don without his lawyer. Until after the trial, they left their talking to their law firm and to the magazine's public relations department—again something they would never tolerate from others.

At one moment that I found especially humiliating for *Time*, Sharon appeared in his usual accusatory manner on ABC's "Nightline." The moderator, Ted Koppel, announced that "on advice of counsel" representatives of *Time* declined to be on the program. "On advice of counsel?" That's what news sources under fire are always telling journalists. It is conventional wisdom that speaking to the press before or in the middle of a big lawsuit could hurt the case. I can imagine such a situation but I—and leading libel lawyers I have asked—have never known one. With modern news media coverage, the opposite is more often true. Winning in court often does not compensate for the damage done outside by a lengthy battering in the press.

By the time the Sharon case went to the jury, *Time* had already been battered outside the courtroom. Though it was legally in *Time*'s favor, the final jury verdict was even more punishing.

Ever since the Supreme Court's Sullivan decision defined actual malice in ways that contradicted the words' ordinary meaning, juries in libel suits have been like sailors in a fog without a compass.

Judges try to guide them to the home port required by law. But they rarely succeed. Proof enough of the confusion is that almost never are jury awards of damages for malice allowed to stand without being reduced; a large percentage of the cases have been dismissed or reversed altogether by judges and by higher courts.

For example, when the president of Mobil sued the Washington *Post* (see pages 102 and 292), the judge explained the law in his charge to the jurors for more than two hours. After they returned a verdict against the

Post, he told them, in effect, that they didn't understand what he had said about actual malice, and reversed the jury from the bench.

In interviews with the jurors after the case, Steve Brill of the *American Lawyer* found their disregard of the judge's complex instructions as appalling as it was typical. They applied no law in reaching their verdict, only their sensibilities, reacting to the misdemeanors of the press. Brill argues that the malice doctrine is not only confusing jurors but misleading journalists because it "does nothing to promote good journalism. Indeed, whenever you get into questions of actual malice what we're really saying is that it's okay to be incompetent, it's okay to be stupid, it's just not okay to have done it on purpose."

Judges are as aware of the problem as journalists and lawyers. Long before their cases were ever assigned to them, both Judge Sofaer in the Sharon court and Leval in the Westmoreland had worked with a group of judges seeking new methods for more effective jury management. Whatever influence such forethought may have had, no other libel trials in this century have ever been so innovative and successful in getting juries to understand judges and the law.

Throughout the two-month trial, Judge Sofaer repeatedly cautioned the jury on the mysteries of libel law and led them through the fog of actual malice. When it came time to instruct them formally, he delivered a two-hour, sixty-four-page guide. It was clear enough line by line. But taken as a whole, it was as unlikely that any jury could meld its unfamiliar variables as it would be to expect an ordinary taxpayer to understand the instructions of the IRS for filling out the long federal tax form.

A sample passage:

> Minister Sharon will have to prove one aspect of his claim by what the law calls a 'preponderance of the evidence,' and will have to prove two aspects of his claim by what the law calls 'clear and convincing evidence.' If you conclude that Minister Sharon has failed to establish any aspect of his claim by whatever burden of proof applies, then you must decide the particular issue on which there has been a failure of proof against him.

Try as they might to do otherwise, judges—even the best of them—tend to write jury instructions in law school prose rather than in the language of jurors. Judges are generally more interested in protecting themselves from being overruled by higher courts than in delivering simple, understandable homilies to the jury. But Sofaer overcame that problem and the shortcomings of legalese with a device as clear as a sixth-grade test: he gave the jury a multiple-choice questionnaire, dividing up the three separate elements in the case. It was a variation on what in law is called a "special verdict," but Sofaer's approach had rarely been used in libel suits before.

Each part had simple questions to check off leading to a final "yes" or "no" answer. The first was whether the *Time* paragraph had actually defamed Sharon; the second, whether what was said was substantially true or not; and the third, if it wasn't, did *Time* know it was untrue when it printed the paragraph? The questions were like gates the jurors had to open. For Sharon to win, they had to go through every gate in sequence and unanimously. If they were stopped at any one, Sharon would lose.

In an even more unusual move, Sofaer got agreement from both sides—after *Time* itself suggested it—to have the jury come back in open court and answer each question separately, before going on to the next question. A "no" on any question at any gate would end the case. Ordinarily, juries in libel suits consider the whole case and give one overall, simple verdict, for or against the defendant, deciding only on damages separately. It takes interviews with the jurors after the trial is over to discover on what grounds they reached their conclusion. The segmented, three-stage device provided those answers in open court. It also produced the most sophisticated verdict in modern libel history—and waves of public humiliation for *Time*.

The first wave hit two days after the jury went out. Sequestered in a nearby hotel, the jurors deliberated for more than fourteen hours before they brought back their answer to the judge's first question.

Sharon used some of the waiting time to fight his last battle of the real war in Lebanon. From a small office behind the courtroom, he was on the phone to Israel arguing against the final withdrawal of Israeli troops. But he lost that battle. The Israeli defense minister who replaced Sharon announced: "After two-and-a-half years in Lebanon we have learned the hard way that Israel should not become the policeman of Lebanon." Sharon would have to do much better in New York.

Late in the morning of the third day, Judge Sofaer mounted the bench. Reporters and participants scurried to their seats, joined by a crowd from the Westmoreland trial who came streaming downstairs. "We have a verdict on defamatory meaning," Sofaer announced, "bring the jury out." On the first question, the jury agreed that an "average reader" would have read the paragraph to imply that Sharon "consciously intended" to permit acts of revenge including the deliberate killing of civilians. Was that damning of *Time*? Not yet. It meant only that the magazine had accused Sharon, rightly or wrongly. There was the basis—only that—for a libel judgment.

But from the evening network news bulletins and in the headlines of newspapers, *Time* sounded guilty. That impression was as wrong as it was widespread. Before a libel suit can be won it must be established that whatever was said or printed was actually capable of causing harm. Not just words creating hurt feelings or expressing harsh opinions, but specific charges that could cause public hatred, ridicule or disrespect. If there is none of that kind of harm, there is no case. At that point in the trial process, the truth or falsity of the statement is not yet an issue for the jury. That was the next question for the Sharon jury to answer.

So far—in the court, if not in the world outside—the magazine was not guilty of anything other than using words that were potentially libelous, a daily occurrence in all journalism. Instead of calmly explaining that distinction to the press and the public, *Time* compounded the confusion by overreacting. It put out a combative prepared statement, minutes after the jury's decision on the first question. (At every step *Time* had two press releases prepared: one crowing, the other disagreeing or complaining.) It accused the jury of not being able to read. "On this charge," *Time* haughtily argued, "the jury completely misread what *Time* said." The jury still had two questions to go and the magazine was already insulting it.

The next question was profoundly different. It was more about journalism than law.

Was the paragraph true? Two more days passed before the jury would answer. Meanwhile, for anyone but court buffs, the magazine already seemed convicted. It had admitted one error on Appendix B—and retracted. Misunderstanding the meaning of defamation, many thought the case was over, that the jury had reached its verdict, when, in fact, it had just begun its work.

For twenty-six hours the jury weighed the evidence on truth. Then it marched back into the jury box and announced it had decided against *Time* on the vital question of truth. When the magazine said Sharon had "reportedly discussed with the Gemayels the need for the Phalangists to take revenge," the jury said *Time* was wrong. The answer was a shattering blow to the credibility of *Time*'s story. Sharon's grandfatherly lawyer, Milton Gould, from the New York firm of Shea & Gould, made the most of it. He had already told the jury that Sharon "may be fat but he ain't crazy." Now he had a more elegant and hyperbolic endorsement: "The verdict answers all the moral and historical issues in the case. The rest is only money."

Outside the courtroom, *Time*'s managing editor, Ray Cave, himself the stepson of a general, was immediately surrounded by reporters. Looking unruffled behind his beard, Cave first got lost in his own press releases. "*Time* is gratified," he started, then pulled back and said, "wrong statement, we had to be ready—ever hopeful." From the right piece of paper he read: "We still believe that the article was substantially true. We have the utmost confidence in our editorial staff and our editorial procedures which have been tested for more than 60 years." The jury had failed *Time* on the latest test, but *Time* was not giving up.

For Sharon, it was the vindication he said he wanted. In one press conference after another he declaimed that now he had proved "they lied, they libeled me." Former Prime Minister Begin, from his depressed Jerusalem seclusion, cabled: "Congratulations for the great moral victory." True, the jury had now said *Time* was wrong, a most serious finding. But contrary to Sharon's rhetoric, it had not so far said that *Time* "lied," only that its story was judged both damaging and wrong. In law and in life, consciously lying is very different from making a mistake. The case at the bar was still not over. The jury had not yet ruled on whether *Time* knew it was wrong, that it knowingly lied, and thus was guilty of actual malice— the last and heaviest gate.

Finally, just after noon, on the eleventh day of jury deliberations, with four inches of wet snow blanketing the city, the judge came from his chambers and again announced: "The jury has reached a verdict." Had actual malice been proved? "To that question," said the foreman, "we find the answer is no."

At the last gate, the jury had balked. It did not believe that *Time* consciously lied. The jurors concluded that *Time*'s reporter, Halevy, its writers and its editors believed what they printed and had no reason to know that it was wrong. In law, *Time* had won. The case was over. But there was a surprise epilogue, seconds later, which would make it even more of a bittersweet victory for *Time*.

Juries characteristically deliver their verdict and are dismissed. Not the Sharon jury. Now wise in the ways of U.S. libel law, it had asked the judge's permission to make a special statement in court. "I allowed the jury to read this statement," explained Sofaer, because "common-law juries have traditionally played a moral as well as a technical role, acting as the community's conscience even as they perform their duties."

The forty-five-year-old jury foreman, Richard Zug, a computer programmer who obviously understood the seriatim verdict program, read the statement to the packed and silent courtroom. The jurors had shown they now knew the law but they also had an opinion as citizens. They wanted to express that view and make it a part of the trial record: "We find that certain *Time* employees, particularly David Halevy, acted negligently and carelessly in reporting and verifying the information which ultimately found its way into the published paragraph." Guilty of bad journalism but not guilty under law.

Consider the moral confusion flowing from the verdict of a scrupulous jury instructed by an innovative judge. Minutes after the verdict, reporters and onlookers jostled for position on the courthouse steps, waiting to interview the winners and losers. But who was who?

Time's chief counsel at the trial, Cravath's Thomas Barr, had too lawyerly an answer. "A lawsuit is very much like a war. Who wins the battles is not very important. Who wins the war is terribly important. The war is over and we won." *Time* itself was still prepared either way. Had the verdict been against it, the magazine would have announced an appeal to a higher court. It wasn't necessary. Instead *Time* released its victory statement: "This libel suit is over and *Time* has won it. The case should never have reached an American courtroom [several federal judges had ruled otherwise]. The article we published was substantially true [the jury said it was not]. When we learned of a relatively minor inaccuracy, we printed a retraction. We remain very concerned about the pernicious effect libel cases such as this are having on the First Amendment rights of the American press."

Sharon was equally off-base. He had unconvincingly said in the past, speaking like an American patriot, "I cherish the First Amendment." Now he gave it his own interpretation. "I feel that we achieved what brought us here. We came here to prove that *Time* magazine lied. And we managed to prove that." The jurors had said the opposite. They had a more sophisticated view. One explained that "we didn't want *Time* to think they're so lily-white that they don't make mistakes."

A passerby taking in the chaotic scene asked no one in particular, "What was the verdict?" A television man answered, "An honest mistake." Another said, "Sharon wins by losing." A third said, "*Time* was found incompetent but not malicious."

They were all right. Two self-righteous opponents had collided head on in court. One was a plaintiff who had embroiled his nation in a devastating war and was seeking the rehabilitation his own countrymen were unwilling to grant him. The other, *Time,* formally adjudged the "winner," was wrong on its facts but protected by law. Reputation in journalism is about being right, not about being within the law. The only sin in journalism worse than being wrong is an unwillingness to admit it. So far as the public was concerned, *Time* had committed both sins.[3]

3. After the New York trial, Halevy was reassigned to *Time*'s Washington bureau, where he got *Time* in trouble again. In a bylined exclusive, Halevy reported that Howard Teicher, the senior director of political-military affairs on Reagan's National Security Council, caused a "flap" in Israel five years earlier when he attempted to publish "a fictionalized account of Israel's nuclear secrets." The actual co-author of the book was an Israeli, Eli Teicher, who promptly launched

I have some sympathy for *Time*'s myopic position. Proud, embattled organizations of all kinds tend to look inward for comfort rather than outward for realism.

Once, from the heights of the Time & Life fortress, I might have taken the same view myself. But the news media can no longer afford such self-indulgence. *Time* continues to say that in its heart it knows it was right even though it cannot prove it. In American law, *Time* was fully justified in its legal stand, although only judges, lawyers and media followers tend to understand that the press is not required to be right or even fair in reporting on public figures. It has only to believe what it says is true and make some effort to check—not much, just some. Yet today many people feel that the media have so much power that they should not easily take cover behind their constitutional protection.

It is a compelling argument. If the news media make a serious, specific factual charge against a public figure, they had better be able to offer proof that it is true. If they cannot—as *Time* could not—whether they believe it or not, they should either not make the charge or withdraw it in the absence of proof. There are crucial exceptions: if the story is of overwhelming, public importance, then the media must be willing to take the chance—and the public obloquy that goes with it—if it turns out they cannot support their charge. *Time*'s offending paragraph was incidental to its main story. It had no such importance.

At the time of the verdict in the Sharon case, some senior *Time* editors argued that observing such a "rule" would destroy the use of confidential sources. Not at all. Those sources are often invaluable. There can be no overall, binding rule about them—just rigorous circumspection. If the charge matters enough, if the sources are reliable enough, the news media must take such chances in writing or broadcasting about public figures and public matters. Among the reasons they must is that publication, or the pursuit of confirmation, can flush out reluctant witnesses or activate law enforcement efforts, as it did in the landmark Watergate stories and hundreds of other less memorable but similar cases.

But charges without proof must be published only with hesitant deliberateness, weighing their significance, evidence, fairness and seriousness.

a $250,000 libel suit against the magazine. In this instance, *Time* didn't wait. Less than a month after the incorrect story, in its letters column *Time* actually apologized: "*Time* confused Howard Teicher with Eli Teicher. *Time* regrets the error and apologizes to Messrs. Teicher." The magazine settled the libel suit out of court but as usual refused to disclose the terms of the settlement. In December of 1987, Halevy left *Time* to write "a book based on his experiences as a reconnaissance battalion commander during the 1973 Yom Kippur War" and also to "act as a consultant to a number of private companies."

Making such charges cannot be a routine practice for the sake of retailing exclusives. *Time*'s controversial paragraph was not taken that seriously in advance by the editors nor weighed on a sensitive scale. Sharon was thought to be "libel proof," a term from another era that invites a cavalier attitude. After the libel suit began, *Time* was caught up in the traditional reflex of standing by published stories. It refused to concede the possibility of error, even on a point in no way essential to the real weight of its whole story.

Sharon was defeated in law. But *Time*—and journalism—suffered a worse defeat by having to invoke the privilege of laws that allow, but certainly do not applaud, inaccuracy or unfairness. A "Sharon verdict," where the press loses on truth but wins on law, became an accepted new term in libel parlance—and a possible new objective for people who wanted to clear their name even if they could not collect damages.

Almost exactly one year later, in Tel Aviv, *Time*—still convinced it was right—quietly settled Sharon's Israeli libel suit. Forced by the settlement to give up its ghostly case, *Time* was required to regret in public "this erroneous report" and more than pay Sharon's legal costs in Israel.

In Israel law—modeled on the British common law—there is no malice doctrine.

11

Verdicts

If CBS had apologized in the first place, none of this would have happened. I consider I won.
—General William C. Westmoreland

Nothing in any way diminishes our conviction that the broadcast was fair and accurate. We continue to stand by the broadcast.
—CBS spokesman

Upstairs in courtroom 318, the lessons of Sharon v. Time Inc. were not lost on either Westmoreland and his lawyers or on CBS and its counsel.

Both cases vividly told more about the American news media than about the rights and wrongs of the wars they refought. One aimed at the workings of television; the other at the operations of print reporters and editors. Each took the public behind the scenes of different journalistic processes. In the Sharon-*Time* case, the words actual malice and malice were spoken every day. In the Westmoreland-CBS case, although those terms were banned, state of mind recurred just as often. Whatever the language, both put the news media on trial in different but related ways.

Judge Leval several times warned the Westmoreland jury not "to be influenced" by the pending verdict in the "absolutely and totally different" Sharon case. Like "two automobile accidents," he said, "they have nothing to do with each other." But no one in Leval's courtroom could avoid the remarkable parallels along with the unfolding method and message of the other trial.

The three-tier jury verdict on Sharon, with the jury's unusual and damaging separate opinion, had acquitted *Time* in law but damned it in journalism. Variations of that outcome were especially worrisome to the leading participants in the other courtroom—not just to CBS but to Westmoreland. Both could win and lose at the same time. Jurors now had a way to abide by the law while going outside it to express their opinion as ordinary readers and viewers.

With the Westmoreland trial heading to its conclusion, Judge Leval left no doubt about the possibility of just such an ending. He told the opposing lawyers that he too would divide up the issues for the jury with a questionnaire. He said he also intended to bring the jury back into open court, as Judge Sofaer had done, to deliver separate judgments on the main issues: defamation, truth and malice. Both sides—for different reasons—felt their clients would be in unpredictable jeopardy from that step-by-step process. They preferred a single verdict rather than, in effect, several. Together, they objected to the judge.

"The record will reflect," Leval wrote in his proposed jury instructions, "it was the joint request of the parties that the verdicts on truth and state of mind be announced simultaneously rather than separately when reached. The court would have preferred separate announcements as done in Sharon v. *Time* Inc., but yields to the joint request of the parties."

By then it was not just atmosphere that connected the two media trials. There was a direct connection. In libel suits, it was now even more possible than it had been to win in the courtroom and lose outside—or lose in court and win outside. As a result, both sides in the Westmoreland case could now be hurt by the same jury verdict—and neither could tell which would suffer the most.

Westmoreland's side knew it had failed to show that CBS had deliberately lied. Burt's attempt to set a new standard for what amounted to fairness, with his "indicia of actual malice," had not worked. His effort to redesign the Sullivan landmark was not good enough. In the end, that meant Westmoreland would almost surely ultimately lose the case as a matter of law. But for Westmoreland himself there could be an even worse personal humiliation. The jury, in answering the judge's questions about truth, could find that the program's charges against him had not been proved wrong. Burt later said that when Westy heard his former officers testify against him, "I think his heart was broken. If he loses the case on truth, it will kill the old man."

If Westmoreland lost on truth, it would have the effect of confirming, in a public judicial forum, that he had acted dishonestly. He would be seen to have violated the code by which he felt he had governed his life since military school. Failing to prove CBS wrong, Westmoreland, in his own words, would stand convicted in the public's mind of "treason and betraying my country." The horror of that condemnation became even more possible because of the weakness of his courtroom advocates and their growing disarray.

The picture was not much prettier for CBS.

While there was no doubt there had been plenty of juggling and disagreement over enemy strength figures in Vietnam, it was certainly not proved that Westmoreland was the leading culprit.

One cable read at the trial from Westmoreland's boss, General Earle Wheeler, chairman of the Joint Chiefs, set the environment in which Westmoreland was operating: "I have just been made aware of figures you now report for battalion and larger size enemy initiated actions. If these figures should reach the public domain they would literally blow the lid off Washington. Please do whatever is necessary to insure these figures are not repeat not released to news media or otherwise exposed to public knowledge."

It was hard to believe, as the program charged, that the Joint Chiefs and LBJ were Westmoreland's victims rather than his models, or at the very least his collaborators. Of course, the law dictated that CBS did not have to prove it was right. Westmoreland had to prove CBS wrong. He would have to persuade the jury with "clear and convincing evidence," not that his command's enemy strength estimates were correct, only that he personally had not "dishonestly" misled his military superiors and the president. In court, CBS said it never meant to question Westmoreland's motives. He could have been acting out of pure patriotism, believing he was doing the right thing. But in the program itself, CBS had made no such fine distinction.

The broadcasters might win a "Sharon verdict"—a legal decision in CBS's favor. The jury might even find the program's charge substantially true. But there was no doubt that everyone thought the program had been marred, in both its content and its methods. CBS admitted as much in the Benjamin Report. Most damaging, the program had been *unfair* to Westmoreland. Even though unfairness technically doesn't count in a libel suit, it counts in the everyday moral reckonings of life, and often in the deliberations of juries.

It would have been no proud moment for CBS if the jury found in its favor formally, then said either in a statement, as in the Sharon case, or in interviews afterward that CBS was guilty of unfair journalism within the law. Besides, in the eyes of much of the world, Westmoreland had become something of a martyr, more a victim of his limitations and the manipulations of politicians than the devious character the program suggested he was.

As a result of the trial and of the belated honor now being paid to Vietnam veterans, he was becoming a sympathetic symbol and leader of the benighted vets, rather than the villain of Vietnam. A CBS victory dance on Westmoreland's grave of "dishonor" was a spectacle that appealed to no one—not even a potentially victorious CBS. The network did not want to be seen, said one of its lawyers, "as trying to pursue an old man and drive a stake in his heart."

Given all these considerations, both sides had much to gain by ending the case themselves instead of putting it into the hands of the jury.

One of the minor catechisms in the theology of journalism is that at public gatherings reporters do not clap. It is against their occupational practice to demonstrate for or against anything except in print or on the air. This is such a deeply ingrained habit that I still find it hard to applaud even a theatrical performance, as if my palms, suddenly brought together, might short-circuit my nervous system. (At a dinner gathering of conservatives, I once tried to explain this to a bright, young Reaganaut sitting next to me. "Oh," he said seriously. "I've noticed that reporters don't clap but I thought it was because they were all Democrats.")

A more important tradition is that the news media do not easily settle libel suits. They fight them, unless absolutely convinced they are wrong or will lose in court. This is not mere stubbornness. By routinely settling, the news media would invite all kinds of rascals to drag them into court in the hope of being paid off by the media, who preferred settlement to the cost and nuisance of litigation. A nobler reason is that the press is supposed to take seriously what it tells the public and not back off just to avoid being sued.

But behind that sensible policy are realities that seem to belie it. In all civil suits, including libel, there is talk of settlement before and during the progress of the case. Judges in chambers try to bring the warring parties together in some resolution or bargain, just as a responsible lawyer or counselor first tries to see whether a marriage can be saved before agreeing to the abrasions of divorce. Lawyers themselves constantly put out feelers. Libel insurers always weigh dollar exposure against the price of settlement (although in most policies, they do not have the last word on whether to settle or not).

From the very onset there were endless attempts at resolving out of court both the Sharon and Westmoreland cases. In both cases the steadfastness of *Time* and CBS against the demands of lawyers for the plaintiffs made settlement unlikely.[1] But in the Westmoreland case, with both sides

---

1. *Very* unlikely in the Sharon-*Time* case. After some early fencing about a settlement, which was "strongly recommended" by Judge Sofaer, *Time* and Sharon could not agree. Long after the trial Sharon's press adviser, Uri Dan, reported that Sharon said he wanted to punish *Time*, not settle: "*Time* published a blood libel about me. How the hell do you settle a matter like this? A blood libel you fight!"

hurting each other and with no certain outcome for either, the hope of resolution began to glow more brightly in the dark cave of the law.

Part of the posturing in libel suits is that once they are started each side preens with confidence in public while looking for ways out in private.

From the first day of the Westmoreland-CBS case, there was much discussion over whether CBS would make any financial settlement with Westmoreland or his lawyers. Westmoreland's lawyer, Dan Burt, made impossible demands for apologies, millions of dollars and abject CBS surrender. But in the two and a half years of drilling in cadence for the grand trial spectacle, each side was also turned eyes-right, glancing secretly toward a possible peace treaty just off the parade grounds.

At least ten or more direct attempts at settlement took place, including interventions by Roswell Gilpatric, a member of the CBS board who had been deputy secretary of defense during the early days of the Vietnam War; Frank Stanton, the respected former CBS president; Paul W. Thompson, a retired general, who had been an executive at *Reader's Digest;* a mediator appointed by Judge Leval, Stephen E. Kaufman, a former chief of the U.S. attorney's criminal division; and, in frequent meetings, the battling lawyers themselves. Even on the eve of the trial, when Burt was saying settlement was as unlikely as "a bear coming down Fifth Avenue in a pink tutu with a reefer," he was negotiating with CBS.

The network proposed—as it had before—a statement saying it never meant to question Westmoreland's patriotism or loyalty. But CBS refused to retract or apologize. Burt insisted on a retraction and a multi-million dollar payment, more for its symbolism, he said, than for the cash. One of the "good Samaritan" interveners suggested a settlement involving a payment of $500,000 by CBS toward Westmoreland's legal fees. CBS viewed any such payments as the wrong kind of symbolism, and would not retract the program's charges except to repeat that it never meant to question Westmoreland's motives.

But after General McChristian and Colonel Hawkins testified, Westmoreland's courtroom demeanor changed from chin-up resolution to slumping, weary disappointment. He was hurt and discouraged, never having expected his old military and West Point comrades-in-arms to stand up in court and damn him. It had begun to look to him, he told friends, like a "no-win situation." Burt also told him he was running out of money and Westmoreland felt that whoever won, there would be lengthy and expensive appeals. He was now more ready than ever for an honorable démarche.

After the court session on the day Hawkins finished his punishing testimony, Burt and the Westmorelands solemnly conferred.

It was a Wednesday, the eve of a five-day court recess. Dispirited, they agreed that negotiations over settlement should be renewed. Burt wasted no time. He called CBS's general counsel, George Vradenburg, and suggested they talk. Vradenburg coolly answered that his calendar was full but that he could make a Friday breakfast date at Manhattan's Westbury Hotel.

Two days later at breakfast, Vradenburg led from the strength he felt CBS had accumulated, and withdrew some of the features of his earlier offerings. He asked Burt for a written proposal. Burt scribbled a suggestion on a yellow pad. Afterward, Vradenburg consulted with Boies and rejected any words of regret or apology. He suggested instead a formula for a joint statement which would "exchange platitudes," to be followed by each side's expressing its own, but mutually agreed upon, views. At that point, he told Burt, they seemed not very far apart.

On the same day, Burt and Boies saw Judge Leval's draft instructions to the jury. Burt said after the trial—and some journalists still accept it—that the main reason he settled was not because he was discouraged by the way the trial was going on the witness stand, but because of the instruction by Judge Leval requiring "clear and convincing proof" for the truth part of the case. His after-the-fact explanation doesn't hold up. To be sure, Burt had argued in his pretrial brief that only actual malice need be established by "clear and convincing proof," not the truth or falsity of the CBS program. But he had added in his brief that "the higher standard would not affect the result in this case." After the trial, he was telling the press exactly the opposite.

In addition, the weight of libel case law and Supreme Court decisions on public figure cases was heavily against him. The "clear and convincing" test has repeatedly been applied by judges on matters of truth; it was also used by Judge Sofaer in his instructions to the jury at the close-by Sharon trial. Nonetheless, Sharon had proved the *Time* story wrong. Burt could not have been caught by surprise that Leval would apply the same traditional standard to Westmoreland's case. Leval at the time also offered Burt an opportunity to argue against the standard. Burt never took up the offer.[2]

Without even telling his own trial staff he was in the process of settling, Burt, after more haggling with Vradenburg, called Westmoreland early

2. Later, in the summer of 1986, the Supreme Court carried the "clear-and-convincing" standard a step further. It ruled that the standard had to be applied by judges even in pretrial proceedings, again overruling a lower court decision by the then Supreme Court justice-designate, Antonin Scalia. Had that Supreme Court ruling been handed down before the Westmoreland-CBS trial, Judge Leval could have been more likely to dismiss the suit without trial.

Sunday morning at a friend's house near West Point, where the Westmorelands were spending the weekend. Westmoreland heard the proposed statement and recalls: "I listened to it and thought it made sense. I know the historians can deal with a case like this but a jury—well, it could have been happenstance, a flip of the coin. I had to decide whether to fight or compromise." He decided to compromise.

On Sunday night, in her home in Carmel, New York, forty-two-year-old Patricia Roth, a grade school art teacher and part-time real estate agent, was at work in her studio. Monday was a legal holiday—Presidents' Day. She would be free of her absorbing duties as a juror in the Westmoreland trial. Suddenly her husband, Bob, shouted from the living room: "Westmoreland has dropped his libel suit against CBS. They just announced it on NBC." Before she could even absorb the news, the phone rang. Another juror shouted: "Did you hear the news? CBS is dropping the lawsuit—I just heard it on ABC."

With the modern, high-speed news media, flash bulletins always come before explanations of the events they signal. The Sunday night news of the settlement was out even before most of Westmoreland's lawyers knew it.

The earliest stories in print and on the air were fragmentary and puzzling. Only the tabloid New York *Post* had a simple judgment: "Westy Raises the White Flag." All the reports agreed on the essential fact that the case was over. Its enigmatic ending would not be explained by the next day's court formalities, with the jury absent. Nor would who "won" and who "lost" became much clearer at the separate Westmoreland and CBS press conferences after the court adjourned. As in many of the most celebrated recent libel suits, the real outcome was in the eyes of the beholders. They beheld whatever they wanted and tried to make it believable to others.

Everybody—judge, CBS, Westmoreland, savants of all kinds, excluding only reporters present—mouthed the evasive cliché of the day. The verdict, they all said, could now be left to "the judgment of future historians," as if Solomonic wisdom had at last prevailed. It was banal nonsense. Few historians, alive or dead, have ever gathered so much original information, had so many catalogued documents, not to say living witnesses, to illuminate a single complex question. The evidence necessary for conclusions was as abundant and available as it would ever be. The verdict of history would be based on subjective values not on objective verification.

"Your honor," said Dan Burt, "the parties have reached a settlement in this case."

At a special sixty-sixth session of the final nineteenth week of the trial, early arriving press and sketch artists were lallygagging in the empty jury box. The atmosphere was more social than judicial. At 11:48 A.M. Judge Leval entered the courtroom, giving no sign of the disappointment he felt that he would not have a chance to charge the jury. Burt read a boilerplate of legalisms, including a four-line stipulation ending the case "with prejudice," meaning that Westmoreland could not reopen it. Leval announced that on the day following the court would have one final session to dismiss the jury.

Opposing armies of lawyers and public relations staff hastily regrouped. They had some explaining to do. They needed to unravel an awkward paradox for the press and the public: how could both warring and bloodied sides be as satisfied with such an unresolved peace treaty as they said they were? Their answers were face-saving cant and bafflegab.

The formal statement, signed by the warriors, was indeed "platitudinous," as the lawyers had agreed it would be. It was so meticulously statesmanlike that it seemed to suggest there never was any reason for battle:

> Historians will long consider this and other matters related to the war in Vietnam. Both parties trust their actions have broadened the public record on this matter. Now both believe that their respective positions have been effectively placed before the public and continuing the legal process at this stage would serve no further purpose. CBS respects General Westmoreland's long and faithful service to his country and never intended to assert, and does not believe, that General Westmoreland was unpatriotic or disloyal in performing his duties as he saw them. General Westmoreland respects the long and distinguished journalistic tradition of CBS and the rights of journalists to examine the complex issues of Vietnam and to present perspectives contrary to his own.

For all the actual and attributed faults of the press, one of its invaluable services is to puncture the balloons of hot air in evasive public euphemisms. At both the Westmoreland and CBS press conferences, the assembled journalists had plenty of puncturing to do.

With the joint statement in hand, reporters arrived for Westmoreland's 1:30 P.M. press conference in the Turtle Bay Room of Manhattan's Harley Hotel. The jammed room had the traditional background music of all such media crushes: the clicking whir of motor-driven shutters accompanied by the chorus of that eternal favorite, "Down in Front!"

One reporter, more conclusive than most, cracked that Westmoreland should be holding this ceremony "on the deck of the Missouri," where the Japanese surrendered. But a smiling Kitsy Westmoreland, eyes rimmed red with sleeplessness, set a more celebratory tone by kissing half a dozen of the trial's regular reporters (including me). Dan Burt, barely tall enough to see over the podium and the tangle of microphones, began his grim task. Behind him to his left—where military aides are supposed to follow—stood the erect and ashen general.

Burt: "Many people said this case did not belong in court. But there was no alternative. I think it helped accommodate within our society conflicting passions on the war, on the press and on the rights of the individual." Then he read Westmoreland's prepared statement, concluding with, "and now let me give you someone who stands a little taller than I do."

Westmoreland, weary and taut, relieved his own tension with a surefire opener. "It's been suggested," he said, "that we might organize a Westmoreland-CBS Trial Watching Association and I understand my wife has been nominated as the first president." A loud chorus of applause and "hear, hear." As to the serious business at hand, he was satisfied with the result he had sought from the beginning—the vindication of his honor that he said he believed the statement represented. His anger had long since been drained by the unintended but inevitable courtroom comaraderie and weariness. "At first you get angry," he later said, "and then you just get numb."

Now that it was over, he was as evenhanded in public as a juggler at a USO performance. "The court action certainly exposed some of the problems and complexities of producing intelligence on an elusive enemy and exposed some of the problems and complexities in producing a television documentary."

Then the puncturing began. A reporter asked, "How can both sides claim victory?" Westmoreland: "If earlier I could have received such language, that would have concluded and ended the confrontation." Burt chimed in: "The issue here was very simple. Westmoreland wanted an apology. He wanted his name cleared. If that statement had not been forthcoming, we would be going back to court tomorrow."

The press was not satisfied. Why did he sue and then settle for so little? "General, do you consider this a win, a loss or a draw?" Westmoreland: "I consider I won by virtue of that statement. I got all I wanted. That is what I asked for originally and when that was forthcoming for the first time it satisfied my request. I wanted an apology. If I had it to do over again—" he hesitated—"I probably would."

And how did he feel about the press? Mellow or, more likely, tired of fighting that old losing battle: "In Vietnam poor reporting was the exception rather than the rule. I could have done a better job dealing with their needs." As for the future, he was willing to let "historians and scholars assess the facts of that war in accurate and non-sensational terms." He had come, he said, "to defend my honor and to affirm constitutional principles, which indeed include the rights provided by the First Amendment. Now I'm going to try to fade away."

His dignified words of satisfaction and resignation were unconvincing. But even the dry-eyed reporters seemed sympathetic to "Westy's" personal plight. Murray Kempton, moved by the human drama unfolding before him, muttered under his breath, "I hate to see the press get away with this." Three months later Kempton would win a long overdue—and his first—Pulitzer Prize for general pungent commentary.

On the west side of Fifth Avenue, in the mirrored Chippendale Room of the Dorset Hotel, CBS waited its turn. Minutes after hearing from Westmoreland and Burt, more than two hundred reporters, producers and television technicians streamed into the room. Their notebooks and tapes were only half full. Now came the other half.

Freed from the burdens of an agonizing lawsuit, CBS was not about to brag. Van Gordon Sauter presided—in his working tweeds, bow tie and loafers—calmly stroking his trim, full beard. At his side was a gratified and grinning David Boies. For his handling of the case, Boies was the only indisputable winner on either side. (A year later he was pictured on the cover of the New York *Times* Sunday *Magazine* as "The Wall Street Lawyer Everyone Wants.") The opening words were brief and banal. The questions were not. Now the reporters were dealing with experienced, smooth media tough guys, not an aging general and his diminished counselor.

Didn't CBS view its agreement as an apology? Boies ducked, denying there was any apology or retraction because no money was paid. Sauter would "not calibrate who won and who lost. The general may read into the statement what he wishes. We stand by the content of the broadcast." He too was willing to leave it "up to historians," as if a thoughtful television documentary, with a resounding conclusion about events that took place fourteen years earlier, was never meant to be viewed as history.

As lawyers will, Boies argued that CBS gave up nothing new, basing his claim on four little words, unnoticeable to all but those who drafted them. The statement, Boies argued, said that Westmoreland performed his duties "as he saw them," implying no disloyalty or unpatriotic spirit. ("That was no apology at all," said retired Admiral Thomas Moorer, one of Westmoreland's most ardent supporters, "you could have said that about Hitler.") Reporters heatedly pointed out that the program itself clearly contradicted that legalistic view.

This was not, alas, an uncommon evasion. Increasingly, the news media seem willing to take cover behind hairsplitting technicalities, ignoring the real overall impression their damning stories sometimes create. And not only in the Westmoreland case. For example, after three years and millions of dollars in legal fees on both sides, the owner of California's McClatchy Newspapers said in 1987 when the Laxalt libel suit (see page 101) was settled: "We are not backing away from anything we said in the story. We never said there was skimming. We said that there was evidence from an IRS agent that there was skimming. We have not retracted, we have not apologized, we have not paid any damages." Laxalt had precisely the opposite view: "This is the day I've been waiting for. The cloud has been removed. We've received everything we wanted."

In many such cases readers and viewers of the stories at issue—like the viewers of the Westmoreland program—were never given the benefit of such doubts originally. In fact they were left with exactly the opposite impression, even though word-by-word, legalistic examination of the texts might justify the media cop-outs. If the story suggests venality or criminality, although it doesn't come right out and say so, that may satisfy the law but it certainly cannot be considered fair-minded journalism. It is close to what the press, full of acknowledged guilt, once called its own "McCarthyism"—passing on accusations without evident proof—and vowed never to do again.

At the CBS press conference, reporters insisted on knowing why Westmoreland was finally now given this "fig leaf" by CBS. Boies had another lawyers' answer: "When a plaintiff wants to drop a lawsuit without any money or apology, I think you ought to let him." The real answer was unspoken and obvious. Both sides wanted a pragmatic way out—orotund principles be damned. Next day a New York *Times* headline writer summarized the irresolution, over Myron Farber's lead story in the paper's blockbuster coverage: "CBS Stands By Documentary But General Claims Victory."

"This broadcast," Van Sauter concluded, resulting in what was "perhaps the most significant trial in the history of television, has stood the test of two-and-a-half years of day-to-day examination." Was he concerned that CBS and the press in general would be "chilled" by such libel suits? Not at all; they were just part of the price of media power. "We live in a very media conscious society."

The casualties on all sides sounded relieved if not exactly euphoric. Westmoreland explained in follow-up interviews that "I figured it was the best I could get." He also displayed the charity of a saint in reassessing his on-air accuser: "I think Mike Wallace was a busy man. He was working on a number of things. I guess I think Mike was a victim of circumstances as I was." Wallace was equally subdued. He said he'd "love to sit down with Westmoreland. I really do feel compassion for him." (More than two years later they were together but did not discuss the case.) Westmoreland added, with almost too much martyrdom, "I am going to enjoy the last few years I have, unless CBS decides to be my perpetual tormentor."

CBS had no such intention. It wanted nothing so much as to forget Westmoreland and get on to other things. In the months ahead, CBS and its news division would have more than their share of other issues, including a change in ownership and a reorganization of the news division as well as of the entire corporation (see chapters 15 and 16).

And how did the hard-working jurors feel about the case they never had the opportunity to decide?

Before Judge Leval finally dismissed them, he told the disappointed twelve, "I think it is safe to say no verdict you or I would have been able to render could have escaped widespread disagreement." Then he followed them into the jury room, where "Judge Pierre," as the jurors among themselves referred to him, thanked each of them. In return, a few of the female jurors embraced him and bussed him on the cheek. Leval also extended an unusual and sensible invitation. He suggested that instead of fleeing the way jurors usually do, they could return if they wanted to the courtroom to talk to both sides as well as be interviewed by the waiting press. All but one, who ran off to tend to her sick mother, were eager to do just that.

When they did they told me and other reporters who interviewed them that they felt cheated—some bitterly—at not being given a chance to render their verdict. The foreman, Richard Benveniste, a thirty-two-year-old casualty insurance underwriter, complained, "It was right at our fingertips—like a fish at the end of a hook that gets away, taking your whole fishing reel." To my surprise, he told me that their deliberations could have taken two to six weeks. They might even have ended with a hung jury, he said, because the verdict had to be unanimous on all three major questions, defamation, truth and state of mind.

The jurors were mixed on the question of whether the program was basically true or not. One juror had seven-hundred-pages of notes, another three hundred. All wanted to reexamine exhibits, tapes and pages of testimony. By a narrow margin, they said, they were leaning toward CBS. Some counted as many as eight votes for CBS, possibly four for Westmoreland. But four claimed they were undecided and the foreman said it could easily have gone either way. At first most were moved and persuaded by Westmoreland's testimony, they said, until Adams and Crile, then especially McChristian and Hawkins, turned the tide against him.[3]

Only one juror said there was evidence that CBS's "state of mind" was dishonest, or lying, i.e. full of actual malice—the words they never heard in court. "I believed," said a forty-two-year-old accountant, "that CBS showed a reckless disregard for the truth. But what is the truth?" he added enigmatically. In their disappointment, several said they thought their verdict would have allowed Westmoreland to come away from the trial better off than he had been in settling out of court. They were all beguiled by Boies' informal competence and humor, unimpressed by Burt's earnestness and put off by his obvious inexperience.

When I asked the foreman whether he thought the program was fair to Westmoreland, he seemed surprised at the apparent naiveté of my question. "Oh no, no, we didn't think the program was fair to Westmoreland." He hastened to add, severely, "but don't you know, as the judge told us, that fairness is not an issue in a libel suit?" They obviously had learned their lesson in law.

David Boies was philosophical: "The best kind of bargain is the kind both sides go away happy with. The second best is the kind both sides go away saying they're happy with."

Media lawyers and almost every newspaper in the country had an editorial opinion about the outcome. Few were crowing. While expectably deploring libel suits as an effective means of expressing grievances, press opinions on the settlement were mostly critical of media performance— including their own.

The Arizona *Republic:* "The public cannot be faulted if it believes that both CBS and Westmoreland were guilty of manipulating facts." New York *Daily News:* "Fair-minded viewers concluded that CBS was overzealous at best—and unfair at worst." Detroit *Free Press* editor and publisher, David Lawrence, Jr.: "It was a gain for CBS and for those of us who care about the media but for us to say we have won some big victory would be perilous. The questions still stand in the public mind about our devotion to accuracy and fairness." Commentator Bill Moyers: "It's not the First Amendment that protects journalists. It's humility."

Don Hewitt, the outspoken producer of CBS's "60 Minutes," was relieved, even jubilant that his friend and his program's star, Mike Wallace, was finally finished with the punishing trial. But Hewitt was unwilling to

3. Early in 1987, Colonel Hawkins, sixty-seven, suffering from debilitating and painful terminal lung cancer, walked into the Mississippi woods, put a gun to his head and killed himself.

be as selfrighteous as he usually is about his own program: "We've got to stop acting as if journalism is a priesthood. We weren't ordained. We've got to stop hollering First Amendment every time we get hit, as if that's the only thing in the Constitution. Other people have rights, too."

CBS News President Edward M. Joyce was taken aback, as were some CBS staffers and the reporters present, by a lavish celebration and dinner-dance that CBS and its lawyers held in a New York night club on the evening the trial ended. Joyce took one look and left in five minutes. Next day he sent out a memo lavishly praising the Benjamin critique and saying to the CBS News staff, "This is a time for us to feel relief but not jubilation." (For unrelated reasons, Joyce was replaced as news president, left the network less than a year later and wrote a bitter book about his managerial experience, *Prime Times, Bad Times,* Doubleday, 1988).

In an editorial about both the Sharon and Westmoreland cases *USA Today* concluded: "There is nothing for the media, the network or the magazine to cheer about after these two controversial cases. Celebrating is as out of place as waltzing in a graveyard. In the aftermath of these two trials, it is appropriate for all the news media to reappraise their performance and values and rededicate themselves to fairness and balance."

Whether they intend to or not, journalists are constantly issuing report cards on public figures.

CBS flunked General Westmoreland in its documentary. Then, after he agreed to withdraw his $120 million libel suit, CBS regraded him. This time, in its statement after the trial, the network gave him "A" in character but stuck with its "F" in military procedure. Both the general and CBS said they were now satisfied. Very statesmanlike—but signifying what?

"Without a jury verdict, it was a waste of time and money," said some. "This never should have been in court in the first place," said almost everybody. And in a triple header, the general, CBS and the presiding judge, one after the other, all said that history should deliver the real verdict not the courts.

Ironically future historians may well find *Time* right in its overall judgment of Sharon, although the jury found *Time*'s specific accusation wrong. Conversely, historians of the future, as many of the present already have, may find CBS wrong in its preoccupation with Westmoreland's culpability. For Sharon, historians will need no further evidence than the Kahan Commission report to conclude that he was like the southern sheriff from another era who opened his jail door to a lynch mob. The sheriff was not the murderer himself but he eased the murderers' way. In Westmoreland's case, he will be—and has already been—considered part of an administration-wide deception of the American public to try to gain support for an unpopular, losing war. But Westmoreland, like McNamara, was an administrator of that policy, not its creator.

Those who say that these cases never should have been in court, that they accomplished nothing and were a useless expenditure of time and money, are mouthing facile clichés. The Westmoreland v. CBS trial, together with the less important and very different Sharon v. Time case, were two of the most significant and, it turns out, worthwhile libel suits in modern American history.

Good for the press, good for the law and good for the public.

Consider first the news media. They have been profoundly affected, despite their recent "victories" in libel suits, or even their hollow public claims that they see no reason to change their basic ways. Their habits and processes have been opened up for the whole world to see, just as severely as they lay bare the work and lives of others.

CBS had taken an important and valuable historical subject, elaborately researched it, then in the end could not resist the temptation to hype what it found. A potentially good piece of journalism was destroyed by sensational overstatement. CBS had aimed its powerful cannon at Westmoreland because its ammunition couldn't reach the real target, President Johnson and his administration. In journalism as in war, such misfires can be brutal.

Meanwhile, *Time* could produce no evidence to support an unnecessary and damaging charge in an otherwise impeccable story. The magazine refused to back down on the point—until forced to do so. Both CBS and *Time* were saved not by the quality of their journalism but by the laws of the United States. But staying within the law cannot be the journalist's central concern. Being right and fair must be. By that vital standard, nobody in the press could take pride in the outcome of either case.

When Ed Murrow pilloried Senator Joseph McCarthy in one of CBS's most powerful "See It Now" documentaries, he announced: "If the Senator believes we have done violence to his words or his pictures and desires to speak, to answer himself, an opportunity will be afforded him on this program." (McCarthy accepted the time offered and did so poorly, calling Murrow the pro-Communist leader of the "jackal pack," that he added to his own discredit.) Such an offer should not be automatic. But when the charge is serious enough and the person at whom it is leveled has real grounds for complaint, television needs to find ways to let people answer. Had Westmoreland been given the same opportunity as McCarthy, there would very likely have been no libel suit.

Even the battered George Crile came around to that view. Almost two years after the trial, when he had become a producer for "60 Minutes," Crile said: "All of us at CBS now feel that we should have gone forward and opened the airwaves to let this be a good, old-fashioned debate. You would have to be inhuman not to have learned certain lessons, not to become a better reporter and a better person."[4]

Sharon had his own agenda—his political rehabilitation. He sued even before he asked for a retraction. But once *Time* discovered—as it did early in the dispute—that its proof on only one of many damning facts about Sharon was either non-existent at worst or shaky at best, it should have promptly retracted the marginal point. Instead *Time* relied on what it felt to be its convictions, its honest intentions and the protection of the law. With motives different from Westmoreland's, Sharon might have pursued this objective in court nonetheless. But he could not have won the case either in law or in the eyes of the world. And *Time* would have lost nothing by retracting, except its stubborn pride in appearing unfailingly right.

One benefit from both trials is that journalists are now more aware than ever before that their methods, accuracy, fairness—even their manner and attitude—may one day be subject to similar minute inspection.

Journalists who covered or followed these trials have been forced to ask themselves how their own work would measure up under such scrutiny. They realize that it is a rare story—especially if it is major and contentious—that on close inspection would not turn out to be flawed by some error or a procedural embarrassment.[5] There is not a serious journalist alive—or maybe even a scandalmonger—who will not be more careful in the future.

Is this the "chilling effect" that weakens the resolve of the news media to report and expose as they always have? Certainly not. There are no signs that the big news media have been scared off difficult but important stories when they have the proof they need to publish or broadcast. More

4. Crile has obviously taken many lessons from the trial experience. He recently wrote to me: "A commanding general should be held accountable for his misdeeds but a reporter should be generous and kind. The Westmoreland interview was so devastating that he ended up looking as if he hadn't been acting out of patriotic impulse. The *Wall Street Journal* had it right when it praised us for opening up the most important field of inquiry into the war but faulted us for having presented a two-dimensional cops-and-robbers story. It is possible for a patriot to do the wrong thing for the right reason but I think we are in agreement that he deserved to have been treated with more respect in the telling of the story."

5. Long after the Westmoreland trial, Judge Leval himself pointed out: "In any ambitious piece of journalism there will be some factual errors. Even if they are slight and insignificant, these will become a source of great embarrassment at trial. Also it is a rare piece of accusatory, investigative journalism that cannot, after the fact, be made to look slipshod or biased."

careful, yes—but what could be wrong with that so long as their constitutional protection remains? If the news media can show professional care and honest conviction that they believe they are right, they are unlikely to have a problem with the law. They may have to face public embarrassment for their mistakes or excesses—as CBS and *Time* did—but not the penalty of actually losing in the courts.

It is true that the very threat of costly litigation has made some smaller publishers and broadcasters turn away from hardball reporting. That remains a serious problem. Libel insurance rates have skyrocketed and some media organizations have had their coverage canceled completely. The CNA Insurance Companies negotiated a payment for less than *Time*'s estimated $5 million in costs, and paid CBS more than $7 million. Several months later, CNA went out of the libel insurance business altogether.[6] But billowing insurance premiums were hardly unique to the press or even higher than the increase in many other liability policies.

The New York *Times* (and now CBS) asserts both its independence and its affluence by carrying no libel insurance, standing the possible costs of its own litigation. That is a luxury few can afford. But because the big media companies are so concerned about the possible erosion of First Amendment rights, perhaps they and their insurance companies should explore further ways to protect the smaller media from harassment and threats to free press values, pooling the financial risks even more than they already do.

A number of changes in the law itself have been suggested, including the British convention of making the loser pay the winner's costs. Other proposed legal remedies include banishing punitive awards because they are uncontrollably vague and invite punishment for unpopular speech. As appealing as any is the suggestion that where actual monetary damages cannot be shown, voluntary retractions after arbitration replace financial compensation. (Most forms of compulsory retraction have been ruled by the Supreme Court as an unconstitutional imposition on the press.)

But national legislative changes in libel practices are unlikely. The news media are wisely reluctant to go to the Congress or the government for additional immunity from the complaints of citizens or government. First there is the constitutional tradition that "Congress shall make no law

6. In the conglomerating world of business where who owns what is often hard to remember, there are many ironies. The Tisch family, which controls CNA Insurance, later acquired a controlling interest in CBS (see page 242). Just as Renata Adler, in suing Condé Nast over an article to which she objected, ended up suing her own publisher when the Newhouse family acquired Condé Nast, the *New Yorker* and her book publisher, Knopf (see page 244).

abridging. . . . .'' Neither, in most journalists' view, should the government make laws helping the press. Even without that caveat, the American news media are hardly considered by the public in desperate need of enhanced powers.

If new legislation offers little promise, the two inventive federal judges in the Sharon and Westmoreland cases have brought about important changes in the legal process itself. Sitting in courtrooms two floors apart, they pioneered a new kind of jury management in libel suits that made tangled legalisms understandable. The need was plain enough. When judges repeatedly have to overrule confused juries, then it must be time for a change.

And so the change came. The root of the problem was, of course, the Supreme Court's creation of the "actual malice" doctrine more than twenty years ago. But perhaps for the first time, both juries clearly understood what the law was and why it was so. In the wide coverage of the trials, the public got a similar education. It is hard to believe that judges in the future will not learn from these two examples.

Will this increase or decrease the number of libel suits? The Westmoreland and Sharon trials have underscored the "heavy burden" imposed on public figures who try to win expensive libel suits. That message was spread across the airwaves and newsprint of the United States. The effect is unpredictable. But it seems likelier that those experiences will discourage rather than invite more such cases.[7] Nobody welcomes libel suits, neither the plaintiffs nor the defendants. Yet in these two cases, each produced unintended benefits. They stimulated—but did not force—the press to reexamine and revise its own standards. At the same time, the novel conduct of the trials created new public understanding of vital First Amendment protections. Taken together, these results far outweigh the earlier and widespread view that bringing either case to court would do nobody any good.

And what of Judges Leval and Sofaer? Leval spent most of the next two years presiding at a Mafia and drug trial widely referred to as the "pizza connection." His experience with the Westmoreland case led him to speculate that agreements between plaintiff and defendant to exclude certain issues and limit rights, offered a more promising route for resolving libel disputes than full trials. Plaintiffs, he said, are more often interested

---

7. The evidence was inconclusive, but in the two years following the Westmoreland and Sharon cases, libel insurance executives reported that the number of libel suits filed against the media fell off by about one-third, although jury awards skyrocketed.

in clearing their names than winning money (see pages 99 and 288. For their part, the media are wary of high litigation costs and huge jury awards for damages.

To satisfy the needs of both parties, Leval suggested agreement to limit the malice issue and place modest limits on money awards (say, $25,000), along with agreed-upon space or airtime to publish the findings in the plaintiff's favor, if the media defendant lost. Text and placement would be approved by an arbitrator. Leval has a persuasive rebuttal to the objection that television and print are reluctant to turn over their space to any outsiders. He argues that the media do just that all the time for advertisers, or by printing the full texts of speeches; and on television, by giving live coverage to speeches and news conferences. Why not so resolve libel disputes that would otherwise be dragged through the courts and are a far greater hazard to the media?

In the April 1988 *Harvard Law Review*, he addressed the subject more formally. Leval suggested that, as a matter of law, someone suing for libel who did not seek money damages, should not be required to prove actual malice. This would benefit both sides, he said. It would relieve the media from having their motives or editorial process exposed and involve only the truth or falsity of the story.

As for Judge Sofaer, he became the most activist legal counselor to a U.S. secretary of state in memory.[8] Asked about libel matters, he expressed concern that the law was being used to encourage sloppy journalism. "The media," he said, "have given too much weight to the law in deciding what they can do instead of deciding what they should do. The media, not the courts and particularly not media lawyers, should set the standards for their own conduct." And he adds a sensible warning: Without a "new emphasis on truth, the law may well change again to the detriment of the press."

8. When the trial was over Judge Sofaer left the bench to accept an appointment as senior legal adviser to the State Department. Freed of his judicial robes, he was interviewed shortly after the trial by the *National Law Journal*. Sofaer, surprisingly for a judge—former or not—said that the best argument against malice *Time* had for itself was the quality of Halevy's journalism. Halevy, he said, was "the kind of reporter who was a bad apple" and there was "quite a bit of evidence Halevy was lying." Judge Sofaer explains: "Your quotation is unfair and out of context. I distinctly remember why I was willing to make the statement I made—in order to explain why I had ordered a seriatim verdict. Had there been no evidence that Halevy lied, no danger would have existed that the jury would confuse falsity with malice. Because some evidence impugning his credibility had been introduced—an obvious fact to any observer—I felt the danger of an improper verdict was very real. A judge should be free after a case is closed to explain the reasons for adopting an innovative procedure."

Experience, it is routinely said, is a great teacher. What lessons are there in the CBS and *Time* libel suits? Plenty—but not enough. They were, to be sure, great case studies, a paradigm of how things can go wrong. But they were far from the only examples. You had to look beyond them—beyond malice as understood not only in law but in life—to grapple with many other conflicts of values between the contemporary news media and the society they serve and disserve.

Where to look? Just about everywhere, every day.

Book Two:

THE NEWS MEDIA AT WORK

12

Adultery and Other Sins

*We tend to think of American journalism as
cognitive. Well, that may have something to do
with it. But I also think it operates the way that
fire does, or water, with a kind of mindless pursuit
of objectives.*
　　　　　　　　　　—John Chancellor,
　　　　　　　　　　　　NBC Commentator

Turn from the formalities of libel suits to the realities of the press at work;
from the media before the bar to the media before its public.

We live in an age of overstatement. Cassandra-like complaints about the
press are the rule, not the exception. Hostile rhetoric exaggerates reality.
Too many events are called crises when they are really just snarls. Natural
advances or unnatural setbacks are too easily termed "revolutions" when
they are more often evolutions. Enough "watersheds" in press history
have been declared to require a fleet of arks, manned by an Annapolis
graduating class of Noahs.

Was the press really as suspect as many of its critics claimed in the mid-
80s? Was it so overpowering, prying, unreliable, dishonest, hyped-up,
unfair? Had the profit engine and the new devotion to Wall Street's security
analysts so taken over that the press was just like any other widget-making
enterprise? Certainly not, no matter what scolds said (many, most painfully, former members of the press themselves). Of course, too many in
the media were indefensible—and will always be. More important, even
the best have an alarming number of bad moments and mixed motives.

By the mid-80s, the American news media, with all their faults, not only
were the freest, most varied and most informative in the world but they
were better than they had ever been. No one could seriously quarrel with
that judgment. (Of general circulation publications, only the weekly London *Economist* has no American counterpart.) Then why all the complaining, the big libel suits, the worrying, the polls, the conferences, the self-
examination, financial gyrations and talk of reform?

It could be that the spurts of bile from the public and the self-criticism by the press flow from disenchantment with big institutions of all kinds. Financiers, defense contractors, politicians, lawyers, doctors, government officials, public utilities, drug manufacturers, insurance companies, airlines, have all become targets of public wrath. In 1985 alone, more than 13 million lawsuits were filed in the United States, one for every eighteen Americans. Everybody is suing and attacking everybody else. Why not the news media?

Lawyer Floyd Abrams thought that was a large part of the explanation. "In some ways," he recalled, "those in and out of the press may view it as reminiscent of the scene in *Catch-22* when Joseph Heller's anti-hero Yossarian explains why he has decided to fly no more bomber missions:

"They're trying to kill me," Yossarian said calmly.

"No one's trying to kill you," Clevinger cried.

"Then why are they shooting at me?" Yossarian asked.

"They're shooting at everyone," Clevinger answered. "They're trying to kill everyone."

"And what difference does that make?"

The novelist's dialogue gives only a partial answer. Like other giant institutions and even individuals, the news media are judged not on their routine behavior. They are rarely applauded for their daily successes. They are deeply remembered for their mistakes, their sensationalism, their intrusiveness, their unfairness—their offenses.

It is not so different in other venues. NASA dazzled the world by getting us into space and to the moon. Yet overnight it was humiliated, damned and forced to reorganize when, after fifty-five successful manned space shots, it allowed one faulty O-ring in a booster rocket to cause the death of seven astronauts. Billions of Tylenol capsules provided one of the most popular headache relief medicines in the world, until seven people died when a few capsules were murderously filled with deadly cyanide. The odds that any single person anywhere else would be poisoned were billions to one, as compared with 620,000 to one for getting killed in a commercial airliner (including from a terrorist bomb). Yet Tylenol in capsule form was eliminated from medicine cabinets forever. It has always been so. "Foul deeds will rise," Shakespeare wrote, "Though all the earth o'erwhelm them, to men's eyes."

The best of the news media had no preponderance of foul deeds to answer for. But they had enough. Their faults were no longer the concern of separated or single communities. Their messages, their steps and missteps, bounced around the globe. It was not unreasonable to judge them so severely. With enhanced power comes the demand for more accountability.

Sure, journalists said, we make mistakes. Some of us (mostly the others) commit reprehensible offenses. But don't just remember the error we made today or yesterday. Don't characterize us by the bums among us or the bad calls we sometimes make. Remember all the good we do, how hard we try, the service we regularly perform. Journalists pleaded for understanding of the hazards inherent in the speed at which they are forced to operate. They wanted credit for protecting the public against the hypocrisy of some public officials, abuse by government, big institutions and other impersonal bureaucracies. They had a mission to inform and reveal, to be the vehicle for the people's need to know, the answer of the powerless to the powerful.[1]

For long stretches, their pleas of virtue were answered not in declarations of agreement but in acquiescent silence. More and more people depend on what they see on television and read in print. It goes mostly unquestioned. "I saw it on the news or read it in the papers, so it must be true" is more an all-American homily than a middle-American delusion (although you can also hear the wise-guy reverse, "Oh, you can't believe anything you get in the news"). The news media provide the public with its information diet, and are taken as much for granted in most American homes as the food on the table. People are nourished by what they are served from the news media menu, until they choke on a bone. The trouble was there were always lots of bones to choke on.

Not surprising, many were embedded in the coverage of the criminal justice system.

In the yeastiest cases of 1984–85 it was no longer just a throng of scribblers writing lurid stories about the Lizzie Borden murder or the Lindbergh kidnapping. A new phase had begun in the 60s with the Billie Sol Estes farm fraud in Texas and the murder conviction of a Cleveland doctor, Samuel Sheppard. Both guilty verdicts were set aside and had to be retried because of what higher courts called "the carnival atmosphere" of the print and the new television coverage.

Some twenty years later, on both coasts of the United States, the media competition to cover three other sensational criminal accusations made the earlier trials look like warm-ups for the main events.

---

1. Although they often seemed insensitive to their own power, unmindful of Madison's warning: "It is of great importance in a republic not only to guard the society against the oppression of its rulers, but to guard one part of the society against the injustice of the other part."

Some hasty police work, compounded by a piece of misinformation given to reporters, was speeded around the world from New Bedford, Massachusetts, creating the biggest rape trial in history. What gave it instantaneous velocity was not the horror of a gang rape of a young woman on the pool table of a local bar. That was bad enough but insufficient to make it the story it became.

It was the report that "cheering throngs" of patrons in Big Dan's Bar had egged the rapists on that really drew the attention of the public. One of the many street demonstrations that surrounded the pretrial buildup featured a sign: "Rape is not a spectator sport." It turned out there had been no "cheering throngs," just a mistaken early police report whose effect on the news media, and then on the public, was so great that a local horror story became a national event.

By trial time it was too late to correct first impressions. CNN—the new twenty-four-hours-a-day cable news network—decided to give the courtroom near gavel-to-gavel coverage for an audience estimated at 25 million homes. The judge asked that the twenty-two-year-old victim's face not be shown to anyone outside the courtroom so that her name would not be reported, a practice most journalists accept in rape cases. She was known simply as "the victim" or "the woman," until two newspapers decided that the lid was off because she was once accidentally referred to by name in court and it was not bleeped out on television. (A Justice Department study later estimated that nearly half the rape victims never report the crime, partly to avoid the humiliation of public exposure.)

At the end of the trial, the judge who had allowed the unobtrusive television camera in his state court, was sadly disappointed. He denounced the publication of the victim's name as "an abysmal error of judgment. It could serve no purpose other than to assist in the voyeuristic aspect and sell a few more newspapers."

To "sell a few more newspapers" or "jack up the ratings" was confidently asserted by just about everyone, except journalists, as the obvious fuel for the media engine.

To serious journalists, this charge was as alien to their thinking as accusing, say, clergymen of donning the cloth so that they could have a steady job. Journalists said their motivation was much more straightforward. In addition to what they pretentiously asserted to be the people's "right" to know (to know everything?), journalists said they also wanted "interesting" stories as much as their lusting audiences did.

In a country whose leading domestic issue was crime and violence, another such story was made to order. Two hundred miles south of New Bedford, in New York City, the case of what the press originally titled

"The Subway Vigilante," bounced back and forth in press and public opinion almost as violently as the bullets Bernhard Goetz had fired from his nickel-plated revolver at four menacing teenagers in a Manhattan subway car.

The early reports portrayed Goetz as a national hero, a symbol of everybody's frustration over unpunished, random crime. He was on the cover of news magazines, interviewed on network news about everything from his childhood and manhood to his diet and dress. His psyche was the subject of dozens of feature stories and editorial analyses. It took a little time but as the facts came out it became harder and harder to separate the victims from the victimized. Included prominently among the delinquents were not just people with sharpened screwdrivers or guns but journalists, politicians and some law enforcement officials. An all too familiar case of "mutual manipulation," said one critic of such media whirligigs.

If rape on a pool table and vengeance in a subway car sent the media into a hyperactive frenzy, so did a cocaine bust in a California motel.

The arrest and trial of the fallen automaker, John De Lorean, again put the press in the public dock along with the defendant, first for building him up, then for wallowing in his downfall. If ever there was a corporate hero created by hype, it was John De Lorean. But as the stories of his rebellious business success at General Motors, of his glitzy life-style and of the sports car of the future that bore his name ballooned airily in the news media, they were deflated with an even louder whoosh.

He was caught white-handed in an FBI sting involving a multimillion-dollar cocaine deal. His trial was delayed by the presiding judge when someone slipped CBS a video tape of the most incriminating visual evidence of his guilt. It was played on the evening news, showing De Lorean gleefully trying to make the buy near the Los Angeles airport in a hotel suite that had been video-bugged by the FBI.

De Lorean reflected on his misery in a *Rolling Stone* interview. His wife, a stunningly beautiful super-model, poured out her own story of love, devotion and trust in her husband to *People* magazine and to Barbara Walters in an interview for ABC's "20/20." (Shortly after the trial, she separated from and then divorced De Lorean.) The prosecutor asked the judge to gag the lawyers to prevent them from talking to the eager press, arguing that the defense lawyer held a press conference every day on the courthouse steps. To which the defense counsel replied, with some logic, that so did the prosecutor and it was too late to stop the trial by media anyway.

At the trial, the key participants spent almost as much time trying to influence the 150 reporters outside as they did the jurors inside. ABC's "Good Morning America" carried media intrusion a step further. Until the judge angrily stopped it, the program's staff tried to line up the jurors for posttrial interviews even before they reached a verdict. In the end the jury found that De Lorean had been entrapped, and let him go free.[2]

Because of the publicity "John's case" said his triumphant lawyer, is a "wonderful test of the jury system and the criminal justice system." He might better have said that both systems survived—as did a third, the free press. In a nation still dedicated to the proposition that progress and the pursuit of happiness remain constant goals, survival has never been enough.

Consider the media's role in a matter of real survival: the coverage of the life-and-death struggles of terrorists and their victims.

In the summer of 1985, the terrorists who hijacked TWA Flight 847 to Beirut knew how to use the media as well as they knew how to fire the AK-47s they carried. They bargained on television with deskbound New York anchormen. They put on menacing shows featuring American captives with guns pointed at their heads. They encouraged media madness at a jammed, unruly press conference, in which both the terrorists and their hostages were forced to retreat from the mob of bellowing press troops. There is no one, other than press fanatics, who would consider the lives and welfare of the victims of terrorism less important than the complete liberty of the media to cover each grisly incident any way they want. Yet repeatedly, fired by competitive instincts—like "dogs in heat," said Peter Jennings—the media put on what has been called "terrorvision."

In his analysis, "Terrorist Spectaculars: Should TV Coverage Be Curbed?" (Twentieth Century Fund, 1986) former New York *Daily News* editor Michael J. O'Neill wrote:

> Instead of merely covering the news, television often becomes a participant. In terrorist episodes especially, it frequently is the central nervous system for all the parties, brokering emotions, sometimes managing negotiations and performing all sorts of other services or disservices.

One of the hardest terrorist exclusives to take was NBC's "interview" with Mohammed Abbas, who was charged with highjacking the cruise ship *Achille Lauro,* during which an American was murdered. After having been turned down by others earlier, Abbas went before the NBC camera only for the purpose of delivering a murder threat. No really tough questions were asked. The price NBC paid for providing Abbas with an

---

2. His lawyers had avoided using the verb entrap because they said it carried the implication of guilt. So they instead used "set up," "put on" and any other circumlocutions they could contrive.

outlet for his deadly announcement was concealing his whereabouts from the police and governments that had been searching the globe for him (though it is surprising that *they* couldn't find him and NBC could).

Very few inside or outside the media condoned NBC's deal or the justification that it was able to show "the real face" of terrorism to a public that needed to "know thine enemy." Nor could many buy NBC's afterthought, amidst public outrage, that it was "worth hearing those warnings first hand" to understand the "venality of Abbas' thinking, the darkness of his mind."

By far the biggest and most ambiguous argument was over the rights and wrongs of relentlessly exposing the private lives of public people. On the radar of public concern, there were early blips in 1984 that would multiply and cover the entire screen within the next two years.

Of course, a warm comforter covered the press. Democracy requires robust debate under the bright, healthy sunlight of information. Public figures willingly surrender their privacy when they seek a position of power or celebrity. But by the winter of 1984, these old homilies seemed to press and public alike more troubling than comforting.

There were many examples of the growing difficulty of distinguishing between the media's self-proclaimed "right to know" and their self-righteous pursuit of vulnerable public prey. One such victim got the most space in print and on television in 1984. She survived but was bloodied and exhausted by the struggle. It could be said she deserved to be challenged by the media. Yet?

Geraldine Ferraro had undoubtedly invited it by becoming the first major party female vice-presidential candidate in history. An exciting first—acknowledged to be so by her Republican opponents.

The opening event of the Ferraro press olympics started routinely enough, given the competitive instincts of the players. On the eve of her departure for San Francisco to become the first woman ever to be so anointed, Ferraro was the unblemished heroine of the moment—remember? Reporters suspected that she was going west on a scheduled Northwest Airlines flight. The Washington *Post,* in a story headlined "The Thrill of the Chase," reported that more than twenty journalists bought tickets, boarded the flight and began searching frantically for her, even in the lavatories. Not immediately finding her on the plane, they then suspiciously looked over every blonde aboard—especially those wearing sunglasses—for signs of a concealed Ferraro. (She had actually left five hours earlier on a private jet.) "It was crazy," one reporter later said, "I rushed up to one stewardess and asked if she were Geraldine Ferraro in disguise. She looked at me, like 'You jerk, I don't even look like her.' "

The bloom on the feminist rose quickly wilted. Ferraro and her husband John Zaccaro were exposed to a searing news media investigation of their financial life together. The whole "bowl of spaghetti," as it was unfortunately and surely inadvertently described one night on the CBS Evening News, was devoured, strand by strand by hungry journalists competing with each other. In print the exposés provided daily sustenance not only for the Popular Press but the Deep Press as well.

On one day, the New York *Times,* devoted one-quarter of its front page to the story. Her husband's humblest real estate tenants were interviewed. One eighty-one-year-old—a real find—complained in cold print that a hole in his bathroom wall had prevented him from taking a bath or shower there for four months. Across the country, the day's discoveries followed Ferraro everywhere she campaigned, magnified by the 5:00, 6:00 and 7:00 P.M. local and network news, filled with phrases like "smoking gun" "and alleged Mafia connections." Newspapers editorialized about "long, dark shadows."

At one climactic televised press conference, Ferraro momentarily won the sympathy of the public not because she was so right or convincing but because by comparison the press pack was so bloodthirsty and boorish. Ellen Goodman, Boston *Globe* columnist, scored the press conference: "Christians 10. Lions 1. The lions, it should be noted were the press."

Many said the press exposure proved that because of her husband's questionable business connections and the shortcomings she revealed, Mondale never should have picked Ferraro in the first place. Her own revealing Chappaquiddick. But the entire chase proved as much about the scattershot methods of the news media as it did about the fragile qualifications of the candidate. Two *years* and six months later, after the House Ethics Committee had already cleared Ferraro, the Justice Department completed its investigation and dropped all civil and criminal charges against her.

New York *Times* columnist, Flora Lewis, summed up a widespread feeling of unease about such media-inflated moral absolutism: "It's considered smart to say 'Never trust a politician.' A code of ethics is essential but it's coming to be applied as 'guilty until proved innocent.' "

"Guilty"—guilty of what? In what certainly looked like a modern record, more than a hundred members of the Reagan administration had plenty of guilt to answer for in the sleaze department. But by 1986, in politics charges by the press against public figures mushroomed to include everything from adultery and pot to plagiarism, wedding dates and the behavior of candidates' spouses.

Laws of privacy in the United States are vague and unsettled. If the laws on privacy are at best unclear, media standards are chaotic and completely unpredictable. For the press what is private or not is largely a matter of individual editorial judgment—or misjudgment.

One view from a couple of a lawyers:

The press is overstepping in every direction the obvious bounds of propriety and decency. Gossip is no longer the resource of the idle and the vicious, but has become a trade which is pursued with industry as well as effrontery. Modern enterprise and invention have, through invasions upon privacy, subjected [people] to mental pain and distress, far greater than could be inflicted by mere bodily injury.

Is that a complaint about the tumble of events in 1984–85, escalating into a national uproar in 1987? Hardly. It was a judgment rendered in 1890 by Louis D. Brandeis, before he ascended to the Supreme Court, and his law partner, Samuel D. Warren. It is not surprising in its antiquity, for basic questions about the human condition remain constant, which is why we still learn from reading the classics. But that condition can be significantly altered by science (e.g. medicine and bioengineering) or technology (the environment and communications). Invasion of privacy has always been a bleat against journalists by the public and politicians. But by 1987 the definitions of what was private and what was not became more of a troubling enigma than ever (see page 15).

First it was Gary Hart, who asked for it. "Follow me" and see if you can catch me womanizing. And then Joe Biden, who got caught passionately making other people's speeches. Both were nailed and driven out of the presidential race as a result of a new political buzzword, the "character issue." The press some say—or that darker word, the media—undid them.

Senator Hart moaned at first ("a false and misleading story") but later recanted to his supporters ("I've let every one of you down"). Senator Biden was right on the edge of blaming the press, then drew himself up short ("I'm angry at myself for having been put in the position," but no, he quickly interjected, "put *myself* in this position"). Gary Hart had no such compunction. When he surprised everyone and reentered the race, he decided his personal conduct was less relevant than his program for America, so he went over the heads of the prying media. As he said in his new knight errant role, "Where character is concerned, I say let the people decide." They decided no and he quickly withdrew.

If the media were not the perps they certainly were the cops on the beat. Hart had to quit the first time after a Washington *Post* reporter, who already had hard evidence of the answer, asked, "Have you ever committed adultery?" Biden might have ridden out his borrowing the words of the British politician, Neil Kinnock. But not when video comparisons were played on split television screens across the country, compounded by another tape of his exaggerating his educational achievements. Then a second Democratic candidate, Massachusetts' Mike Dukakis, after his wife preemptively struck by announcing that she had been addicted to pills but was cured, admitted to the nation that his staff had done something routine in presidential campaigns: they had provided one of the damaging Biden videotapes. His "confession," as well as his wife's, saved him.

These disclosures inevitably forced other candidates under press pressure to deny or quickly confess to their own rumored violations of the seven deadly sins, including how two of the most God-fearing happened to marry women decades ago who were pregnant at the time. Then suddenly the ground shifted. A new question arose: "Have you ever used marijuana?" It became the question of the week after the forty-one-year-old Supreme Court nominee, Judge Douglas Ginsburg, was discovered, not by the FBI background check but by inquiring reporters, to have tried pot eight years before, as had millions of other Americans and thousands of journalists, some of whom were asking the embarrassing questions.

Strange to report that in these cases there was not the usual feeling of either triumph or self-righteousness on the part of journalists. The best of them were more troubled than gloating. Why? After all, the killing wounds were self, not press, inflicted. Zealousness in the face of public hypocrisy, some of them said, was a press service not a sin.

In years past, reporters and editors had easy clichés to answer the question of how to deal with the private lives of public figures. The rule was that if an official's personal habits didn't affect performance on the job, it wasn't news. So a political *Who's Who* of sometime liars, adulterers, alcoholics and ailing public figures were immune to exposure until after they died or were so conspicuous in their failings that reporting them was unavoidable.

But like most rules on complex subjects, that one didn't work. So a more impressionistic personal standard of taste was invoked. Yes, we know that stuff but "it's just not our kind of story." Not our kind that is until someone else ran it—and someone usually did. Then everybody had to cover it because now news of the news about national figures any place becomes news everyplace. Times were once very different. George Washington communicated by quill pen and dispatch rider. Today, public figures can be talking to and seen by the whole world when they open their mouths or keep them closed—especially if they do either unwisely.

It's not that media or public morals have changed so radically. The press has. Once it was no more than a regionally limited voice. But national publishing by the new electronics and, above all, television changed all that. The basic characteristic of the press is its new clout—not just enhanced but different. As a result, the new characteristic of public figures is their vulnerability. Some say both characteristics create more perfect democracy. Everybody now learns everything about public officials. Let the people judge on the basis of complete information.

But it's not so simple. Hypocrisy and fake moralizing abound, by the press, the politicians and the public. How fairly and carefully the press uses its new capacity is as up for judgment as is the total disclosure that now is a fact of life for all politicians. In the end, the public will judge whose character deserves more opprobrium. With hypocrites in both the press and politics, and a voyeuristic public in the middle—enjoying and deploring the spectacle—there is no assurance of who will be judged the good or the bad guys. In the final analysis, as someone once said of such dilemmas, there is no final analysis. Only constant questions and judgment calls.

W. H. Auden put it poetically:

> Private faces in public places
> Are wiser and nicer
> Than public faces in private places.

Private? The very essence of the American government and legal system is its openness. What had changed was that openness had taken on a new meaning.

What are they supposed to do, ask many journalists, when the news is out there, when a drama is unfolding, or when charges are made of unacceptable conduct or possible violations of the law by public figures? If the media hold a story or refuse to run it altogether, their sources often threaten that the story will be peddled to the competition. If they decide to wait to check the story or circumstances further, they run the risk of losing or sharing it. If they go to too many sources, they may be spreading the word or allowing a counteroffensive cover-up to be mounted.

If the media uncover potentially damaging personal information about public figures, why not let the public be the judge of whether it matters or not? When they have information about criminal activity or the whereabouts of criminals, they face another dilemma. If they go to the police they will become agents of the government, untrusted by future sources who may have valuable information. If they tip their hand on a question of foreign or military affairs, they may be engulfed in usually specious pleas that their disclosure will be dangerous to national security.

All possible. But the dangers of being used, of being sanctimonious morals police, of being unfair or inaccurate by rushing into print or going on the air questionably or prematurely, are more damaging to a news organization's reputation than the possibility that by passing or waiting the organization may be beaten to the story.

Being first is no excuse for being manipulated, half-cocked or wrong. The media's triumphs give the press pride in how good they can be at their best. The glow of their big successes, however, does not brighten their failures when they are at their worst.

If there is no absolute cure for these failings, the media could at least try to stop playing so many games of follow the leader, "catch-up" and "gotcha." They could try to control their hyperactive professional reflexes before they rush to judgment by overplaying questionable charges. In many cases they could give the subject more of a chance to answer; they could also do more than just report both charge and reply, and in some cases even make the judgment that the accusation is not worth inflating, even though someone else may choose to inflate it. And they could stop measuring importance by what other news they have on a dull day or a quiet season.

Possible? Not really, say most journalists. It's the built-in system, the momentum of the media, their assigned role to go headlong after the story. But that traditional banality covered up a roily public disenchantment.

Unfortunately, the polls and surveys provided no convincing answers to just how the public felt about the press.

Does the public trust the media? Put all the polls and surveys together and the sensible answers are sometimes yes, sometimes no. Does the public find them fair, biased or credible? Again, the same kind of division, numbers varying by an insignificant swing to one view or the other, often depending on what happened yesterday or the day before.

Ask abstract questions on complex subjects to which people have not given much thought before you ask them, and you get responses that are not worth much after they answer. (Illustrated in a *New Yorker* cartoon in which a television commentator says on the evening news: "The latest research on polls has turned up some interesting variables. It turns out, for example, that people will tell you any old things that pop into their heads."[4])

Is freedom of the press important? Nearly 100 per cent of Americans

4. Ruth Clark, one of the country's best-known media pollsters, reported that the most persistent complaint about newspapers was that the ink came off on the readers' hands. More seriously—and more preposterously—a national poll reported in February of 1987 that 60 percent of the 1,006-person sample trusted their spouses; 54 percent said they trusted television anchors; 40 percent trusted their auto repairman and 38 percent trusted President Reagan. Not reported was how many people trust the polls.

believe it is. Break down the freedoms into some American legal components: Should the courts prevent or fine the news media for publishing or broadcasting biased or inaccurate stories about public officials? Should newspapers and television be required by law to present all sides? The public unknowingly but overwhelmingly votes "yes," favoring press restrictions that would please a dictator.

By agreed-upon trade practice, each poll is accompanied by an announcement that the "margin of error is plus or minus 3 to 5 percent" or more egregiously by a "potential error" in that tiny range. Sounds impressive, but the statements are also misleading. They mean only that the margin for *sampling* error (that is, whether the group was representative of the whole population) could be off by that much. It says nothing about the incalculable margin of real error in the offhand answers or the conclusions of the real poll itself.[5]

In 1985, puzzled by the conflicting evidence, Los Angeles' Times Mirror Company reached for yet another poll—this one its very own. The company commissioned the Gallup Organization to take the biggest national news media survey-poll of all (more than 4,000 interviews), and then go back and reinterview the sample to double-check key findings.

The overall conclusions were reported in early 1986 and trumpeted in full-page newspaper and magazine ad campaigns. The results were advertised as reassuring to the media. But the bad news was as abundant as the good, full of warnings. One analysis of the poll was titled, "They Don't Hate the Press As Much As Was Feared," concluding "but when the conflict is between the press and individual rights, the press loses every time."

The public was shown to "maintain a favorable disposition toward the press." Not very surprising, given the amount of time and money people voluntary spend getting news messages on television or from print. But contrarily, large numbers of those polled in the Times Mirror study were very critical and suspicious of such news media behavior as yielding to pressure groups, unfairness, invasions of privacy, political bias. They seemed to be saying that journalism was a necessary but much too fishy business.

While the press grabbed for the good news in the survey, the director of the project himself reported: "Is the press too interested in bad news?

5. Recently the New York *Times* began adding a final paragraph to its explanation of its opinion polling methods: "In addition to sampling error, the practical difficulties of conducting any survey of public opinion may introduce other sources of error into the poll." And the Washington *Post* cautions: "Sampling error is only one of many potential sources of error in any public opinion poll." Amen.

Sixty percent say it is. Too willing to invade people's privacy? Nearly three-quarters feel that way. Try to cover up its mistakes? Fifty-five percent say so. Unconcerned about the people it covers? A plurality believe that, too.''

Even if you believed the numbers down to the last digit, the pollsters suggested the media should take pride in their impact but no comfort in their practices. Not very reassuring conclusions about the climate surrounding the news media.

President Reagan offered a small, half-joking reminder of the assumed, almost casual resentment that Americans directed against this new media force. Reporters at a "photo opportunity" in the Cabinet Room of the White House violated the no-questions ground rule and shouted questions to the president. Reagan, not knowing there was still a live microphone in front of him, turned to an aide and said, unsmilingly, those "sons of bitches." It was said offhandedly, not to be taken seriously.

But the Great Communicator's epithet was clear evidence that those media sons of bitches, whether triumphant or not, had got more deeply under the American skin than ever before. It was not his first nor his angriest thrust at the press. He had a louder shriek welling up inside of him. It would come bursting out when, midway through his second term, he confronted the worst credibility crisis of his presidency (see page 226).

The American press has been railed at throughout American history. Journalists have learned to expect the attacks and dismiss most of them. They know their own built-in faults better than their detractors. If they cared, they did what they could about their shortcomings and went on with their work. The Lord's work, the more earnest among them thought. Their critics, though, had always viewed journalists more as devils than apostles.

By the mid-80s, you could argue about how widespread or important the resentment was. Was it a majority sentiment or a minority view? A fringe obsession or a widespread complaint? The polls offered only conflicting and confusing numbers. There were no clear answers. Only one certainty: the argument itself was intense enough to command attention.

Some of the criticism lumped everyone in the media together, assigning bad motives to good journalists, assuming that similar instincts co-exist in a dissimilar lot. Some critics paradoxically—if not ignorantly—accused all news media managers of being interested only in profits. At the same time, their staffs were said to be bent toward liberal, antibusiness objectives that were at odds with the same corporations that employed them. Editors, producers and reporters were charged with a carefree publish-and-be-damned attitude that most had not held for years. "Journalistic ethics" were widely thought to be a laughable oxymoron not a professional concern. Ethics are an invisible theory; behavior an observable fact. The facts of journalism too often obscured the theory.

Midst all the broadsides, there was one centrifugal truth. As good as American journalism was, everybody knew it was not good enough. Neither were its critics. But they could no longer be shrugged off.

13

Some Raps . . .

There is a difference between what we have a right to do and the right thing to do.
—Potter Stewart,
Supreme Court Justice, 1915–1985

Critics have a luxury that those who must make decisions do not.

Second guessing is easier than having to decide in the first place. To go or not to go, to print or not to print. To damn, to praise or just to stand by. Complex, hard choices and shades of gray end up as judgment calls that appear black and white. John F. Kennedy once said of his Rambo-like senior air commander, "If you gotta go to war you want Curt LeMay in the lead bomber. You just don't want him to have anything to say about whether you gotta go or not."

Decision-making in the news media is not clear-cut. Only the biggest decisions are made from the top. The others, which make up most of the daily news fare, are decided by a linked chain of people who have differing values, standards, experiences, motives and responsibilities. The head of a news organization is more like the conductor of an orchestra than the pilot of a plane. Some of the players hit dissonant notes no matter how much they are auditioned and rehearsed or how sternly the baton waves over them. The bigger the orchestra, the less control the conductor has over each player.

Journalists and their bosses, more than in most occupations, must make hundreds of decisions a day affecting other people's lives. For years those hard choices were mostly made by rote. But as the power of the press was amplified in the modern news media, the old habits no longer served. The change was fundamental. It required a retraining of some of the most deeply embedded press reflexes.

Yet the public has no reason to excuse the faults, only to judge the results. Behavior is fairly judged by its consequences more than by its intention or motives.

American law does not guarantee or even mandate, a good and fair press. Nor can it impose any speed limits.

It guarantees only a free press. Journalism's best defense against restraint from outside is more selfrestraint. But journalists do not gratefully take suggestions from outsiders for modifying their ways. They rebel against their critics. The more preachy the critics become about what the news media should and should not do, the less effective they are and the more they are resisted.

There are too many different kinds of journalists, too many close calls and hard choices to make, too many new situations to confront, too many conflicting objectives, to write a *Summa Theologica* for the news media, although hundreds have been churned out. When working journalists hear moralizing speeches about their work, or attend symposiums, they are like fire fighters at a civics lecture. They may be very uplifted but they have real work to do and all that theoretical chatter isn't helping them.

So not much is gained by the usual finger-pointing at the most egregious practices committed in the name of a free press. Conscientious journalists try all the time to curb the most blatant offenses (e.g. fraud, plagiarism, fiction masquerading as fact, clear conflicts of interest). Those offenses are the easiest to handle. By one count, at least seventy-eight newspaper people were fired or suspended between 1983 and 1985 for what were called such "ethical" violations. As for journalists without a conscience, they simply don't care and are beyond remedy.

The whole aura that journalists embrace is a more fruitful subject for scrutiny than composing still another handbook of dos and don'ts.

Head on, cast a realistic eye at the journalist's two icons: pursuit of truth and devotion to the public weal.

Both need to be cut down to size. Both are too pretentious to be believed and too contrary to the facts of actual performance. Both also nurture the kind of hubris and illusion that invites unbridled license where in many cases little is warranted.

Beyond the simplest of facts ("the police arrested . . . ," "the meeting started at . . . ," "the bombing took place . . ."), truth is an assessment. It is not to be confused with either honesty or accuracy. Truth goes beyond describing and trying to make sense of exactly what happened. Good journalism makes an earnest effort to report and explain what happened, putting it in an orderly and understandable context. Truth is mostly speculative. It is a judgment at the end of a long road of inquiry, which an opinionated journalist, like anyone else, is entitled to make and defend with conviction, unless or until some contrary truth convincingly challenges it.

"News and truth," columnist Walter Lippmann wrote more than a half century ago, "are not the same thing, and must be clearly distinguished. The function of news is to signalize an event, the function of truth is to bring to light the hidden facts, to set them into relation with each other. There is a very small body of exact knowledge, which it requires no outstanding ability or training to deal with. The rest is in the journalist's own discretion."[1] Nor should belief in the pursuit of an illusory truth confer a special status. Columnist Ellen Goodman points out that journalists too often behave as if "in the pursuit of deceit, deceit is okay, that we have a right to use untruths because we are going for a greater truth." *Time*'s essayist, Roger Rosenblatt, puts it most pungently: "When journalists hear journalists claim a 'larger truth' they really ought to go for their pistols."

Consider how wrong many of the most informed journalists can be.

Political pundits, for example, have been less reliable than astrologers in the past twenty-five years, even with the best of polls. Who could have known that Lyndon Johnson would have accepted a vice presidency, or that having succeeded to the presidency, as a result of an assassin's bullet, he would not seek a second full term? Richard Nixon, written off politically by the press and himself after a disastrous 1962 defeat in a California gubernatorial election ("You won't have Nixon to kick around any more") came back to be president in 1969, only to resign the office and be succeeded by a pleasant, lumbering congressman from Michigan, who had as his *vice* president—imagine that—Nelson Rockefeller. (Before he accepted the appointment, Rockefeller cut a deal with President Ford that he be allowed to spend weekends in New York!)

Did many truth-seeking political savants in the press expect, when he started out, that Jimmy Carter would make it to the White House from the Georgia state house? A movie actor from California who became governor was considered by most of the press to be "unelectable" when he first sought the presidency. In his second presidential election Reagan carried forty-nine of the fifty states. And who would have predicted that Gary Hart would reenter the presidential race after his public humiliation?

Journalists are incessantly asked who they think will be the nominees or the next president. Four years before any first-term election since the end of World War II, almost every one of them would have been wrong. They can predict only from month to month, always excluding the unknown,

---

1. Lippmann's analytical insights were more impressive than some of his discretionary truths, including his judgment that Nazi Germany represented no threat to Europe and that Franklin Roosevelt had no talent to be president.

which in fact has determined our political lives during that period. Often they cannot even do that.

The venerable columnist and writer, Max Lerner, said in an interview just before the 1984 Democratic convention that nominated Geraldine Ferraro: "I try to cut through a lot of baloney when I write. There's no way Mondale will have a woman running mate. It's not going to happen yet." And politicians don't make it any easier. Onetime Texas Democrat turned Republican, John Connally, once said about his presidential aspirations: "If you nominate me I will not run. If you elect me I will not serve. But if you beg me—I might."

On the eve of the 1964 Republican convention, I myself confidently wrote for all to read that no matter how many delegates he counted, Barry Goldwater would not be nominated as the candidate of his party. Within five days he was. I also turned away accusations of rampant corruption in the New York City police department told to me by a sententious young sergeant whose name, Frank Serpico, became almost as well known three years later in annals of crime-fighters as Dick Tracy's. A colleague of mine similarly rejected, without even looking, a thick pile of papers offered to him as evidence of "war crimes" by an agitated whistle-blower named Daniel Ellsberg. The New York *Times* months later made legal and journalistic history by publishing them as the Pentagon Papers.

At times there are stories that journalists—often mistakenly—think can't or shouldn't be written. Once in the late 60s, I was on an overnight patrol in Vietnam with a National Guard company of amiable, middle-class young soldiers from California. As we moved toward the shore of the China Sea through high grass, we were fired on. Two of the Americans were badly wounded. When the company came upon an ancient Vietnamese man on their flank, they attempted to question him through their Vietnamese interpreter, who barely spoke kitchen English (true of most of the army's field interpreters). They got nothing from their captive. So while *Time's* correspondent David Greenway took pictures, and the company took a smoke break, the laughing GIs turned their hefty scout dog loose on the terrified prisoner. He was chewed bloody from arm to neck until he "confessed." The GI medic then patched him up. Neither Greenway nor I ever reported the incident, nor sent in the pictures (which I still have). Too grisly, we decided—and how to explain it? Any more than the fact that embittered U.S. soldiers had been collecting the ear lobes of dead Viet Cong long before anyone reported it.

The day after Spiro Agnew was picked to be Nixon's running mate, another Time-Life correspondent, Charles Eisendrath, who had covered him for the Baltimore *Evening Sun,* described Agnew to me as a "hack

Maryland politician on the take.'' ''We can't use that'' I said, even though Eisendrath assured me that such reports were common knowledge among Maryland reporters. We never pursued it, until Agnew was discovered to be taking cash bribes in his vice-presidential office. Correspondent Jonathan Larsen reported that we should follow up on talk he heard that Missouri Senator Thomas Eagleton ''sinks into depressed states so severe that, according to friends, he has taken shock treatments to get himself out of them.'' We let it pass and inquired no further until four years later when George McGovern was confronted with the same information and dropped Eagleton as his vice-presidential partner on the Democratic ticket.

And, oh yes, when a Chicago correspondent suggested *Time* do a story on a new magazine called *Playboy,* I rejected the suggestion on the grounds that such ''college humor'' would never last.

Dumb? Lazy? Venal? Lacking in guts? No just routinely ragged. Every journalist has such tales. ''Don't be so humble,'' a wise friend once said to me, ''you're not that great.''

It is hard enough to know what to go after, even harder to be right about what you find and try to explain it. Unless it is the simplest and most straightforward story, to believe that journalism is the pursuit of truth is a pretentious dream bearing little relationship to a checkered reality. Whose truth? Which truth? How much truth? As the news media expand and their technology amplifies them into louder and more dominating national voices, assertions of truth need to be left more for the public to thrash out and less for the press to declare. Truth is a field for theology, formal logic, science and zealotry. In journalism it is enough to try to be honest and accurate without cloaking that pursuit in the mantle of truth.

There is no area where journalists need to be more honest than about themselves. They know how little and how much they know. They know where they get their information. They know how fragile or one-sided it can be. They are aware of their biases and potential conflicts of interest, which are rooted more in ambition and careerism than in commerce or crookedness. They know how many mistakes they make, large and small. They rarely let the public in on those secrets or reveal the tricks of the trade. They worry that such candor would undermine their authority and credibility, which is shaky enough without confessions or revealing exposure. Much as I myself once thought otherwise, good journalism is not a holy order, endowed with spiritual values in the service of the public. It is an occupation—one of the most gratifying.

Posturing aside, journalists neither choose their occupation nor engage in it as a career to do public good. That can and should be its by-product.

Although they often dress themselves in fancier raiment, most journalists have workaday motives not unlike those of people in other jobs. They may enjoy their work more and it is quite true that, as they are often told with wide-eyed envy, they "lead such interesting lives." They treasure their go-to-hell independence of everyone but their own bosses. They are stimulated by their need to inquire and are enrolled in a permanent graduate school of education for which they are paid, some modestly, others lavishly. They enjoy the access and leverage they have on events and public policy. They enjoy the power, though they rarely say so.

Most people work to earn enough to survive, or ideally to live the kinds of lives they dream about. Some small fraction of the population actually revels in the work itself, viewing the income as an ancillary benefit. Most journalists are in that fortunate group, not for the good they may accomplish but because of the personal gratification their work gives them. Nothing wrong with that—except for the halo they often wear around their heads as an adornment to the press badges they wear around their necks.

Journalists go astray, at the expense of their work and the public interest, when they vest themselves with a special aura of superiority, as truth seekers in the service of the republic, custodians of the public morals. That self-image is a breeding-ground for arrogance, cynicism and pretension. It kindles an apartness that encourages them to patronize the lives, work and pretensions of others. That posture makes them feel like superior judges. They should be expected to pay the price of their privilege with superior standards of conduct and work. Too few do.

As a group journalists are as ragged in the integrity of their work, as questionable in their judgments and as driven by their own demons as the people they report on in the public and private sectors. The worst excesses of other enterprises are curbed by public exposure and laws. The news media rarely expose themselves; their professional behavior and its results are further beyond the reach of the law than any other occupation.

In their defense, journalists are eternally caught in a conflict embedded in the very nature of their work. People in the news—and not only politicians—always try to put their own "spin" on stories. Those who seek press favor exaggerate the accomplishments they are claiming. Those who want to manipulate press attention cover up, mislead, hide and lie. Reporters, editors and producers acquire the hard shell of cops working on the vice or bunco squads. They have heard every story, seen everything and believe no one at face value. Everyone they deal with is a potential con artist. "People who see something derogatory written about themselves, *always* say it's false," says Robert D. Sack, a media lawyer who has written a basic text on libel, "and they believe it passionately, of course, because it reflects badly on them. Whoever says about an unflattering statement, 'You're right—thanks, I needed that.'?"

The Washington *Post*'s editorial page editor and columnist, Meg Greenfield, who is just as often critical of press behavior, explains:

> Our cynicism is easy to account for. We would be crazy to approach public life in any other way. The political history of our time has been, it seems to me, a chain of surprises and inversions of accepted truth. Each can only deepen the journalist's gut certainty that he is at least half of the time taken for a ride when officialdom opens its mouth.

Refusing to "go along" rarely creates popularity. So be it, say journalists. They want respect not love. But they too often get neither because the media are so often wrong, unfair, arrogant, prosecutorial, cheaply sensational or pursuing success at the expense of the higher values they espouse. They also abuse their immunities, taking refuge behind legal protections that are intended to assure free speech, not to create a privileged class of free speakers.

We expect and welcome righteousness from clerics but not from journalists. With news people such pieties can create behavior patterns that are not needed to get their work done and that damage their standing. Knowing both the shortcomings and virtues of their occupation, they would do better to look at themselves and their subjects from the perspective of information seekers rather than as carriers of holy writ or public prosecutors. They are professional eyes and ears, unlicensed agents who attempt to report and explain what should be known.

That more modest view of the journalists' role need not diminish them or destroy their espirit. Journalists do need special access. They need to be free of intimidation and awe. They need to awaken people in the middle of the night, persist in their questioning and doubting in search of real rather than surface information. They need to question motives, hidden agendas, concealment. Often they need to invade people's privacy. Many of their assaults against the sensibilities of others are essential. But too many journalists now consider such activities their God-given right and exercise it with swaggering abandon.

They would do better to think of it as a burden instead of a perquisite of their special position. They need to question their own ability to be right and fair as much as they question the honesty of everybody else. Such a process of constant self-examination would not have to make them timid, paralyze them or even interfere with their hectic deadline demands. It can and should become an important and built-in part of their thinking.

That perspective would help rather than hinder journalists in overcoming one of their biggest embarrassments, the stories in front of their eyes they often miss.

Against their record of triumphs in the 80s is an equally long list of failures. In New York City the press failed to uncover the fiscal crises of the 70s and the corruption of the 80s. The media did not discover some of the biggest and worst scandals on Wall Street or in defense contracting. They were not the discoverers of rampant drugs and gambling in big-league sports. Before the Challenger space shuttle exploded, they cast an unchallenging eye at the management of NASA. In Washington, influence peddling has been alive, well and appalling for years, without much media monitoring until it became too blatant to ignore.

The AIDS epidemic was at first ignored then overplayed by most of the press ("Now, No One Is Safe from AIDS").[2] Voters in Illinois pulled the lever for candidates with crazy programs but nice-sounding names before the media ever persuasively told them about the radical LaRouchian revolutionaries for whom they were really voting. Senator Moynihan, Nathan Glazer and a few academics raised their voices about the breakup of underclass families long before the media put it high on the national agenda. Kiss-and-stab White House memoirists told stories in best-sellers that many journalists said among themselves were old stuff, even though the revelations were news to most of their readers or viewers.

Scores of people from several government agencies at home and abroad were involved in the secret Iranian arms dealing, yet it was first exposed by a small Lebanese weekly not by the U.S. press. Many reporters were well acquainted with the National Security Council's operative, Lt. Col. Oliver North, but completely missed the shenanigans that made him the centerpiece of the Reagan administration's biggest scandal.

Journalists have as many failures to answer for as successes to preen over. They would be better off displaying the grace of their undoubted power than wielding it as a club. Their work would be more effective, not less so, if they adopted the tone and viewed themselves as fallible as ordinary citizens, with an occupational necessity to try to report and fathom meaning. They need to be especially aware that *their* product can have broader consequences than the work of bankers, carpenters, lawyers, artists, doctors or even judges, who can be reversed and overruled. Journalists who are carefree ("I just report"), cynical ("Let's get those bastards") or uncurious ("Everybody knows that") can often do infinitely more harm than good.

2. See *And the Band Played On* (St. Martin's Press, 1987), by the San Francisco *Chronicle*'s enterprising reporter Randy Shilts.

Many of them have taken as their bedrock oath that they just publish or broadcast the news. They neither make it nor are responsible for its effects. The consequences are somebody else's concern, not theirs. That may have been acceptable in earlier times, when their voices were weaker and geographically limited. But such a cavalier and shallow notion no longer works. Journalists cannot declare that they just shoot the shells, that where they explode and the damage they do is not their business. Their shells are too powerful now to allow them to ignore the consequences of hits and misses, on individuals, institutions and on a society that grants them such freedom to fire at will.

For daily journalists, in print and television, the built-in hazards of speed and the ticking clock of deadlines will always lead to error. The publisher of one of the best dailies in America recently said to me, only half joking, "Even in my own paper, I've *never* read a story in which I was directly involved that did not have mistakes in it." Not big mistakes, just weeds on the fairway. The problem of finite accuracy is not limited to daily journalism. It abounds in current books and magazines as well. Two of the best-known authors in America have told me that after one of their best-seller books is published, the mail they get corrects not fewer than fifty and as many as two hundred factual mistakes they made, despite their efforts to avoid them.

For accuracy's sake, it would help if newspapers backed up their reporters in the field more. Correspondents are under the gun to meet tight deadlines and are unequipped with home office information resources. A long-standing conceit is that the best reporters can get everything right. Impossible. The copy desks of bigger news organizations would do well to equip themselves with more fact checkers to correct mistakes as time allows, rather than rely solely on the memory and resources of reporters in distant outposts.

The weeds sprouting in an otherwise correct story give the whole story a bad name. In the public's mind, even good stories in print are no more respected than their smallest mistakes. Old newspaper saying: "A story is only as good as its dumbest error."

Even those who get favorable treatment tend to be unimpressed by the accuracy and depth of the reporting on activities in which they are involved.

Anyone who has ever served in government, or close to the top of other pyramids of power, or anyone who is a national celebrity of any kind, becomes disdainful of the quality of media coverage. Hodding Carter, a journalist before and after he was assistant secretary of state for public affairs, echoes the views of many with similar professional experience: "I cannot think of a single story with any real meaning in which there was not either a failure of emphasis or fact.''

Thomas Jefferson's view of the press is remembered for his lapidary pronouncement that if he were forced to choose between ''a government without newspapers or newspapers without a government, I should not hesitate to prefer the latter.'' But like Washington and Adams before him, and all the presidents after, Jefferson was no admirer of the press of his time. For him, press freedom was more a philosophical imperative than a personal preference. ''Nothing,'' he said, ''can now be believed which is seen in a newspaper. The real extent of this state of misinformation is known only to those who are in a situation to confront facts within their knowledge with the lies of the day.''

In my own experience in the public and in the quasi-public sector, and in being interviewed about my work, I have been very lucky. In hundreds of such stories, I can remember only a very few that were really wrong. Nor have there been many that I considered impressively right—mostly satisfactorily close but very few exactly so. I also have an even rarer piece of good fortune. I have almost never been misquoted, or quoted badly out of context. But neither have I often been really quoted in my own words despite the quotation marks around them. What usually appeared just carried approximately the correct meaning even though not in my language (unless the reporter was using a tape recorder or chose to read the quote back to me). Television interviews that have lasted half an hour and are edited down to five-to thirty-second bites, can be even less satisfactory.

Ask press people how they feel when they or their activities are reported on. Almost without exception, they will be as disparaging, or more, than those outside the news media. They know how shallow, misleading or just plain uninformed much of what they read and see about themselves can be, even when the stories are entirely favorable.

Among other problems that journalists at work have are their manner and their manners. They now need to mind their manners more—for quite practical reasons.

I have never known a reporter, editor or television producer who consistently accomplished more by bullying than by persuasion, backed up by homework and knowledge. It is possible—no, necessary—to be relentlessly inquisitive while not being disrespectful. Courtesy is no sign of weakness. Tom Paine once wrote (and Barry Goldwater rewrote as a presidential campaign slogan): ''Moderation in temper is always a virtue; but moderation in principle is always a vice.''[3] It should be printed on every journalist's press card.

---

3. Goldwater's version: ''Extremism in the defense of liberty is no vice. Moderation in the pursuit of justice is no virtue.''

Better journalistic manners are not a genteel social amenity. They have become a necessity. Before television brought the sights and sounds of news in the making, journalists were read but not seen. The ink-stained among them protested loudly—and still do—that, damnit, reporting has become a show for television. Much of it unavoidably has. The cameras are not just showing the subjects of the news but those reporting it as well. Reporters at work are frequently not an appetizing or impressive sight.

Not just crises make their blood run hot. The New York *Times'* R. W. Apple reported on the announcement of the first major breakthrough in nuclear arms control in years:

> In the briefing room at the White House this morning, President Reagan managed to read one spare paragraph announcing that [the U.S. and U.S.S.R.] had reached an agreement in principle. And then—bedlam. For what seemed like five minutes but was probably only about two, the place sounded like a cattle-auction barn. Five, ten, twenty reporters shouted questions to the President—all at once, all incomprehensible, with the stentorian voices of the television correspondents failing, for once, to drown out the squeakier notes of their ink-stained peers. Poised as ever, obviously delighted to have good news to announce, the President managed a series of one-liners despite the din.[4]

Presidential press announcements are not the only place where the world now sees the pushing shoving swarm, entangled in their gear. Recall the horde of newspeople encamped amidst their debris in the Barbados airport ("Who would want that undisciplined rag-tag bunch accompanying our troops invading Grenada?"); crawling over the lunch table set for American hostages at a staged terrorist press conference ("What a time for the press to be fighting each other"); staked out from dawn to dawn, going through the garbage and interviewing the children outside the house of a White House aide accused of accepting petty gifts ("Is that really necessary?"); shoving the microphone in the face of an unsuspecting victim of tragedy ("Have they no sensitivities?"). They are all on view.

Now in lawsuits reporters' outtakes, notes and office memos are also on display. The solution is not to destroy raw material that has not been published or broadcast. It is to have more defendable outtakes, more reliable notes, better procedures and motives that do not horrify if they must be disclosed. We demand such rectitude from the people who govern us. Why not from those who dominate us with their airwaves and presses?

4. Network television question shouters tried to justify their aggressiveness on the grounds that Reagan has held fewer press conferences than any president since Eisenhower first allowed filming of them. True enough, but the remedy of screaming questions was unappetizing and rarely produced any information of value.

Not that there should be objection to bulldog investigative reporting or intimidating, tough, direct questions, personified these days by, say, the directness or even pushiness of ABC's Sam Donaldson.⁵ They are needed. For a relevant public purpose there is no such thing as a rude question, only questions rudely asked. For many years, the bitterly nasty verbal battle, created in Vietnam at the daily U.S. military briefing (the "5 O'Clock Follies") and becoming even uglier at the White House press briefings after Watergate, went unseen by the public.

Now when the event is big enough, everybody can tune in to the noisy, hectoring back and forth.

Reporters trying to make news by tripping up or roughing up the briefers, in the hope of getting from them more than they have been instructed to tell. Or pouncing with relentless demands on an official or instant celebrity in the middle of an unexpected, confusing crisis. Journalists point out that it is even stormier in the British House of Commons, the Israeli Knesset or the West German Bundestag. The televised press conference is the American equivalent, journalists say, the most visible way public officials can be called to account. They are right. But politicians have to answer to the electorate, which can defeat them. Journalists can be frowned on only by their bosses or public opinion. In one of his better known epigrams, Oscar Wilde said it: "In America the president reigns for four years and journalism governs forever."

Presidential press conferences are tame by comparison with many other forms of press combat. In the early days of the Reagan administration, reporters reluctantly accepted a new White House rule they presumably first learned in grammar school. They would have to wait to be recognized instead of jumping up and outshouting someone else trying to get the president's attention. A small amenity. It helped and should have been initiated long ago by the White House press corps itself. Yet despite dozens of proposals, reporters themselves have rarely been able to agree on any better format for mass press conferences. They mistakenly view even minimal experimental attempts at planning or collaborating with one another as illegitimate acts in restraint of the free press trade.

5. As Donaldson himself told *Newsweek:* "If you send me to cover a pie-baking contest on Mother's Day, I'm going to ask dear old Mom why she used artificial sweetener in violation of the rules, and while she's at it, could I see the receipt for the apples to prove she didn't steal them. I maintain that if Mom has nothing to hide, no harm will have been done. But the questions should be asked. Too often, Mom, and presidents—behind those sweet faces—turn out to have stuffed a few rotten apples into the public barrel." Does he really mean it? I doubt it. But his interrogatory trademark comes close.

Press conferences, media circuses, herd coverage of political campaigns and other press jamborees, are a public show of media unwillingness to be ruled. They are right about that. But they are wrong in their unwillingness to create any better patterns of conduct among themselves. Voluntary efforts at new, self-imposed standards of decorum and order need not mean surrender, restriction or meekness on the part of the press. There are now too many in the pack, too much equipment, too many different objectives, for journalists to go about their business as usual. Too often they confuse freedom of the press with freedom of access and conduct in all situations.

Independence and individualism need not mean mob rule. Yet most journalists are as chary of getting together and creating their own standards of behavior as they are of accepting restrictions that could thwart their legitimate goals. Self-imposed restrictions are hardly inconceivable. On extreme occasions in the past, the media have voluntarily given up rights the law allows for values they themselves recognize as more important. After the urban riots in many cities during the late 60s and early 70s, the media collaborated with local governments to create standards of coverage that helped reduce inflamatory tensions. They adopted similar standards after the press mayhem of a terrorist radical Moslem outbreak in Washington, D.C. In kidnappings, it is common practice now to hold the story if there is real danger to the victim in prematurely disclosing the crime. Most newspapers do not publish the names of rape victims or juvenile offenders.

U.S. Circuit Court of Appeals Judge Irving Kaufman, a leading defender of unrestricted press freedoms, pleads for just such restraints from the media themselves, less they be restrained by others:

> There is no question but that the broadcast and print media have, of late, been the subject of severe reprobation. They are perceived by some as aloof and arrogant, insensitive to human needs and concerned only with the profits reaped from sensationalist coverage. When the public sees TV cameras recording the anguish of shocked parents who have just been informed their son was killed in Lebanon, the image of press indifference is reinforced. When major newspapers and magazines are compelled to acknowledge the products of reportorial fabrication, the press' reputation for truthfulness—and the strength of its claim to special constitutional status—is diminished. When aggressive reporters pose loaded questions more newsworthy than the response they expect or receive, people are apt to be repelled by such oppressive reporting techniques.

14

. . . And Bum Raps

[Journalists] are a sort of assassins who sit with loaded blunderbusses at the corners of streets and fire them off for hire or for sport at any passengers whom they select.
—John Quincy Adams

Much criticism of the media is invalidated and ineffective because it is so often driven by the biased anger of self-interest. When in doubt or in trouble, blame the press.

Everybody does it. All those who find themselves in the news play the media game, naturally trying to put the best face they can on every episode in which they are involved. How many in the public eye have not misled, obscured, covered up, exaggerated, distorted, lied or manipulated for reasons of self-interest when talking to the press? No wonder reporters are taught to be suspicious, to believe no one. News executives and journalists themselves are no different when they are the subjects. The public has every right and reason to treat them with the same wariness with which the press treats others. It is a tug of war between the way things actually are and the way those involved want them to appear to be—reality against policy.

Politicians are hardly the most reliable sources for assessing their real objectives. Cigarette companies are not the best judge of the hazards of smoking. Playwrights cannot attest better than critics to the merits of their latest works. Publishers will tell you their business is booming just before their publications fold. Public relations people and lobbyists are paid to serve their clients' interests, not the public's or the press's. Taking information at face value is not a journalist's job, nor is it any service to the public.

That's why the most recurrent complaints about media performance come from those who want the news reported their own way.

Lyndon Johnson told his biographer, Doris Kearns:

> There's only one sure way of getting favorable stories from reporters and that is to keep their daily bread—the information, the stories, the plans, and the details they need for their work—in your own hands, so that you can give it out when and to whom you want.

In his angry book chronicling his experience as Jimmy Carter's press secretary, Jody Powell compared the attitude of the free media to that of the embattled politician:

> Both have a tendency to become overly defensive when under attack. The 'circle the wagons; everyone is out to get us syndrome' in the White House is a generally familiar problem. The 'circle the typewriters; the First Amendment is at stake' phenomenon in the press is at least as common, almost as serious in its consequences, and much less well recognized or understood.

A weak and wavering governor once complained to me "I don't see the person you described when I look in the mirror every morning." Of course he didn't, but his constituents, who were quoted in a *Time* article, did. A banker, who was accurately but painfully characterized by dozens of people interviewed, told a reporter, "That's not the way I am, people don't think of me that way." How could he possibly know? Nixon, in a historic embarrassment, announced on television before a group of editors, "I'm not a crook." Congress had a different view of the unindicted co-conspirator. Eleven years later, before a similar group, Nixon was more conciliatory: "I have no enemies in the press whatsoever. There has to be an adversarial relationship. I don't think the press has changed, and as far as I'm concerned, I probably have changed some. When they give it to me I give it back in kind and that's just the way it's going to be."

What about matters of public safety, national security and secret international affairs?

Despite government protestations to the contrary, there are repeated examples of reporters and their editors who have not compromised real national security information when they were convinced of the harm they could cause. Journalists in Teheran knew that the Canadian embassy was hiding American hostages, never reporting it until after they were freed. The dramatic Israeli Entebbe rescue was not reported until after it was over, although several reporters knew about it. The unstoppable Seymour Hersh cooperated with the CIA director in not revealing a secret American effort to raise a sunken Soviet submarine in the Pacific, only to find himself beaten to his story by others. Some reporters knew of the U.S. plan to bomb Libya and withheld their information. The surprise Bolivian drugs raids in which U.S. troops and helicopters participated were not reported until the Bolivian press disclosed the plan. The Washington *Post,* at the request of the CIA director and the president, held back some of the details the paper knew about secret information an accused American spy gave to the Soviets.

Any fair balance sheet that attempts to weigh the evidence of government accusations that the press violates national security against evidence that the government itself far overclassifies and, above all, leaks secrets, comes out favoring the press, not the government. The courts have always found that to be true. No working journalist in this century as a result of work or access has been convicted, either of espionage or of violating national security laws.

Most of the information classified as secret and top secret by the government needs no such restriction. Satellites, electronics and spying operations leave very little unknown by foreign intelligence services. The press tends to be last in line, rather than first, in exposing really important military secrets. When reporters come upon material on the borderline, they are likely to check with government sources before rushing into print or broadcasting. They also frequently modify what they intend to print or broadcast if they are really convinced that security is at stake.

Government officials who plead national security to reporters are not very convincing. For its part, the press tries hard not to be simply the parrot-like purveyor of government policies—domestic or foreign, peaceful or warlike. Its role is to be the describer, not the enhancer of government actions.

Very few were surprised—except at the naked ineptitude of the operation—when the Washington *Post*'s Bob Woodward, of Watergate fame, exposed a three-page National Security Council memo putting into effect a policy of "disinformation" (read, lying). The plan was to convince the Libyan leader, Muammar Qadaffi, that he was about to be attacked by the United States. The government led the press to believe that there was increased Libyan terrorist activity, at a time when it had, in fact, fallen off. The government's objective was to make Qadaffi nervous about the possibility of American retaliation.

Secretary of State Shultz sounded more annoyed that the plan was discovered than he was about its intent. "Frankly," he said, "I don't have any problems with a little psychological warfare against Qadaffi. It's very easy. You people in the news business enjoy not allowing the United States to do anything in secret. So we can absolutely bank on the fact that, if the fleet does something or other, you'll scream. And Qadaffi will hear it. The fleet may or may not be getting ready to do something." The New York

Times' A. M. Rosenthal had an entirely different view of the government's deliberately lying to the press: "We should leave that garbage to the Russians."

The press, in this case, had conclusively caught the government in *flagrante delicto.* This, more than the fact of the deception itself, accounted for the unanimous media indignation. Both in government and in the press, everyone expects government officials to mislead, give their own "spin" to stories, deceive when they think it suits their own or the national interest. Every administration has done it. What made the Qadaffi deception so egregious, was that the lying was inscribed in a memo. It was dumber as a process than it was unique as a practice.[1]

The Qadaffi disinformation plan was compounded in quickstep by a series of deeper presidential disasters converting President Reagan, said the London *Economist,* from a "six-year wonder" into a "six-week mortal."

The reversal resulted from the administration's fumbling, secret shipment of arms to Iran—a country the president had described earlier as one of those outlaw states run by "the strangest collection of misfits, Looney Tunes and squalid criminals since the advent of the Third Reich."

The Janus-faced gambit was first unmasked in an effort to embarrass the United States by Iranian officials. They gave the story not to the American press but to a tiny (circ. 25,000) Lebanese Moslem weekly in Beirut. When it later turned out that millions of dollars in profits from the arms sale had been laundered through Swiss bank accounts and were intended for the contras in Nicaragua, by every reckoning it stripped away the Teflon that had coated the Reagan presidency.

White House chief of staff, and chief spin controller, Donald Regan, unselfconsciously told the New York *Times:* "Some of us are like a shovel brigade that follow a parade down Main Street cleaning up. We took the Reykjavik summit and turned what was really a sour situation into something that turned out pretty well. Who was it that took this disinformation thing and managed to turn it? Who took on this loss of the Senate [to the Democrats in the 1986 election] and pointed out a few facts and managed to pull that? I don't say we'll be able to do it four times in a row, but here we go again and we're trying." The effort failed, and shortly thereafter Regan was forced to resign. When the Iran-contra story finally broke the shovel, President Reagan reacted as embattled presidents before him had. He blamed the press.

1. And caused the State Department spokesman, Bernard Kalb, to resign. Kalb, who had been a correspondent for the New York *Times,* CBS and NBC, explained: "Faith in the word of America is the pulsebeat of our democracy. Anything that hurts America's credibility hurts America. You face a choice—as an American, as a spokesman, as a journalist—whether to be absorbed in the ranks of silence, whether to vanish into unopposed acquiescence or to enter a modest dissent."

Watergate had exposed a presidential cover-up. The Iran-contra affair, at the very least exposed Reagan's ignorance and lack of control over his own government.

He and his administration were attacked from all sides. His personal popularity and approval ratings plummeted. Congress and the press were in full pursuit. Every television network gave live coverage to two of his key aides who took the Fifth Amendment against criminal self-incrimination before a congressional committee. Suddenly Reagan's uncharacteristic personal anguish became impossible to miss. On November 26, 1986, the day before Thanksgiving, he exploded.

Hugh Sidey, the *Time* columnist who has specialized in covering the presidency since Eisenhower, was in his Washington office. Sidey had little hope for the request he had made late the day before to talk to President Reagan on the phone. Reagan's morning schedule, his secretary told Sidey, was fully booked. Then he and Mrs. Reagan were immediately taking off to their California ranch for Thanksgiving.

Minutes before Reagan boarded the helicopter on the White House lawn, Sidey's office phone rang. The White House operator announced the president was returning his call. With no prompting from Sidey other than his saying "These must be difficult days for you, Mr. President," Reagan replied calmly and without the anger in his voice that his words belied. "There is bitter bile in my throat," he said. Then the bile came pouring out, not in tone but in the words all over Sidey's yellow note pad. When published, Reagan's shriek flashed around the world: "I've never seen the sharks circling like they now are with blood in the water. What is driving me up the wall is that this wasn't a failure until the press got a tip and began to play it up. This whole thing boils down to a great irresponsibility on the part of the press."

Reagan's tough communications director at the time, Patrick J. Buchanan, followed by digging up that rotten old chestnut: "All newsmen should remember that they are Americans first and newsmen second." To which, as might be expected, shouts of "traitors, traitors," were heard in the hall where he was speaking. At the same time, in television interviews, Buchanan was crediting the administration with the exposures. "The leads and breaks," he said, "have come from the President himself." "The left," he added to another cheering crowd, "is not after the truth. The left is after Ronald Reagan," helped by the media's "sensational headlines and scavenger hunts."

This time very few, other than partisan, knee-jerk media bashers, could blame the press. Even the newly appointed special presidential adviser on Iran, David M. Abshire, said at the time: "The administration is taking and will take criticism of why its foreign policy went wrong. It will be severe and harsh criticism, we know that, as it should be.''

The story had, after all, been put out by the Iranians to an out-of-the way Beirut weekly. The president himself and his attorney general, Edwin Meese, announced the contra connection. To be sure, the American media and the Congress then went full-throttle after the facts—as they should have. The momentum had started. The chase was on. The questioning was relentless:

- *UPI's Helen Thomas:* "Mr. President does that mean you never knew anything about contra funding with Iran sales money?

- *NBC's Chris Wallace:* "You have stated flatly and you stated flatly again tonight that you did not trade weapons for hostages . . . ?''

- *ABC's Sam Donaldson:* "Polls show that a lot of people simply don't believe you. Your credibility has been severely damaged. What does it mean for the rest of your presidency?''

- *CBS's Bill Plante to a briefer:* "He is the president of the United States. Why doesn't he know?''

- *Unidentified shout:* "Why not dispel the speculation by telling us exactly what happened, sir?

Those are the kinds of questions that presidents expect and get: polite and respectfully expressed, but as direct and up-front as they can be. The questioners were not the source of the trouble. It was not media creativity or even initiative that ravaged Reagan's presidency but the mistakes and contradictions in the plan itself, and possible violations of the law. If at times the press had plenty to answer for, so did the politicians and the public who so readily smashed the imperfect media mirror instead of looking at the reality it could be reflecting. In the Iran-contra affair, many of the harshest critics of the media provided current evidence of that old cliché: they struck the messenger for so harshly bringing bad news.

Many former (and present) government officials agree that the real sources of such tensions are indefensible policies or lack of discipline within the government, not a lack of concern on the part of the press[2]

2. For example, Henry Kissinger, in an *American Heritage* interview long after he left government, said: "I have contempt for individuals in government who turn over to the press classified documents in their trust. But I don't have contempt for those in the press who receive them. I do not think the media should censor themselves with respect to information that has come their way, provided that they did not commit the act of theft or get somebody else to steal the document. However ill I think of the thief, it is not the media's responsibility to police

Government officials would like to conduct their affairs and make their plans with less press and less public scrutiny. But in our "open society," they know it is virtually impossible. "Your job requires you to pry," Secretary of State Dean Acheson once wrote to James R. "Scotty" Reston, "and mine requires me to keep secret." Among the faults of the news media, undermining national security is not one.

Certainly the most vocal complaint against the news media is that their work is biased toward a liberal and left point of view. The charge of a left-wing bias was also a deep undercurrent around the Westmoreland-CBS trial.

At the most extreme, polemical form, two examples of the accusation are:

• Senator Jesse Helms:

> The real threat to freedom is on our TV screens every evening and on the front page of our newspapers every day. These newspapers and magazines and television programs are produced by men and women who, if they do not hate America first, they certainly have a smug contempt for American ideals and principles.

• *National Review* publisher and rightist lecturer William Rusher:

> I charge that the major media of the United States are a bunch of slanted liberals, who have deliberately, systematically, over a long period of time delivered the liberal line to the people of the United States.

Such exaggerated charges, by far overstating their case, do the conservative cause no good. They miss their targets and disqualify themselves from being taken seriously just as extreme left-wingers do when they call everyone opposed to them "reactionaries," or worse, "fascists."

Much harder to deal with is a more sophisticated—and more persistent—assertion that is summarized in an essay-pamphlet by the New York *Times* television critic, John Corry (Media Institute, 1986). Although he is writing about television, Corry is plainly describing the whole news media envi-

themselves in that regard." What about the Pentagon Papers case, taken all the way to the Supreme Court by the administration Kissinger served: "At the time I was outraged by the whole procedure, which seemed to me to threaten vital and delicate negotiations in which we were engaged. On sober reflection I would go along with the distinction I have just made."

ronment:

> Television does not consciously pursue a liberal or left agenda, although it does reflect a liberal to left point of view. This is because the point of view is fixed and in place, a part of the natural order. What determines much of what a journalist calls news and how he approaches it is not so much his faith in a political creed as it is the intellectual and artistic culture that shapes his assumptions.

To be argumentative one might answer: Tell that to Walter Mondale, Jimmy Carter or Geraldine Ferraro. But that reply is too simple, proving only that losing politicians of either party always place some or much of the blame on the media.

The issue of the political bias of the media is so charged emotionally that it produces dozens of conflicting studies, biographical and political profiles of journalists as well as pseudoscientific content analysis or even Rorschach-like Thematic Apperception Tests on how journalists interpret the news. The statistical research is no more conclusive or revealing than opinion polls on people's attitudes toward the press.

Pass over the questionable finite numbers and just take the sums. They are, with caveats:

- In the modern national media, most journalists are white college graduates, more likely to be educated in the East than in any other single region of the United States. They are better educated than the general population (they would have to be to do their job). In national elections since FDR's New Deal, they have tended to vote much more Democrat than Republican. On such key social issues as abortion, nuclear power, church and state, the environment, equal rights, and social programs, they tend to be aligned on the "liberal" side of the issue, though less so in a Reagan-dominated period, when conservatism is a main current rather than a tributary.

- Their headquarters are in New York City, but as distorting as that may be, no single location in the United States is its equal in human diversity. In origin, the CBS anchor (Rather) originally came from Texas, NBC's (Brokaw) from South Dakota and ABC's (Jennings) from Canada. Other anchors and commentators have been no less varied in their origins: Cronkite (Missouri), Brinkley (North Carolina), Mudd (Washington, D.C.), Chancellor (Illinois), Sevareid (North Dakota), Moyers (Oklahoma). As anyone would expect, it is absolutely true that they know one another, are more attuned to the power centers of the East than to the wheat fields of Kansas or the sunsets of Hawaii. But they self-consciously try to overcome that limitation by travel and trying to keep their eyes, ears and minds open. Of course, they do not entirely succeed—but is there a better alternative? CNN originates and is headquartered in Atlanta, and two new television news services for local stations come from Minneapolis and Chicago. Others similar services originate from regional headquarters around the country. There may be something to the unavoidable northeastern tilt, but not much.

• The three most influential dailies in America are the New York *Times* and Washington *Post,* whose editorials are consistently on the liberal side, and the largest, the *Wall Street Journal,* which leans even harder in the opposite direction. The most widely syndicated political columnists—James Kilpatrick, William Safire, George Will and William F. Buckley, Jr.—are all conservatives, with liberal columnists not coming close to their combined circulation. (Jack Anderson, with the biggest syndication of all, specializes in exposés, with no apparent political tilt.)

Despite conflicting and weighty numerical analyses on both sides of the question, no one has ever demonstrated convincingly to me that political campaign coverage leans unfairly to one party or the other. Conversely, it remains true that in editorial endorsements, Republican candidates nationally continue to fare much better than Democrats, but such endorsements seem to have no discernible effect on the final result. Voters are plainly more affected by events than endorsements. "There is about as much ideology in the average Washington reporter," said David Broder, one of the best of them, "as there is vermouth in a very dry martini."

On the networks, the news coverage does not have any *party* political consistency no matter what their leanings on social policy. Of the commentators, NBC's John Chancellor and longtime (until recently) CBS commentator Bill Moyers are liberal, while ABC's George Will was conservative. As for David Brinkley, Ted Koppel, Robert MacNeil and Jim Lehrer, who have their own television programs, not even right-wingers accuse them of political bias.

A far more serious criticism of television in elections is that political commercials, which increasingly dominate campaigns, have escalated in both cost and nastiness. The charge is true enough, as evident in the 1986 and 1988 elections when political advertising reached an all-time high in cost and an all-time vitriolic low in content. But it is pointless to blame the existence of television as a communications medium for that, any more than obscene phone calls are the fault of the modern telephone system.

If there is a solution to the partial degradation of U.S. elections by paid television commercials, it could best be explored by the television networks and stations themselves. Television now bans cigarette, liquor and most advocacy advertising. A voluntary ban on paid political commercials is not beyond imagining. Instead networks could allocate free public service time to qualified candidates or parties. The loss of revenue to the television networks and stations makes such a swap unlikely. Many would also oppose it on grounds that it would restrict paid-for free speech. But reasonable public pressure is growing to take elections out of the hands of media consultants and candidates who have the most money to buy media time, with all the related fund-raising pressure. Some change is obviously in order, either in television practice or in mandatory government restriction of paid advertising in campaigns.

By the time of 1988 presidential campaigns, the combination of a crazy-quilt primary system and television coverage made the question, "Is this any way to elect a president?" almost as pressing as the choice itself.

Ah, but critics say, never mind their commentators and editorials, how about the bias evident in the stories the media pick and choose to play? How about the media's carping negativism and failure to accentuate the positive?

Hard as what makes news is to define, there is no doubt that a functioning nuclear plant is less an event than one that explodes, even as a volcano at rest is not as newsworthy as one spewing lava on the surrounding population. Nor are full bellies or full employment worth reporting as often as hunger and widespread unemployment. The South African government's halting steps to modify apartheid get less daily attention than its constant oppression of blacks. War makes more news than peace, murder on the campus more news than meetings of the college French Club. Misdeeds are covered more intensively than good deeds. News by definition is more the interruption of the orderly flow of life than the routine, although the latter is now more frequently reported in life-style stories both on television and in print.

"The media," says Elliott Abrams, an intellectual who served as Reagan's hard-line assistant secretary of state, "tilt toward the visually interesting and exciting stories. They will choose the Philippine protest over the Rumanian practice." True enough—because the Philippine protest represents potential change while Rumanian Communist tyranny remains an encrusted horror.

Journalists do tend to be more sympathetic to those who have little power than to those in power. They are indeed skeptical of authority, as they should be. They are naysayers rather than yea-sayers. They are doubting and distrustful of those who want to influence them and, yes, they are more interested in exposing than affirming, more stimulated by dramatic bad news than by routinely good news.[3] They tend to spotlight problems rather than solutions. The public and the democratic process are

3. "Show me a country," says Senator Moynihan, "whose newspapers are full of good news and I'll show you a country whose jails are full of good people."

far better served by a press whose modern skepticism—to be sure, at times overwrought—grew from its Vietnam and Watergate experience than by the powerful press in the era before, which was characterized by a smug entangling alliance with government.

Irving Kristol, the neo-conservative eminence, says that the popular media "focus their dissenting energies on social policies affecting those portions of the population who, for whatever reason, are faring poorly." They do this, he argues, "since sanctimonious compassion has always been a key element in their professional self-definition." Their sanctimony is indefensible, but the media's compassion is essential to the role society, the Constitution and the courts have assigned to them, providing a check on the power of the majority.

Does that make journalists left-wingers whose political biases constantly are reflected in their broadcasts or publications? Hardly. It does often position them against the political mainstream, whatever that happens to be. They see as their role—as the Founding Fathers could be said to have defined it—to check the power of government rather than to cheer it on. The evening news, for big-city mayors or presidents, is a depressing daily report card on how little is working really well in their domain. But that is the price of their broad responsibilities, not necessarily the fault of the media.

Political critics of the news media would do better to zero in on specific examples of bias or bad judgment when they occur—as they do—and stop undermining their case with political generalizations that neither reflect media performance nor impress the performers. When a Soviet "commentator," who can be no more than an official propagandist, is invited to discuss a presidential speech for eight minutes in prime time, the network deserves to be rapped. When authentically good economic news is covered with the main emphasis on how bad the economy still really is, there are grounds for complaint.

But apart from the media's useful and intentional perversity, even the *Times'* John Corry agrees that their slight tilt toward the left is evidence more of a cultural background than a political creed; more a loyal opposition to whoever is in power than an embedded political ideology.

Consistent political bias is the least of the built-in faults of the news media. They are guiltier and more vulnerable in other areas. Press freedom, explained Yale President Benno Schmidt, then dean of the Columbia Law School, does not now and has never depended on the First Amendment alone, or even primarily. It "depends on the spirit of tolerance in our society and the extent to which society as a whole understands the role of the press. Most important is the current social and political climate which is unfriendly to the press, viewing it is an uncaring, unresponsive big business.''

In 1985, just how big a business it had become needed no amplification. Not only had the atmosphere in and around the news media changed, so did its structure as a business. It was certainly not business as usual.

In the same year as the Westmoreland and Sharon trials, along with scores of other major collisions between media performance and public expectations, media takeovers were an equal attention-getting upheaval. In that year *all* three television networks and a fourth potential one, plus scores of newspapers and major magazines, either changed hands or got new controlling owners. ''An immense clearance sale,'' columnist Russell Baker wrote, ''Everything must go. Newspapers, television networks, magazines. All for sale, and money the sole object.''

15

Dollars and Angst

We are witnessing a frenzy of activity in business, and on a scale never experienced before. But it isn't activity that appears to be creating new viewers, new products or new jobs, or for the most part, new competitive leadership—at least, not so far.
—ABC Founder Leonard Goldenson, after selling his media conglomerate, 1986

This century's milestone innovators in the media were motivated more by passion than profit.

Driven newspaper proprietors: California's William Randolph Hearst, St. Louis's and New York's Joseph Pulitzer, Chicago's McCormick, [1] New York's Adolph Ochs (and in a special way, *USA Today's* promotion-minded Allen H. Neuharth). Inventive magazine creators: Time-Life's Luce, the *Reader's Digest's* DeWitt Wallace, the *New Yorker's* Harold Ross, *New York* magazine's Clay Felker. In size and national impact, the biggest of them all, television: RCA's David Sarnoff and CBS's William Paley (and in another special way, CNN's Ted Turner).

In the aftermath of their pioneering came huge fortunes. Their creations were the result of ideas and instinct, not market research and spread sheets.[2] None could have survived—or would have been so widely cop-

---

1. Who tore off the banner headline atop page one in his paper, reporting the dropping of the first atom bomb on Hiroshima, and sent it to his managing editor with a buckslip ordering him forthwith: "Find a remedy for this."
2. The idea for *USA Today* was projected and surveyed in advance to the point of exhaustion and widespread internal disagreement. A vain, bullheaded Neuharth went ahead anyway. The paper's ultimate success bore little relationship to the detailed demographic projections. Time Inc., which for years has done elaborate market research, was wrong in almost every one its projections. *Fortune* was published into the teeth of the 1930's depression. *Life's* tremendous and unexpected early success came close to bankrupting the company by far underestimating its circulation and ad rate. *Sports Illustrated* took ten years to overcome its start-up dive.

ied—without the financial rewards that came from the success of their inventions. But it was their creativity and products that made their fortunes. They didn't follow the crowds or use market research to find out what their potential customers wanted. They led them—some to lower depths, others to new heights. Not a single major innovation and success in publishing or broadcasting has ever come from finding out in advance by pretesting what the public thought it would buy. The customers didn't know what they wanted until they were given it. (In a 1939 questionnaire, Gallup asked people whether they wanted television; only 13 percent of those questioned said they had any interest in this futuristic new product.)

Profits were the result, not the primary stimulus. Outside the world of communications it was the same. Akio Morita, the near-genius founder of Sony, explained that his plan was "to lead the public with new products rather than ask them what kind of products they want. The public does not know what is possible, but we do." The same was true of Henry Ford's first automobiles, but not the company's much later Edsels; Thomas Edison's electric light bulbs, not the utility giants that lighted them; George Eastman's Kodak and Edwin Land's Polaroid cameras, but not when one tried to imitate the other.

At Time-Life, in my own experience, we pursued our special new brand of journalism in a way that we knew and found exhilarating. In our wake came large profits. In Time Inc. language, it was the "church" (editorial side), which led the way, supported by an unresentful "state" (the business side), which enhanced and assured our profitability. Not even the leaders of our "state" wanted or thought then that it should be the other way around. The editors were not even *allowed* to see market research, then used only for advertising and circulation promotion. ("Every *Time* reader either has an inside toilet or wants one," was the editorial wisecrack about reader research.)

As the news media became bigger and bigger business, the innovative traditions led by creative editorial dominance began to erode. The media were an attractive investment, as was proved unmistakably in the mid-80's by the biggest outbreak of media takeover fever ever, raised to new heights not so much by the media brokers as by Wall Street investment banking houses "packaging" deals.[3]

The 1985 media takeover round started in an unbusinesslike way. It was pure spleen.

---

3. Proudly announced in financial houses' traditional tombstone ads, e.g.: "*Scientific American,* Inc. has been acquired by Verlagsgruppe Georg Von Holtzbrinck GmbH." In 1986 for *all* U.S. industry, there were 3,300 takeovers worth $175 billion.

North Carolina's Senator Jesse Helms, the most obstinate right-winger on the Hill, was fed up with what he called CBS News' "liberal bias." At a time when corporate raiding and takeovers of big businesses had become almost daily billion-dollar events, Helms backed an organization called Fairness in Media. The group's announced purpose was to gain control of CBS and become "Dan Rather's boss." Helms urged like-minded critics of CBS to buy stock in the company. Together they could put their money where the network's mouth was. It quickly turned out that those with Helms's conviction lacked the resources and those with the resources lacked his conviction. His open, ideological attempt to move in on CBS disappeared into the night as vacuously as it had arisen on the far-out horizon.

But others whose more conventional motives were profit and expansion went on a media acquisition rampage. It had less to do with pride and point of view than with revenue and return. Collectively, the total revenues from the entire media industry (television, radio, newspapers, magazines, 40,000 books a year, even including movies), added up to less than the gross revenue of the two companies on top of the *Fortune 500* lists. General Motors and Exxon were bigger than the whole media bunch put together.[4] But company for company, the media conglomerates were still rich prizes.

Newspapers sold for ten to fifteen times their operating cash flow. Television stations went for similar ratios. In other U.S. industries even the most successful companies usually sold for one-third to half those prices.

All the new tricks of the financial trade were put to work. Junk bonds, leveraged buyouts, spinoffs, consolidations, white knights, poison pills, greenmail. The financial merger-go-round had little to do with politics, news or influence, but it gave enhanced visibility to the "news business." The primary governing laws in that business were always thought to derive from the First Amendment, and only secondarily from the rules and regulations of the SEC or even the FCC.[5] In the takeover game, the secondary became primary. It was reminiscent of that old piece of folklore

4. In number of employees as well as gross revenue. GM alone has 811,000 employees worldwide. All of television—including networks, local stations, cable and public broadcasting—has about 80,000. Daily and weekly newspapers plus magazines employ 574,000 in all departments.
5. In broadcasting, takeovers were accelerated beyond any time in history by a change in two FCC rules. One abolished the "anti-trafficking" rule requiring in almost every case that stations be held for three years before being sold. The second almost doubled the number of stations allowed under one ownership to twelve AM radio stations, twelve FM stations and twelve television stations.

from Detroit in which a senior auto executive was said to have told his staff: "This company is not in the business of making cars. It's in the business of making money."

Within a nine-month period in 1985, three major acquisitions and one full-scale attack engulfed media companies once controlled and dominated by their creators. Now, despite their troubles with the public and the government as well as their special constitutional status, the news media lived under the roofs of companies that were among the most financially attractive in the United States.

Seventy-nine-year-old Leonard Goldenson, who had built ABC from the "Almost Broadcasting Company" into a network conglomerate, agreed to sell for $3.5 billion. The buyer was Capital Cities Communications. It was one-fourth ABC's size and had grown from a seedling radio and television station in Albany, N.Y., into a seven-television-station, twelve-radio-station, fifty-five cable-system broadcast company, which also owned ten daily and twenty-eight weekly newspapers (including the Kansas City *Star* and *Women's Wear* Daily). It was a friendly takeover and, like the others to follow, was calculated more to please Wall Street than to influence Main Street.

In anticipation of its new bosses' wishes, ABC began cutting its news and corporate staff even before the merger was completed. The new owners were said to operate "lean and mean," the new buzzwords of approval in the financial world. Despite the sums involved, the very blandness of the deal in broadcasting terms suggested how impersonal, even abstract, who owned what had become. That was not true of many of the other moves.

Ted Turner, the high-spirited Atlanta yachtsman, baseball-team owner, entrepreneur and founder of CNN, accelerated his upwardly mobile media drive by making an extraordinary offer. His Turner Broadcasting System, one-eighteenth the size of CBS, filed to buy CBS for a paper figure that might be as high as $5.4 billion. Nobody could really tell the price because the bulk of the payment was to be in the future. His bid involved a promise down the road that his new combined enterprise would reward CBS's stockholders at more than the market value of their holdings at the time of the offer.[6]

6. Turner expanded globally into news, entertainment and movies with daredevil financing. He was described by one network executive as "the Peru or Mexico of broadcasting. The banks can't afford to foreclose on him." In 1987 Turner got financial help from another quarter: he agreed to sell a large share of his company to a group of cable operators (including Time Inc.) for $550 million, which threatened Turner's control of the company.

CBS cried everything but rape and fraud. It successfully fended off Turner's attack, plus another assault from arbitrager Ivan Boesky (who later pleaded guilty to fraudulent insider trading in other transactions). To block the raiders, CBS bought back $954 million worth of its own stock in the open market, taking on the strain of huge new debt. Not that CBS at that point was unwilling to play the game. It just didn't like these new partners, or owners. CBS always held in reserve a different kind of merger. If it ever needed to keep Turner—or anyone else—off its back and out of its board room, CBS could merge with some white knight rescuer, possibly Time Inc. or General Electric.

But GE had other plans. It spectacularly put itself into the same game by buying RCA (and its NBC network) for $6.3 billion, the largest buyout then in history outside the oil industry. As soon as the takeover was completed and against the advice of the successful NBC management, the new owners, "following corporate practice at GE," filled the vacancy of president of RCA's broadcasting activities with one of their own. No matter that Robert C. Wright, who had risen in the GE ranks from plastics to finance, had little broadcast experience.

One of Wright's early decisions was to bring in an outside consulting group to examine the efficiency of the news division. The leader of the consultants attempted to reassure wary news people by explaining that he was not hired to cut staff. He had a more elegant view, worthy of a bumper sticker on his company's cars: "There either has to be more work with the same number of people or the same work with fewer people."[7]

The CBS game was still alive, when up to the gambling table stepped an ever higher roller of media dice, Rupert Murdoch. The Australian-born press lord had already become the dominant figure not only in his own country but on Britain's Fleet Street. There he owned the wildest, largest daily tabloid in the West, the *Sun,* the huge, scandalmongering weekly *News of the World,* and for the prestige and influence, his more recently acquired *Times* and *Sunday Times* of London. When Murdoch first entered the American scene in the early 70s, he made his usual splash by creating the national *Star,* to compete at the bottom of the trash barrel with the weekly *National Enquirer.*[8] He also picked up Texas papers, then moved northward.

7. When the predictable study was finished by mid-1987, the New York *Times* reported that the consultants "found there are too many employees on the NBC division payroll, their salaries are too high and their time is wasted too often, according to network officials familiar with the report."
8. When Murdoch first came to the United States he visited me in my Time-Life office, accompanied by two Australian aides. He had heard I was aware of some

He spread his formula of sex, scandal and sensational junk food to New York. (His usual method, the London *Economist* said, was to "buy them up and tart them up.") Murdoch bought the New York *Post* and brought an uninhibited team from down under (in both meanings) to run his noisome tabloid. ("We go for the shiny and the jagged," said one of them.) Then on to Boston, acquiring Hearst's failing *Herald*. And Chicago, where he arrived as the buyer of the Marshall Field family-owned *Sun-Times* with such a clang that he drove out much of the paper's senior staff. Along the way Murdoch picked up a string of magazines and weeklies, including *New York* magazine and the *Village Voice*. (The *Voice's* profits were attractive but not attractive enough to overcome the paper's countercultural bent that was so distasteful to Murdoch that he sold it to the proprietor of Hartz Mountain, a pet food and products company.)

Personally, Murdoch was a bright, socially charming, energetic and unpretentious "family man." His private personality bore little resemblance to his public prints. Anyone who knocked his racy school of journalism, he labeled a snob. "Too often, he said, "tedium is the message." He was just giving his readers and the politicians in power the cards they wanted—from the bottom of the pack. Most working journalists who criticized him preferred anonymity. Understandably, inasmuch as he had become one of the biggest employers of journalists in the world. Outside the U.S. alone, he controlled one-third of Britain's and close to two-thirds of Australia's newspaper circulation. Many politicians had the same reluctance to cross him. His childhood friend and the former Australian prime minister, Malcolm Fraser, said elected officials were "too scared" to criticize Murdoch.

As much as he enjoyed shirt-sleeve editing, Murdoch was no koala bear in high finance. He tried and failed to buy control of Warner Communications, making a tidy $40 million profit when he sold his Warner stock. So he teamed up with Marvin Davis, a Denver oil potentate, with a wallet as fat as his waistline. Murdoch bought half of Davis's 20th Century-Fox movie studio as the first step to his next and boldest move.

of the best writing and editing talent in the U.S. He said he was about to start a weekly newspaper called the *Star* and needed an editor. Could I suggest someone? I asked what kind of a paper it would be, so that I could orient my thinking. He accurately described the mass-circulation, non-news weekly he had in mind. I told Murdoch, an engaging personality and a shrewd, tough businessman, that I was not well acquainted with the kind of editor he was obviously looking for but that, as a friendly gesture to a foreign press lord I would inquire overnight. I did and the next day produced the name and credentials of a clever gossipist, James Brady. When I passed the information on to Murdoch he told me that confirmed his own thought and he hired Brady as the *Stars's* first editor. I plead guilty of co-conspiracy in Murdoch's early debasing of the American scene.

Foreigners are banned by law from owning more than 20 percent of American broadcast properties. Murdoch simply changed his citizenship and became a naturalized American. He had been an in-and-out "permanent resident" for ten years, so it was easy. That qualified him to become the buyer (without Davis) of the Metromedia chain, whose six owned-and-operated television stations made it one of the largest broadcasters in the United States and potentially a new fourth network.

Within two years he would have to sell both his New York and Chicago tabloids to comply with the law that prohibited new cross-ownership of a television station and daily newspaper in the same city. He did sell the *Sun-Times,* to an investment group headed by the paper's publisher. Murdoch had bought the paper and its syndicate for $100 million and sold it for $145 million, holding onto the syndicate, which he later sold to Hearst.

But he was working to have the cross-ownership rule waived for his New York *Post,* on the ground that there were no buyers for his money-losing paper in the city he now called home. But in a move as devious as the publisher they opposed, Democratic senators Ernest F. Hollings of South Carolina and Kennedy of Massachusetts, attached a nearly invisible rider to a massive catchall spending bill, forbidding the FCC to grant Murdoch any further extensions of the cross-ownership rule. An appeals court later declared the rider unconstitutional but it was *too* late. After wailing loudly at the injustice of being singled out for punishment by his political enemies, Murdoch sold the *Post* for $37.6 million to Peter S. Kalikow, a New York real estate developer with no publishing experience.

Conversely, back in Australia, Murdoch's television expansion was challenged because Murdoch, now a U.S. citizen, ran afoul of *that* country's rule banning more than 15 percent ownership of radio and television properties by *foreigners.* He had solved that by having other members of his family keep their Australian citizenship.

The buying of profitable stations, the full ownership of 20th Century-Fox and the abandonment of the shaky dailies was not only a net gain for Murdoch. It could also be for American journalism. It was less likely he could ply his brand of journalism on the news programs of Murdoch's Fox Broadcasting Company stations than in the newspapers he had owned. Murdoch himself acknowledged that. "Television is today's new mass medium. It's taking over the role of newspapers. I think a newspaper should be provocative, stir 'em up," he said, "but you can't do that on TV." Well not as much, anyway. After he signed affiliation agreements with more than one hundred stations, he announced his opening schedule of tabloid television: two sitcoms, one "action adventure" and "The Late Show Starring Joan Rivers."

As for CBS, it was taken out of "play," as they say on Wall Street, when its management invited what it thought was the benign intervention of the New York investor and Loews Corporation chairman, Laurence A. Tisch. He started buying stock in mid-1985 and later accumulated close to 25 percent of the company, which made him the dominant stockholder by far. Before very long, Tisch's presence was not looking so benign. The company started making almost as much news as the CBS News division was covering.

The network had been losing out to NBC in the entertainment sweepstakes. Its profit projections were down. Its bottom-line oriented management, led by Thomas H. Wyman, who had come from Pillsbury and its "jolly" Green Giant company, pressured the CBS News division, along with everybody else, to cut its costs and boost ratings. Wyman was advised by his own staff to handle news differently but replied that everybody at the network had to share the same burden of CBS's downturn. That was not the way CBS had earned its preeminence in news. Gene F. Jankowski, president of the CBS Broadcast Group in charge of all the network's programs (information and entertainment), said with obviously mixed feelings: "The other networks are treated like networks. We're treated like a value system."

The cutbacks and emphasis on ratings in the news brought waves of public complaints from the high-spirited and free-talking CBS News stars about sacrificing news values for entertainment. The CBS News operation, once the standard-setter for network television, became the focal point for widespread public criticism and internal dissent. If ever proof were needed that network news and public affairs determine the reputation of a network no matter how insignificantly their losses and profits directly affect the bottom line, the CBS turmoil provided it.

Finally the pressure on Wyman got so great that he badly misread the signals. At a tense meeting in September of 1986, the fourteen-member board, once supportive of the Wyman management, refused to back him again. Wyman resigned and the board brought in as acting chief executive none other than Tisch, and more surprising, Paley, who by then owned only 8 percent of CBS, as acting chairman.[9] According to the notes of the board meeting, the "shortcomings" of Mr. Wyman's management of

9. Van Gordon Sauter, by then strongly identified with the turmoil, left the next day. A month later, Howard Stringer replaced him as president of CBS News, the third executive to have that post in under a year. Stringer, born in Wales, an Oxford graduate and a naturalized American, had worked at CBS for eighteen years, including as executive producer of the Westmoreland documentary. The board later elected Tisch, sixty-three, president and chief executive officer; Paley, then eighty-five, chairman.

CBS" included: "A record of unsuccessful acquisitions, inattention to the talent and creative aspects of the business, particularly in the flagship News Division, inability to control overhead costs, failure to anticipate declines in operating earnings and other factors."

It was a momentary signal that CBS might be changing its direction, that broadcasting was indeed more than marketing, cost control and high ratings in the news. To restore morale in the news division, Tisch tried to make the change very plain. "While this is supposedly a profit-making institution," he said soon after the board meeting, "it also has an obligation to the American people and I take that obligation very seriously." Then he added: "The news is a must. Whether the news loses money or makes money is secondary to what we put on the air. I can't picture any point at which profit becomes the main thought in deciding on a news program."

His words at the time were cheered; but his follow through was even more loudly lamented. He seemed to say what he believed but was less sure of what he really believed in his world of broadcasting.

Within months the news stars in Tisch's eyes (and in his life) lost their sparkle. At least on the face of it he ignored his earlier promises. Tisch's old experience in other kinds of business (insurance, real estate, tobacco, investment) overtook his new experience in news. He was startled, he recalls, when, along with CBS News President Howard Stringer, he toured the network's European bureaus. Hearing the standard gripes about being unappreciated and underused that foreign correspondents always make to visiting bosses, Tisch was distressed at how much the bureaus cost and how relatively little they seemed to contribute to the evening news. To spend $100 million a year for twenty-two minutes a night of evening news seemed to him both wasteful and excessive (although by one measure, roughly $275,000 a pop was considerably less than what a network entertainment half hour costs and only slightly more than it costs an advertiser to shoot an elaborate thirty-second network commercial).

Tisch immediately proposed cuts of between $30 and $50 million in the CBS News operation—beyond even those undertaken by the other two networks. His order brought another round of firings, closing bureaus and again loud public protests from CBS News stars, some of whom offered to cut their own salaries. Overnight Tisch was viewed as the potential destroyer rather than the hoped-for restorer of the preeminence of CBS News. The new anxiety was summarized in the title over a column Dan Rather sent to the New York *Times* in the middle of the uproar: "From Murrow to Mediocrity?"

It was a year of megatransactions not only in broadcasting. Newspapers and magazines were also appealing targets.

Mortimer Zuckerman had made a fortune in the political hotbed of Boston real estate. From the proceeds, he bought the *Atlantic Monthly*. Then he broadened his horizon and enhanced his life-style among the publicly powerful even more by buying the third-largest national newsmagazine, *U.S. News & World Report*, where a succession of editors came and went like designated hitters in a playoff game.

In ten years the Gannett newspaper group, by far the largest in the U.S., had grown from seventy-seven newspapers to more than ninety and was still expanding. It added to its stable the Des Moines *Register* and the Detroit *News* in 1985, for a total cash outlay of close to $1 billion. Chicago's Tribune Company paid more than half a billion for one Los Angeles television station. (In the two years following, more than four hundred television stations around the country changed hands.) Ziff-Davis Publishing Company sold two dozen consumer and trade magazines to CBS and to Murdoch for a combined price of more than $700 million. (Two years later, CBS sold *all* its magazines for $650 million.)

Time Inc., which had in the past always created its big magazines, changed that publishing strategy. It overcame its northeastern, urban heritage when it bought *Southern Living, Progressive Farmer* and a confederacy of smaller properties in 1985 for $480 million. The Time Inc. city slickers announced they had no plans to try to run the magazines editorially, just profit from them. "We're taking a hands-off approach," said a Time Inc. executive. "All we want to do is watch them grow." (In the two years following, Time Inc. abandoned its biggest new ventures in publishing—*TV-Cable Week* and *Picture Week,* plus half a dozen other possible start-ups—and continued buying magazines more than creating them.)

Then the enshrined but declining *New Yorker,* always proudly independent, eccentric and profitable—an inviolate, sheltered preserve for its writers and editors—was bought for $168 million by the Newhouse family. They already owned Condé Nast magazines (*Vogue, House & Garden, Glamour, Gourmet, Vanity Fair* and others), plus a string of twenty-seven mostly undistinguished daily newspapers and the very distinguished Random House and Alfred A. Knopf book publishers, along with other cable and publishing properties.

The Newhouses vowed not to go near the work of the *New Yorker's* editors or touch the contents of the magazine. That ironbound rule had been carried forward by the *New Yorker's* editor, William Shawn, for thirty-five years. He reasserted his Magna Carta by reminding the magazine's readers (and new owners) of a remarkable piece of publishing abstinence. No one in the family that had owned the magazine from its founding to its sale, the magazine said, "ever made an editorial suggestion, ever commented favorably or unfavorably on anything we published or on any editorial direction the magazine was taking." The Newhouses took the same holy vows of silence, as the spiritual price of their new sacristy.

But not for long. The new owners quickly made a decision reflecting what many of the magazine's readers had known for years. The *New Yorker* had drifted into becoming more supportive of its indulged writers than appealing to its frequently bored readers. Before very long, the tradition-bound business side of the magazine was shaken up. Then, in a noisy public uproar, seventy-nine-year-old Shawn was overruled on the choice of his successor. Despite Shawn's objections, S. I. Newhouse, Jr., retired him and made an inspired change. Newhouse brought in a talented outsider, Robert Gottlieb, editor-in-chief of Knopf. The magazine's staff and writers bitterly and formally protested "the manner in which a new editor has been imposed on us." In an astonishing letter to Gottlieb, 154 of them asked him to turn down the job. They wrote: "It is our strange and powerfully held conviction that only an editor who has been a long-standing member of the staff will have a reasonable chance of assuring our continuity, cohesion and independence." At least they were right about its being a "strange conviction."

During the same period, old family newspaper ties were alchemized into nuggets of pure gold for the heirs of their founders. Two successful, prestigious dailies, family-owned and dominated for generations, were swallowed up by public companies: The Binghams' Louisville *Courier-Journal* (by Gannett), the Baltimore *Sun* papers (by the Times Mirror Company), the last for $600 million, the highest price ever paid for a daily (the price included about $150 million for two television stations and two small magazines). At the same time, the Pulitzers' St. Louis *Post-Dispatch* was racked by a bitter family fight and barely avoided a takeover by a real-estate tycoon.

Less than thirty years have passed since shares of newspapers were first listed on stock exchanges. Yet of today's first rank dailies, only the Sulzbergers' New York *Times,* the Grahams' Washington *Post,* the Knight-Ridder papers, the Chandlers' Los Angeles *Times,* Dow Jones' *Wall Street Journal* and the Taylors' Boston *Globe* remain, for the moment, firmly entrenched in the hands of their founding families. These owners can confidently assert editorial values beyond financially pleasing anonymous stockholders or conglomerate executives. It is no coincidence that these families publish most of the best newspapers in America.

"The Media Bulls Are Running," one headline said. Others described the period as "The Buyout Binge," or "Media Madness."

The sales and takeovers produced few cries of indignation or complaints of press concentration. They were just part of a big money game that enabled buyers to acquire companies by making, in some of the deals, a small down payment. Many used credit, pledging the assets and part of the future cash flow of the companies they were buying. Not entirely different from buying a house with a huge mortgage. It was old stuff in housing, but relatively new in building media companies.

In the scramble, the new owners routinely promised to protect unchanged the integrity and independence of their editorial or news operations. For the broadcasters that represented a tiny part of their total fare—although the most visible and prestigious. As for the rest of their program schedules, did it really matter to the public who owned the networks? They were all financially dependent on their station ownership, prime-time entertainment programs, daytime soap operas, and game or talk shows. In those departments they were indistinguishable from one another.

The news and public affairs programs, they all repeated, with a bow to higher values, would go on as usual. Or benefit, they also claimed, from new infusions of good business management, hardscrabble cost control and fresh funds from their giant parent. Any "downsizing," they said, using another of the euphemisms for cutting costs, would simply make their operations more efficient and up-to-date in fulfilling the public's needs in the changing television environment.

The media had grown from a nicely profitable, creative business into a gigantic investment opportunity. It was becoming harder to think of them as different from any other business in free enterprise America. But there was a crucial difference. The part of them—a small part in many cases—that was the press, remained the only business enterprise singled out for special mention in the Constitution.

16

Prophets and Losses

*In the end, cheap will turn out to be very
expensive.*
—Les Brown, Editor-in-Chief,
Channels

Sound business is as essential in journalism as it is in any enterprise. The more secure the profits the better and more independent the journalists can be. Competition for a bigger and more permanent share of the market is a driving force that affects every enterprise. How and where it drives is another matter.

No rational business person—and all three networks as well as most newspaper groups are now predominantly in just such hands—could closely examine a major news operations in the United States and not find excesses. Like the military or fire departments, the scattered news forces around the globe at times offer more protection than action. The hazard in severely cutting back, or not keeping up with ever-changing costly new technology, is that they will not be there when they are most needed to cover the unforeseen or respond to an emergency.[1] Correspondents, producers and crews will be parachuted into unfamiliar new terrain acquiring spot footage without the background and insight that comes from long familiarity with the subject. The best newspapers and news magazines have the same cost problem as the networks. But the reason they are the best is that they make just such investments on the margin.

"I think," says Walter Cronkite, now a member of the CBS board, "that they are going the wrong route—almost a diametrically wrong route—in cutting back on foreign bureaus, foreign correspondents and domestic

1. Mocked in another *New Yorker* cartoon showing a television anchor saying: "Owing to cutbacks in our news department, here is Rod Ingram to guess at what happened today in a number of places around the globe."

bureaus and domestic correspondents at a time when there are a lot of possible growing competitors in world coverage.''

Not that news operations can or should be immune to cost control or the elimination of waste. But across-the-board budget reductions or the traditional efficiencies recommended by outside business management consultants more often affect quality in news organizations than they may in more conventional business operations. Cut back to its apparently efficient bone, journalism can suffer not by overworking complaining journalists but by cheating the public and hence damaging the service.

In broadcast or print journalism, reflexively trimming costs to improve profits and short-term stock prices or going for hype and sensationalism are as insecure a foundation for success as counterfeiting is in making money or witch doctoring is in medicine.

Look first at newspapers.

Memories persist (from old movies) of wild-swinging dailies hawking extras on the streets and on city newsstands. In those days, the more lurid the coverage or the splashier the headline the more copies were sold. In America that kind of *Front Page,* street-smart incentive hardly exists any longer. In all but a very few communities, newspapers are local monopolies, minting profits no matter how good or lackluster they are. Out of 1,700 dailies in the entire country, in only 20 cities is there still head-to-head competition, as opposed to 500 cities that had competition sixty years ago. As for news magazines, they are 90 to 95 percent sold by subscription.

Successful newspaper groups vary in their strategies.[2] Knight-Ridder (with 31 dailies and a record seven Pulitzer Prizes in 1986, six in 1988), the Times Mirror (11 dailies), the Tribune Company (7 dailies), Dow Jones (23) and the New York Times (26) all pump money and talent into their acquisitions to improve their papers and their profits. "We are totally convinced," says Knight-Ridder President James K. Batten, echoing the views of the other groups, "that good newspapers are profitable newspapers."

Gannett (92), Newhouse (26) and Thomson Newspapers Ltd. of North America (136 small dailies), manage the new papers they acquire differently: they keep their eyes more on the business than the editorial side.[3]

2. Close to three-quarters of all U.S. dailies are now under group ownership, controlling 80 percent of daily circulation.
3. The late S. I. Newhouse started the group by buying the Staten Island (New Jersey) *Advance.* He began accumulating other, bigger dailies without ever reading them, converting his lack of editorial interest into a press philosophy. "Freedom of the press," he told me, "means that I let my editors print whatever

Because they give more attention to cutting costs and raising ad rates than to what they print, none has outstanding papers in their combined collection (until Gannett acquired the Des Moines *Register* and Louisville *Courier-Journal*).

But whichever way they go, even monopoly papers cannot stick to antique ways. None can stand still and rake in money without making an effort to improve or keep up. There are too many comparisons to be made. Readers, viewers and listeners no longer need depend for their news and opinion on local or dominating press barons. They are surrounded not by a monopoly but a panoply of competing—and often louder—voices from within and outside their immediate neighborhoods.[4] As for advertisers, they also now have too many other media alternatives, especially television, to allow local newspapers to coast along, fat and happy.

Once the backwater of most of the country's dailies, local business coverage has been stimulated by the national presence of the *Wall Street Journal*, business magazines and new financial news services. News weeklies showed newspaper editors that organizing and departmentalizing news was better than just throwing it all together. Radio and television's instant bulletins and headline coverage make it necessary for newspapers to explain and expand on the news, not just report it. Syndicates and news services provide a full menu of world coverage and commentary.

The special sections in the New York *Times,* Los Angeles *Times,* Washington *Post* and now most other papers, spurred editors who had been satisfied with stodgier, more conventional coverage to broaden their horizons (while increasing their advertising to suit their special sections). The creation of Gannett's *USA Today* did nothing to deepen content. But it did transform the presentation of news across the country and demonstrate that crisp and popular need not mean crummy.

Today, struggling and failing dailies are those that try to trap their readers into thinking they are getting something they are not. Scare

they want so long as they can make money in their own towns." The Late Lord Thomson of Fleet, when he owned more than 80 papers in the U.S. and Canada, as well as the *Times of London,* had a similar attitude. He said to me one evening in a Bond Street dining room, "Luce interests me. He's made money publishing in a way completely different from me. He *cares* what his publications say. That's not my job. My papers can say what they want so long as they succeed."

4. One example, among many, is New Orleans where, the daily is Newhouse's monopoly, all-day New Orleans *Times-Picayune.* But as media financial analyst, James K. Glassman, points out, the community hears competing voices from "seven major TV stations, 20 radio stations, two business tabloids, one monthly magazine, one city-wide weekly and a number of suburban papers," to say nothing of national magazines and newspapers.

headlines ("Deadly Cancer on the Loose"), hype ("Sword Maniac Chops Ex-Lovers Head Off"), the private lives of the rich and glamorous ("Princess Caroline's Baby May Land Husband in Jail"), the unkept promises of fake sensationalism ("Terror from the Skies"—an air conditioner falling from an apartment house window) are a recipe for daily newspaper malnutrition not for robust health.

There is no need to be stuffy, bluenosed, humorless or commercially unrealistic to understand the distinction. No bridge is long enough to connect the best big daily in the United States, the New York *Times*, with one of the worst, Murdoch's New York *Post*. In the eleven years since he bought the *Post*, when Murdoch sold it in 1988, he said the paper had lost more than $150 million; the *Times* in 1987 *alone* made close to that in profits.

It is not a contest between élite and popular journalism.[5] There is a profitable place for both as well as in between. In the argot of the newspaper business office, there is more to be gained "upscale," where the readers are more faithful and the advertising more effective (in motivation not just income). "Downscale" readers (in appetite not just taste) tend to be fickle and advertisers unrewarded. As for American magazines, few are more profitable than *Time*, *TV Guide* and the *Reader's Digest*, all different, all popular in different ways, none sleazy.

In print, there is every reason to practice good journalism to make good money. There is no need to be tawdry to be popular, nor to feed people's worst appetites to be successful. Quality journalism, in whatever form, and success in its conventional form, can be partners, not adversaries. There is more to be gained in reaching upward toward the top of the line than in plunging downward expecting to improve the bottom line. A pious hope? No, a balance-sheet fact. John Morton, a leading financial analyst of newspapers as investment properties, confirms that businesslike view: "In the long run quality will win out."

The economics of television news is different. The grandfather of network television, CBS's founder William Paley, said in television's early days that if network television news and public affairs ever become a profit center, we're in trouble. In that respect he didn't have much to worry about. For television, both local stations (many owned by the networks)

5. In Britain the distinction is clear-cut between what are known as the "populars" and the "quality" dailies. The big Fleet Street tabloid populars, as wildly sensational as any in the world, each circulate more than one million copies daily. None of the "quality" dailies come close in readership. The line between the two groups in the U.S. press is hazier and the circulation of some best quality papers surpasses that of some of the worst populars.

and network entertainment programs have been deep wells of profitability in past good years. Network news is not.

Network news and public affairs divisions are small percentage contributors to profit or loss. Without successful television "magazine" shows, they are more loss than profit. Network television's biggest revenues and profits (except for CNN and Public Broadcasting) have come from the stations they own and from movies, sports, soap operas, sitcoms, entertainment specials, game shows and whatever the public wants, registered by Nielsen ratings. In print, the equivalent to television's staples of fun and games—comic strips, crossword puzzles, bridge, horoscopes, humor, advice and offbeat columns—is a small sideshow, not the main act.

Dollar ups and down in network news and public affairs are marginal compared to successes and flops in entertainment and other programming or station ownership. Although the bookkeeping is complicated, network news and public affairs rarely show a profit. Each network spends from $250 to $300 million a year for all news and public affairs, about $100 million allocated to the half-hour evening news alone. (Public Broadcasting's hour-long "MacNeil/Lehrer NewsHour" costs $21 million a year.)

Network expenditures for other programming is more than $1 billion dollars a year each. In recent years, NBC has been the top-rated network in both entertainment and news. With an income of more than $400 million, it has also been the most profitable of the three commercial networks, though it loses an estimated $50 million a year on news and public affairs.

Where the economics of print and broadcasting really differ is in how they monitor and react to their measures of success or failure.

A slight momentary rise or fall in a newspaper's or magazine's circulation rightly goes largely unnoticed and unreported. Not so for television news circulation. If a network's nightly news rating forges ahead or to the top by a fraction of a point, it is likely to take out full page ads bragging "We're Number One" and throw an office party to celebrate the event, no matter that it can slip back the next week.

The ratings race in network evening news is now mostly a delusion. Who's up and who's down is not necessarily dependent on how engaging the anchor is or on the appeal and content of the news program. Network news ratings can be as much influenced by what the local station has on the air just before the network news or just after it, what the pull of the entertainment programs is, how many affiliates are on the line, whether the audience is in urban centers or smaller communities, or what the news of the day or week is. (Magazine and newspaper newsstand sales are most affected by some of the same factors, and also the weather.)

Zany as it sounds, the ratings of the network and local news shows in

1986 were as influenced by whether the station had the "Wheel of Fortune" game show as they were by any other single factor. One station manager explained: "You try to do everything right journalistically and you succeed to a certain extent, and then the most successful game show in the history of the land comes along and cuts your head off. It's unbelievable." (ABC acknowledged the commercial priority of game shows in its biggest market, New York, in late 1986, by moving its network news to 6:30 P.M. It pitted the "Jeopardy!" game show against CBS's and NBC's 7 o'clock evening news. "Jeopardy!" quickly outrated both networks' news.)

Nor are Nielsens and Arbitron ratings the report card on performance in network news that they are taken to be. Even if all the ratings measurements were reliable, finite indicators of which news programs were attracting the most viewers, the variation among the three networks is rarely more than a trivial fraction, often less than one (a shift of a few households in the entire sample!) or at most two points. In an election poll, the outcome of such a spread would make the election "too close to call," outside the sampling error of plus or minus 3 or 4 percent.

Add to that the fact that the ratings have been in the past based on what were generally agreed to be unreliable "diaries," kept erratically by 2,600 families who were paid to mail their retrospective reports in every four weeks; plus speedier Audimeters, connected to 1,700 "representative" households across the country. The latter indicate only whether the television set is on and to which channel it is tuned, not whether it is being watched or who is watching. The national sample of who watched what network *news* program can be even more contracted, a group so undefined and small as to make a shambles of its reliability for fractional measurements.

Then why are ratings for national news programs taken so seriously when they are obviously so unreliable? The networks have trapped themselves. By accepting such measurements and bragging about them when they are up, the ratings have become *the* standard for charging advertisers no matter how absurdly irrelevant infinitesimal point spreads on the evening news are.

In early 1987, Nielsen announced it was replacing its diaries with new "people meters" to be placed in 2,000 households, expanding to 4,000 by 1988. Nielsen described them as "an electronic device that household members push when they begin and finish watching television"—if they don't forget.[6] Underscoring the absurdity of ratings standards, for network

6. One company planned to use a high-tech meter that measures the body heat emitted in front of the television set, claiming to register the number of actual

news, the new people meters overnight changed all the ratings, including pushing the CBS News and Rather from an embattled third place to first, with NBC and Brokaw going from first to third. The spread was at times less than one point.

In television, news ratings are more a vanity standard than a direct lift or blow to the bottom line. True, a single rating point on network news can be worth as much as $19 million a year in ad revenue. But compared to the total ad sales, which for the three networks average about $2.2 billion each, the gain from a questionable single news rating point comes out to less than 1 percent of the network's total ad revenue.

Above all else: Network news is now housed in bigger parent companies than ever before. The news and public affairs divisions' net contribution in profit or loss are a tiny percentage of the profits from station ownership or the money they can make or lose from hits and flops in entertainment. The opportunity for significant changes in the bottom line from news alone is minimal. But the effect of the news and public affairs programs on the network's total reputation and audience is unmeasurably large.

The news flagship is consistently the only distinguishing characteristic networks have. It can build a loyal following that creates the habit of staying tuned and watching the network's other programs. In effect networks in the past have subsidized the news, with the eternal hope that it will be successful enough to cost them less but with little hope that by itself it will earn them more. News and public affairs programming have been their practical, dollars-and-sense, loss leader concession to corporate reputation in the wasteland.

If that sounds either naive or too abstract to believe, how can anyone explain that all three networks, at great expense, still instantly cancel all other programs for hours, even a full day, when there is a breaking news event of major importance? Or that all carry presidential speeches and press conferences, when one network would be sufficient? Or that they spend millions covering unexpected summits, earthquakes, catastrophes, special congressional hearings or such events as political conventions. Is there any other business where some employees, such as the anchor people, now make multimillion-dollar salaries in enterprises that consis-

people present in a room with a television set. If the heat exceeds the number of people who should have punched in, a message flashes on the screen: "Who is in the room?" answered by pushing the correct buttons. One critic of this device points out that there is no way to reply that some of the heat is being generated by the presence of a large dog. Or how about an overheated wrestling match on the couch!

tently lose money? Why make any of these investments when the profit from them does not justify the expense and effort?

The answer is obvious. At stake is the reputation of the network's entire operation with advertisers, the public and the government. Cheapening the content or cutting back on the quality and time of news and information may help profits marginally for a moment. But there is no experience in the history of television to indicate that such trashing will do anything but hurt overall profits in the longer run.

Still, the ratings game is relentlessly played with network news, abetted by newspaper coverage that runs ratings box scores almost as faithfully as it does stock market tables. The networks would be far better off, and so assuredly would the public, if—as they once did—they ignored minor variations in network news ratings and confined their preoccupation with ratings to their entertainment programs. The differences in network news ratings are now too small and erratic to matter in measuring viewership or appeal.

More for less may please Wall Street. But it is unrealistic for long-term media success. "Lean and mean" may save a foundering media enterprise, but those currently fashionable attributes alone cannot *create* a really successful media product. As Paul M. Hirsch, professor of business at the University of Chicago, wrote in 1987:

> While Wall Street loudly applauds cost-cutting moves, such as firing productive employees, it puts the same "restructured" companies into dangerously high levels of debt, forces a mono-maniacal preoccupation with short-term earnings and promotes asset sales and layoffs rather than growth, innovation, reinvestment of earnings and research and development.

In today's financially oriented environment, it is worth recalling that on the eve of publishing the instantly successful *Life* in 1936, David Brumbaugh, a soft-spoken accountant who became Time Inc.'s chief financial officer, wrote in a memo: "Never in our history have we come out of any tight spot by a choice of conservatism or economy, but always by expenditure of more money and more effort to gain greater income at greater expense."

Both financial health and public responsibility demand a constant effort to try to improve the quality and service that network and local television journalism offer. Yet there always lurks the thought that in the end, network news could change its course and turn toward the lower not the higher road. Local news certainly once did that, and in many cities it has still not recovered. Network news, under shortsighted management could. But it has not, despite frequent premonitions of disaster.

When sports wunderkind Roone Arledge took charge of ABC News, there was just such apprehension that he would translate his spectacular success in sports programming by hyping his network news, forcing the other networks to follow him into the cheap seats.

Arledge did no such thing. He did, as predicted, transform television graphics and was quickly and usefully imitated by the other networks. It was a needed improvement. Everything looked better and was easier to follow. He made a nightly feature out of Ted Koppel's informative and profitable "Nightline," second only to Public Broadcasting's "MacNeil/Lehrer NewsHour" as the most explanatory daily news program on television. He rescued NBC's David Brinkley from ennui and possible premature retirement, and at the same time transformed weekend television news with ABC's Sunday morning "This Week with David Brinkley." He moved Peter Jennings from the barely visible exposure of a correspondent to become the most thoughtful evening news anchor. All of these moves raised ABC's reputation from a cellar of disdain to a peak of grudging admiration, even at a time when its entertainment programming had slipped into a ratings slump.

In an earlier time, Murrow and his recruits laid the foundation for the quality and pace of television news and public affairs.[7] A later trend-setter had a different impact almost as pervasive. He was, surprising to say, a producer, CBS's Don Hewitt.

Hewitt, a brash, outspoken news populist, directed some of the first network news, early political convention coverage and the first presidential political debates in 1960. Eight years later he created "60 Minutes," a video magazine, which he says was modeled after the actual picture magazines, *Life* and *Look*. Hewitt's new program hung on with its blend of exposés, features, interviews in fourteen- to fifteen- minute segments. The way to win high news ratings, says Hewitt, is "to walk the fine line between news and show business. You have to get close enough to touch it with your toe, but never cross it."

"60 Minutes" tiptoed on that fine line, maintaining an arguable balance. At first it got ho-hum and worse reviews. It slogged along at the low end of the ratings scale until 1975, when CBS moved it to 7:00 P.M. on the network's popular Sunday night schedule. In that spot it flourished, rising

---

7. Murrow was purer in memory than in practice. He was not above swallowing hard, and uncomfortably doing on the side a highly profitable weekly interview program called "Person to Person," which in the mid-50's was not much loftier than the 80's "Life Styles of the Rich and Famous." One writer described it as "the higher Murrow vs. the lower Murrow."

to the top and becoming, remarkably, one of the most commercially successful programs in the history of broadcasting. Today its claimed $70 million in revenues offsets some of the losses of the entire CBS News division.

"60 Minutes" is a feature program, making no attempt systematically to respond to or cover the news but often making news through its own enterprise and its sure sense of the topical. Much of its early success stemmed from its prosecutorial, hammering pieces. Mike Wallace was and remains the program's original trademark interviewer (so much so that "Mike fright" became a term used by businessmen who were often his subject).

"60 Minutes" is rarely oracular. Instead it conveys the feeling that it is everyone's protector against deceit, fraud and just plain nonsense on the American scene—the Paul Revere and overwrought Diogenes of television. But it also combines those qualities with wry feature stories, moving interviews, skillfully presented discoveries of subjects on and off the stream of more traditional news. It is a crackling and enterprising news variety show all packed into fast-moving short segments, touching the interests of large audiences and creating controversy over the outrages it tries to expose—as well as having at times committed some outrages itself.

With its well-known stars (Wallace, Harry Reasoner, Morley Safer, Ed Bradley, Diane Sawyer and humorist Andy Rooney), it also attracted some of the most enterprising field producers and an audience on Sunday night large enough to make it one of the top ten shows on the whole television ratings scale—occasionally even first.

The unequaled success of "60 Minutes" with its feisty new format and drawing power was instantly imitated. Only ABC's "20/20," which earns less than half of what "60 Minutes" does, and ABC's "Nightline," which grew out of a nightly update during the Iranian hostage seizure, succeeded. All three networks have been trying ever since to create profitable magazine shows after "60 Minutes" demonstrated it could be done. Despite more than twenty such efforts ("American Almanac," "Weekend," "West 57th," "Monitor," "1986," etc.), none has lasted or reached its ratings and financial goal.

But by demonstrating that television news features, many with a cutting edge, could draw big audiences and make big money, Hewitt inadvertently gave network executives new hopes and expectations for the kind of profit in public affairs they once made only in entertainment programs. It created an appetite for *big* profit in news, which was considered virtually impossible in an earlier time when public affairs on television was thought to be an imposed duty not an inviting dollar sign.

The effect went beyond attempts to recreate the success of "60 Minutes.'' The program left its mark on network news short features and investigative reports, in the pace, timing and even the style of much of television news. Its influence on public affairs television was a mixed blessing. For all its popularity, ''60 Minutes' '' short pieces have neither the time nor the inclination to explore at length many important national and international subjects. (''If you can't tell it in fifteen minutes,'' says Hewitt, ''it doesn't deserve more than that.'') These were once the function of longer documentaries, which never made a profit and remained in the ratings doldrums no matter what their value.

Hewitt finds the very word *documentary* an invitation to boredom. But his magazine format and longer, deeper documentaries or ''specials'' on the network are not imcompatible. Not every subject can be covered or explored in fourteen-minute television magazine bites. When newspapers began running life-style feature sections, they were much criticized by purists as non-news fluff. Not so, any more than television magazine programs with high, if popular, standards should be so dismissed. The difference is that when newspapers and news magazines added such coverage, they did not abandon their heavier fare as television increasingly does.

The morning network news and entertainment shows are another matter. They have a total audience of close to 20 million: NBC's ''Today''—the only one of the three continuously under the news division—ABC's ''Good Morning America'' and CBS's ''Morning Program,'' the last a tacky variety show launched in 1987, whose co-anchor said, ''we think there's more to life than news,'' was dropped within eleven months. They can also make a good profit when they are doing well. They too have unintended side effects on network news programming, as one NBC producer explained: ''If you're the head of a news division, the prestige show, the one that really matters to you, is the nightly news. However, when you go to the affiliates meetings, the one they want to talk about the most is 'Today.' It plays heavily to the bottom line,'' and can contribute as much as a $30 million profit to the network.

In broadcasting, time, not space, is money. As a result, in network news, time—not content, pictures, pizzazz or even competitive ratings—is the real villain.

Networks and their affiliates deserve the damnation they get for the amount of time they offer the public nightly in national and international news. On a regular, daily basis it remains pitifully little.[8] Twenty-two

8. CBS's Vradenburg argues that is ''not true as to CBS. From 1983 through 1986, from 33 to 35 percent of our broadcast time has been devoted to news and public

minutes a night, plus on the morning shows, ABC's "Nightline," bulletins for big breaking news, weekend programs, "magazines," (other than "60 Minutes" and "20/20," most notably, CBS's 9:00 to 10:00 A.M. "Sunday Morning," with Charles Kuralt), specials when the news is big enough, and occasional documentaries.

For purely financial reasons, the networks are forced by their affiliated stations to be miserly with their evening news time allotment. In the early days of television, the networks dominated the affiliates, who received 30 to 40 percent of their revenue from the networks. No longer. The affiliates depend on the networks for less than 10 percent of their revenue and achieve profit margins of 35 percent to 40 percent, compared to network highs of 18 percent. Now the networks quake in the presence of their affiliated stations' new financial power.

Around the country the affiliates refuse to give up another half hour of profitable "station time," from which the locals keep all the ad revenue instead of the fraction they receive from network shows.[9] So they fill that time with syndicated entertainment or local news programs, preventing the network news from expanding to an hour. The syndicated "Wheel of Fortune," the most successful half-hour game show ever on television, or other "family" programs, make far more money for local stations than an added half hour of national news. So the wheel turns.

It is not often said, but it should be, that in their field and within the prescribed time limitations, the network evenings news programs are no

affairs. In light of the return of the morning time period to CBS News and the addition of '48 Hours' to our schedule in January 1988, I believe the percentage may increase next year." *Broadcasting,* the industry trade magazine adds: "What goes around comes around. In early March of this year, headlines around the nation exclaimed that CBS News was taking a 10 percent cut in its $300 million budget and reducing staff by about 200 jobs. Eight months later the fiscal cut has been restored, probably with a bonus, and the news division is hiring again to help launch two new programs—the revamped 'Morning Program,' once again under the wing of CBS News, and a new weekly prime time program, '48 Hours,' to debut early in 1988. The program will be fashioned after several so-called 'instant documentaries' that the network produced over the past year." The Washington Post's" television critic-reporter, Tom Shales (see page 275), obviously puzzled by a widely reported new burst of CBS News euphoria in early 1988, asked: "Did Laurence Tisch, once vilified by many in the news division, have an experience akin to Ebenezer Scrooge, visited in the night by ghosts who converted him into a pussycat?"

9. In 1981, the possibility that the evening news would go to an hour, was thought to be important enough to make a front-page headline in the New York *Times:* "CBS Will Expand Nightly News to One Hour." But shortly after, when the affiliates met, they beat back the network's intention. There are no foreseeable prospects of the affiliates' opposition changing.

less scrupulous—and wander off course no more often—than most news-papers in America.

Because of its brevity, television is an easy target for general condemnation by critics. Its impact on events and on the largest news audience of all is instantaneous. Surprisingly, diligent readers seem to complain as often or more about specific stories they see and don't see in print as viewers do about what they see on the air. You hear more about television because its voice is louder, its cryptic news more assailable and its audience many times larger than that of any single print outlet. Above all, it is subjected to constant criticism in print—which print journalism itself is routinely spared.

Although television is rightly knocked on all sides for giving so little time to what the public needs to know to be informed, much of the blame is misplaced and misunderstood. It is not the endemic fault of television's network journalists. It is the confines within which they work and the pressure on them to be Number One.

Take the nightly evening news on all three networks. They have their bad blips and blunders. All go by at head-spinning speed often with too little explanation or background. (The *average* interview on network news lasts no more than eleven seconds.) They have been veering toward softer, life-style features, thus too often compressing beyond comprehension much real news and information. They are no longer mostly a headline service. They have come under the influence of money-making television magazine programs, with more enterprise, offbeat and personality stories. Anyone can criticize or cavil with the mix and presentation. Their news judgment can often be questioned. (Who has not raised the same questions about print news?)

But each of the three network news programs makes an earnest effort to report the important news of the day, not just what their surveys tell them their viewers want or the stories for which they have film footage. Taken together, they still are the longest-running, high-rated programs in television. They are the national background music of the American dinner hour. Examined closely, they are now about equal in quality, with CBS, under its anchor and managing editor, Dan Rather, often having a more critical edge. All three vary from night to night, but viewers turn to one rather than another for reasons of personal preference rather than for real differences in what each offers. Their audience is so large and the time allowed so brief that they are constant targets for darts, especially among more serious news buffs.

Some television people bring it on themselves by the way they describe their work. Within the network news divisions, many television journalists too easily agree, in an often self-inflicted wound, that they are in an entertainment medium.

They are. Entertainment does happen to be the house where television journalists live. Profits from entertainment pay the overhead and rent for most network news and public affairs, as advertising does for most general circulation newspapers and magazines. But the place journalists occupy in television's mansion need not make them entertainers any more than their counterparts in print are advertising salesmen.

Successful publishers erect a high wall between their news and advertising departments. So does television news. Not that television news executives don't watch their ratings as closely as theatrical producers keep track of ticket sales at the box offices. Television news chiefs change producers, correspondents and anchors at the drop of a point. They redesign their graphics, makeup, lighting and trench coats, take Q-rating "likability" polls, hire media consultants, rebuild their sets, redefine what they consider important, all to be more appealing to their viewers.

So in different ways, do publishers and editors, although they are less volatile and tend to go more by instinct than reader surveys. At the borderline in television, news and entertainment often intersect. But they do in print too. Coverage in both mediums is always more than what people need to know; it is also what they *like* to know. All newspapers and news magazines run non-news, light-hearted feature stories, living and life-style departments. In their news, editorials and special sections, they try to be interesting, useful and entertaining as well as informative and serious.

Television does put a much higher premium on looks and pictures. But it is no more wrong to try to improve its appearance, delivery and appeal than is striving for more readability and impact in print. Unless, in either medium, form and style bury content. In television it too often does, especially in local news.

Until the early 80s and the Reagan-appointed FCC chairman, stations and networks were required to run a minimum quota of public affairs programming. Stations had to file logs with the FCC, proving their public service. They also had to make lengthy reports on how they were discharging their community responsibility in the "public interest." In 1983 those requirements were virtually all dropped. Now it is up to every station and network to make its own decision on how much and what quality public service programming it should run.

More than fifteen years ago when the FCC pushed local stations to devote more time to public affairs, the stations began experimenting with local news programs. At first they were a throwaway, a dismal flop by any standards. To make up for their losses, a few discovered profitable tabloid trash, mostly under the tutelage of media consultants who figured out what they said the audiences most wanted. The programs were laced with sex, crime, happy talk known on one station as "Kickers, Guts and Orgasms"—a pileup of as many as thirty stories in thirty minutes, bimbo journalism.

The word that bad news could made good profits spread across the country like an epidemic. It was a short-term binge and we are still suffering from the hangover. But now in most cities the local news runs one to two hours, usually preceding the half-hour network news. Even more important, local news standards in many cities are rising—although the pattern is erratic and most still have a long way to go before they get rid of such regular fare as an "exclusive interview with a grieving mother," consumer segments scare-titled "Killer Salad Bars," or the murder or fire of the day. Many stations have lately been discovering that community service is as important to ratings as community sex.

Whether local news programs are getting more reflective of their communities, more enterprising, less provincial and more expansive still depends on where you live. Paradoxically, a few of the biggest urban centers often have the poorest local news. New York, the networks' headquarters, and Los Angeles, their entertainment center, tend to be surprisingly bad. (Conversely, cities like Minneapolis, Dallas, Miami, Boston, Salt Lake, Chicago, Seattle and others, especially those owned by Westinghouse, have some first-rate stations.) There is also a concealed disgrace in some of the worst local news operations. Close to one-third of television stations are owned by newspapers—some of the biggest and even the best dailies in the country. Most of their parent publishing companies regard their stations simply as cash machines. Many of the newspaper owners pay little or no attention to what goes on the air and avoid any responsibility or on-air identification with the name or the standards of the newspaper group that owns them.

But whether the news programs are good or bad, virtually everywhere the economics of network and local news is changing.

News has now become the single most profitable programming on local stations' regular schedules, accounting for up to half of their total revenues, justifying an investment of as much as one-quarter of local stations' total expense budgets. Profits from local news go directly to the station instead of being shared with the network, as they are in programs supplied by the networks. Local news is also—as it is on the networks—the only same area and affecting the total audience flow toward that station or network.

With advancing portable technology, the launching of RCA's Satcom II satellite, greatly reduced rates, station-owned satellite dishes and a wider choice of television news services for national and international news, local stations and station groups are no longer totally dependent on the networks. They have also started to ask the networks for more news feeds tailored to fit into local coverage. Stations in many areas and growing group operations are now crowding the networks to change their formats rather than simply accepting whatever news package networks have to offer.

"CONUS" (for Continental U.S.), based in Minneapolis with more than fifty affiliates, is a new television wire service, of sorts, using satellites for news gathering and distribution. It offers distant feeds to its local station subscribers from dishes on $200,000 to $300,000 roving "Newstar" vans uplinked to satellites. After lean start-up years, CNN has moved into the black, providing competition with the networks from its invaluable round-the-clock news coverage, plus CNN's Newsource special service to local stations. Westinghouse's Newsfeed, Lorimar-Telepictures' NIWS, Florida's News Network and the Tribune Company's Independent Network News, are part of the growing number of television services, including regional microwave co-ops in New England, the South and Far West.[10]

The five NBC-owned-and-operated stations advertised "a very special news unit—investigative reporters and production crews covering major stories around the world from a local point of view," using each station's "mini-truck that is not only a satellite transmitter itself, but has radios, telephones and access to research and wire copy, whenever and wherever there's a story—like tracking down Mengele [the Nazi war criminal] in the jungles of Brazil or a menacing hurricane along the gulf coast, covering the arms talks in Geneva or catching the downfall of Marcos in Manila."

"Local point of view" or not, no local station, even with co-op news services, has the resources and talent to cover the variety of national and international stories the way the networks can. Nor are they as able to withstand the heat and pressure from government, politicians, advertisers

10. The AP reported that for coverage of the 1988 Iowa caucus, the first and least representative nationally of state presidential nominating contests, "television satellite trucks have become as familiar as grain trucks on the Iowa campaign trail. By some estimates, there will be 50 satellite trucks parked in downtown Des Moines the evening of Feb. 8, half the number of such trucks in the nation." To cover the media-created event, more than 2,600 journalists were accredited.

or other powerful special interests as confidently as the networks do. Now-retired CBS Producer Bud Benjamin describes the trend in a telling parody:

> Another development that is interesting, and on the rise, is local-station coverage of important national and international events. I always love those sign-offs: "This is Harry Honcho, Action 11 News, at the Geneva Summit." Followed by the anchorman saying something like: "We'll be back in a moment for our special tonight: Punk Bowling."

The outcome of this new shift from dependence on network news to local station initiative, is still uncertain. It could cheapen or enhance news and public affairs coverage. There are dire predictions that within the next few years network news could become more like broadcast wire services providing stations with footage for local adaptation. Possibly, but not if network news upgrades its coverage, in a way local stations cannot, rather than trivializing it the way so many local stations do.

The best division of labor for the public would be for local stations to improve their community and regional coverage, relying on networks and other new television news services to provide stations with enhanced, more explanatory national and international coverage. Viewers seem to consider local and network news in a complementary rather than a competitive relationship.

Despite cynical observations to the contrary, it turns out that in network and local news as well as in print, excellence in news and public affairs is cost effective rather than an expensive luxury. Long-range financial health is more likely assured by large doses of quality in the news divisions than by hype and ratings elixirs, or by measuring bottom-line performance the way entertainment programs are judged. Networks, with mass audiences as opposed to print's smaller universe, cannot ignore the need for a larger common denominator. But in the relatively small financial part of their operation that is news and public affairs, neither can they afford to ignore the benefits of public service. It is not just good citizenship. It is good business.

No one need be so unrealistic or so overflowing with idealism as to ignore the financial realities of broadcasting and publishing. On the contrary. A passion for quality can be rooted in the evidence that it is an essential path to success in profits as well as in public admiration. During the long stretch when CBS was the dominating network in both news and entertainment, Richard Salant, president of CBS News in that period, recalls: "Not once in 16 years did I have any pressure about ratings." Television news, he points out, "can never be cost efficient." It was never meant to be. It is a service offered as the price for occupying public airwaves—a cost not a profit center.

For years networks had proprietary bosses who were broadcasters, CBS's Paley, NBC's Sarnoff, ABC's Goldenson.

Now all are part of larger corporations, with executives and controlling stockholders who are business people. Responsibility is spread among committees, divisions, boards. The stock price ratings that Wall Street produces are every bit as tyrannizing as Nielsens. Similarly, newspapers and magazines—with a handful of exceptions—have passed from family and proprietary ownership to corporate control, in which the need to satisfy hungry stockholders can become paramount.

Political economist John Kenneth Galbraith described the evolution:

> There is a highly predictable sequence in the development of a great industrial enterprise. It begins as the reflection of the imagination, energy and technical or other competence of some person, and it is strongly identified with a family name. But this does not last. In a generation or two, if it succeeds and expands, it becomes an impersonal bureaucracy of its top management. It is not that the offspring of the founder reared in wealth and committed to self-gratification, are incompetent, although that is frequently the case. It is that any considerable enterprise, public or private, is an expression of organized intelligence. The large firm doesn't yield in its complexity to the average available business brain or even the best.

"I fear," said Leonard Goldenson, "that one of the most insidious by-products of the current merger mania may be the loss of a sense of stewardship, a value to which those of us in broadcasting have always been acutely sensitive. Because our business is more than a business. It is a public trust."

It is harder and harder to know who is in charge, whom journalists are working for, what the objectives of their bosses and parent organizations are. In a period when individual leadership is declining and group thinking is ascending, it is bootless to rue the "good old days," when to journalists the "bottom line" still meant the last line on any page of a story. In fact, although journalism then may have given more pleasure to journalists, it was neither as valuable to the public as it is today nor as powerful.

The new managers should look hard at the responsibilities to that public they have inherited, even though the FCC no longer measures their performance. They might remember the public service penance they had to do for years after the rigged "$64,000 Question" quiz scandals in the late 50s. It brought a tidal wave of opprobrium and new regulations.

The responsibilities of news and public affairs programming are more important, and, in the longer run, more financially fruitful than the demands of stockholders for short-term increases in stock prices or quarterly and annual rises in profit margins. To earn the privilege and profit from their freedom, the news media companies need always be reminded that the real proxy holders of our press are 240 million stockholders of our democracy bound together by our constitutional tradition, not the comparatively few shareholders of corporate record.

17

Two Reforms

A press that wishes to maintain its privileged position can do so only by regaining public confidence, which at the moment has declined. The first step is to respond less arrongantly to those who criticize its performance and less defensively to those who challenge its autonomy.
—Judge Irving Kaufman, 1984

It is often said that where there is no solution there is no problem, only a situation. In the words of the nine-year-old son of a left-wing British publisher:

> Life is an awful bother.
> There's murder, pillage and rape,
> Even with the Labour Government.

Such realism, even from a child, implies no resignation or paralysis, no helplessness against the drift of events. It simply defines the limits of the possible. Many of the shortcomings of the enlarging and protean news media will never be remedied either to the public's or the journalists' satisfaction. There always will be new trends and offenses, new accomplishments and redefinitions of what needs to be done and what can be done.

But these changes cannot be left entirely to the conscience and wisdom of individuals. Nor should government, a major party at interest, be expected to play a key role. In the interests of democracy, government should be prevented from such intervention. Although the courts are forced to intervene more and more, judges rightly shun the role of making decisions that the people, the press and government should make themselves,

There is no shortage of suggestions or demands for proposed changes in news media rules, regulations, economics and even in the laws.

The most obvious medicines for news media ailments are prescriptions for rules of behavior, written into codes of conduct for the press. Most news organizations now have such guidelines. They often seem as clear, if not as simple or as elegant, as the Ten Commandments. The codes are useful, especially for novices, and should be expanded as well as kept up to date, based on new experiences. But they rarely answer the hardest questions or apply automatically to the closest calls.

The Westmoreland documentary violated CBS's News Standards. That embarrassed the network, although the fact of the violations was not admissible in court. Had the guidelines been followed to the letter, they still would not have changed the program fundamentally nor prevented the libel suit. As for *Time,* it is awash in policies, rules and standards that are known to the staff. But its rules would not have eliminated the error that in the end forced the magazine to retract and apologize, as well as to suffer public humiliation.

What about press councils, like the long-standing British Press Council, the recently exhausted and abandoned National News Council or national, state, regional and professional groups?[1]

Such organizations have added some non-binding moral pressure on the media to look at themselves more critically and suffer the public consequences of their failures. But unless news councils or their equivalent are supported by the leading news organizations financially and especially by prominent coverage of their findings, they will always be ineffective. They have neither enough visibility to satisfy the public's desire for an outlet to vent its complaints nor enough repute to overcome the major media's reluctance to be second-guessed by any tribunal, even one of their own creation.

Lawyers have enforceable codes of ethics and committees of the bar to carry them out. Yet there is no licensed profession in the United States which suffers more hostility and disparagement than lawyers. Doctors are similarly circumscribed, yet medical malpractice charges and Medicare insurance fraud have never been more rampant. Business is buried under regulations and government bodies to enforce them, yet scandals in the

---

1. The National News Council was initiated and principally financed by the Twentieth Century Fund, also the sponsor of this book. Only one state, Minnesota, has a news council.The month following the settlement of his libel suit, General Westmoreland told the National Press Club: "The chilling effect of a libel suit on journalistic enterprise is a valid concern. On the other hand a letter to the editor has little effect except perhaps to satisfy the writer who wants to get something off his chest. There is a need for something in between, something like a National News Council." The National News Council was still in existence but impotent when Westmoreland filed his libel suit against CBS.

leading, blue-chip corporations—in investment banking, defense, consumer products—have never been more prevalent. Despite tough, ethics-in-government laws, corruption and its legal companion, influence peddling, flourish in municipal, state and federal government.

From all that experience in other American power centers, there is little reason to believe that self-regulation or more widespread formal surveillance by the news media themselves—or, heaven forbid, the government—could ever satisfy public dissatisfaction with press performance. There must be a more effective way. There is.

But what is achievable? What should the news media do? What could they do? Never mind idealized, unreal reforms. Never mind most academic seminars, papers and doctoral quantifications that make working journalists eyes glaze over. Never mind making assumptions about the press, the public and the government that are exhortations rather than realities. What is really possible?

A lot.

For the news media, there are two immediate and effective reforms to deal with their worst faults and the public's greatest frustration with them. Neither requires new laws, economic changes or transformations of journalists' work habits. Just a change in attitude expressed in two new practices. Both would have discouraged—and might even have prevented—the Westmoreland and Sharon libel suits.

Only two such overall reforms? Yes, two.

The biggest possible improvement flows easily from two unique immunities that the press now enjoys. Abandoning and replacing these two rigidities, whatever else the press did or did not do, could make the biggest continuing difference in how the news media function within democratic America. These anachronistic twins of special privilege, born of, and nurtured by, the press itself are:

- First, the news media's failure to report energetically and critically on themselves and on each other just as they do on the rest of the world.

- Second, their reluctance to give the public adequate ways to reply after the press has spoken.

Neither of these special liberties is suggested, much less dictated, by law. Nor do they make any sense, except as old, unjustifiable habits. Remedying both habits would have major consequences for press and public alike.

The first is the easiest to change and the more important. It takes no elaborate planning or invention for the news media to cover and criticize their own performance and practices with the same determination and enterprise with which they report everyone else's.

The press is rightly fond of repeating Justice Louis Brandeis' homily that there is no better disinfectant for excesses in a democracy than sunlight. Yet for all its history, the press has wanted that sun to illuminate everything and everybody but itself. The open society the news media demand and create stops at their own closed doors. A few examples:

The *Reader's Digest,* the largest monthly magazine in the world (circ. 27.8 million), is published in a quiet, campus-like atmosphere in Chappaqua, New York (the postmark on its mail is "Pleasantville"). Apart from its contents, the magazine is renowed for the tasteful, tranquil atmosphere of its offices, the tradition of gentility and paternalism of its late founder-owners, DeWitt and Lila Wallace, and the benign invisibility of their successor establishment trustees, including Laurance S. Rockefeller.

One day early in 1984, the board summarily fired the *Digest's* long-time editor, Edward T. Thompson, with no warning, no explanation and no sweat. He told friends that there was a vague, unspecific hint that a few of the articles he allowed to be printed did not entirely please the board. The public learned about it, if at all, in a short report explaining nothing, at the bottom of the last page of the business section of the New York *Times.* The firing of the editor of the world's largest monthly was not mentioned on the air at all. One or two equally uninformative stories then trickled out in other papers. That was all, until weeks later when the *Columbia Journalism Review,* the New York *Times* and *Fortune* reported the struggle for control at the top of the publication that reaches more American households than any other monthly. Compare that to the coverage of firing the head of the biggest company making any product as pervasive.

The Washington Post Company had five different presidents and its magazine, *Newsweek,* five different editors in ten years—a record for senior management changes in a major thriving media organization. The *Post* itself reported the changes in one- or two-paragraph, scorecard fashion, listing only the names and numbers of the players. The rest of the daily press noted the news, if at all, as personnel items, and, of course, it was not considered material for television or radio. (The *Post* showed no such reticence in covering changes at other papers, including those at its chief prestige competitor, the New York *Times.*)

The *Times* is even more elliptical about its inner machinations and workings—as exemplified by a triple header in 1985. In the first instance, the *Times* exercised its proprietary prerogative and suddenly dropped an establishment baiting local column by Sydney Schanberg, who had worked on the paper for twenty-six years as a reporter, editor and Pulitzer Prize

winning correspondent. (Columnist James J. Kilpatrick says of such decisions: "An editor is subject to a publisher, and if the publisher says 'Kill
the piece,' that's it, sweetheart, the piece is killed.") Schanberg was
asked, the paper said in a two-paragraph story on page 18, to "accept
another assignment" to nowhere.[2] The *Times* received hundreds of protests and requests for explanations (it printed two without comment). It
offered no reason or coverage in its pages of the uproar within and around
its own organization.

At about the same time, the *Times* also got locked in a bitter arbitration
with one of its byline science reporters, in the course of which seventeen
prominent *Times* staffers—including five Pulitzer winners—complained in
a letter to the publisher about the paper's tactics. Nothing of the bruising
dispute ever appeared in the *Times.* Nor could anyone read in its pages—
until another New York paper picked it up—that the *Times* had a small,
mysterious outbreak of Legionnaire's disease, which has always been
news when it happened elsewhere. (It did find room for a report on a glitch
in its telephone system that briefly interrupted its classified-ad taking.)

Then in the fall of 1986, when the announcement was made that the
executive editorship of the New York *Times* was to change hands (Max
Frankel for retiring A.M. Rosenthal), the *Times* itself ran the bare-bones
story on the bottom of page 1, with no history of Rosenthal's reign, one of
the most consequential newspaper editorships of the twentieth century.
The paper devoted three times as much space to an earthquake in El
Salvador, not to say a half dozen stories on the local and congressional
elections a month away.

All of this and other self-serving abstinence was especially surprising
for the *Times,* not just because of the indispensable excellence of its other
coverage and the fact that it had begun covering the rest of the media more
than all but a few other dailies. For self-coverage it had a memorable
model from its own past. In 1964 the paper assigned its longtime chief
labor correspondent, A.H. Raskin, to do an independent story and analysis for the paper of what went wrong within its own managment in the
newspaper strike that shut down the paper for 114 days. After his no-
holds-barred story was published, labor relations and top management at
the *Times* were reorganized.

At the *Wall Street Journal,* something close to a civil—and barely civilized—war had erupted between the conservatism of the staff of its
editorial page and the different views of many on its news staff.

2. After a vacation, Schanberg, whose story covering Cambodia had been made
   into the acclaimed movie, *The Killing Fields,* resigned and was hired as a
   columnist by *Newsday.*

It was an internal collision on the largest daily in the country, over policy, perspective and what the paper should be doing, saying and covering. Similar tension in the government or in any leading corporation would have rated front-page feature coverage in the *Journal* and stories in other papers. When the argument was at its height, no reporter from any other daily and no broadcasters—many of whom knew all about it—thought it worth reporting.

None of these personnel matters or disputes involved drugs, alcoholism, private lives of malfeasance of any kind. They did involve some of the biggest opinion makers in the world. The silence or sparse coverage in the daily press was not unusual. It was expected. It was not even a conspiracy, just a habit. Daily newspapers and broadcasting cover business, politics, foreign affairs, theater, movies, advertising, television, book publishing, art, entertainment, crime, war and peace with the intensity and commmentary all deserve. They display little interest in their own news—and barely any in the workings of other print news operations.

Knowing something other than the barest facts about a departing or new top editor of the New York *Times, Reader's Digest, Newsweek* or *Time*, a change in the policies of the *Wall Street Journal* or the top command of the Times Mirror or Washington Post companies, has more consequence for millions of Americans than the election of the first woman mayor of San Diego (routinely profiled in the East), or the charge—later dismissed—that a California congresswoman violated election laws, a tussle on a middle level of the Commerce Department, or an attempt to oust the mayor of Loganville, Georgia (pop. 3,000)—all of which rated interesting stories in national newspapers.

Yet ongoing daily coverage of the print press has been rare, unless it is business news, a big libel suit, criminal press fraud, a press created morality play with a dramatic ending, a yeasty family fight over a newspaper in Louisville or a big media business takeover, a noisy and juicy quarrel at an elegant magazine like the *New Yorker*. Most of the daily press and broadcasting hardly cover or even try to explain who is in charge and why, and with what effect, in the same way that they report corporate news and the inner maneuvering in government, politics or any other major institution. Newspapers, led by the Washington *Post* and New York *Times*, began to cover intensively and with good results the network takeovers in 1985 and the changes that followed. But the effort of the media to cover themselves had barely begun—and neither television nor dailies were giving other news organizations that kind of regular coverage.

The press is also not above engaging in the kind of censorship of its own operations that it finds intolerable and worthy of exposure in others.

In its full-page annual review of the 47,000 letters it received ("Looking into 1985's Mailbag"), *Time* covered twenty-two different subjects. On the topic of the press, the article mentioned that in 1985 "many readers charged the media" with being soft on crime, inflating the significance of Reagan's visit to the German war cemetery at Bitburg and encouraging terrorism by giving it too much publicity. But, astonishingly, it said not one word about any letters it received on its own Sharon libel suit. Along with the Westmoreland case, the two were by far the most reported news media stories of the year. Were there no letters to *Time's* editors on the Sharon case?

Well, in fact, there were. Hundreds of them—more than three hundred alone the week following the verdict, two-thirds of them condemning *Time*. The editors' tortuous explanation to me for the omission was that most of the letters "did not enhance or illuminate this volatile issue and it would not have served any useful journalistic purpose to reintroduce this inflammatory subject." They have never displayed such reticence on other "inflammatory" subjects in which *Time* was not involved.

I single out the *Times,* Washington *Post, Wall Street Journal* and *Time* not because they are the worst. They are the best in most respects and are making strides toward covering the rest of the news media as well as creating new standards of conduct for their own staffs. Yet they remain among the worst when it comes to reporting on themselves. Take the *Times* again, in other respects the best of them all. In a long business story about its acquisition of a gigantic new cable television system, the *Times* alone failed to mention that it bought the system from the first pioneer cable operator ever to be sent to prison for bribing local officials to get franchises. True, he had served his time. But no other account elsewhere of his success in cable failed to mention his earlier felony conviction. And when the New York Times Company three years later lost a $51 million civil suit in a dispute over the price of the acquisition, it printed not a word about the court's judgment against it.

Similarly, when the paper's columnist William Safire wrote a one-sided, piqued and self-serving attack on the investigative methods of a federal special counsel, the *Times* impressively printed a story the next week giving the other side. It explained the special counsel's methods as well as those of the five other such chief investigators who had been appointed under the Ethics in Government Act. All to the good. But as balancing as the second story was, it self-consciously neglected ever to mention that Safire's column had been the news peg and reason for the story. Such an omission would have been inconceivable if the accusation had been made by anyone else but the *Times'* own columnist. Trying to be fair was admirable. Concealing its own role in the argument, was a privilege it granted itself and not others.[3]

There are smaller examples of trivial deceptions, which in other industries, would be the subject of consumer protests and mislabeling complaints. How can you tell whether you are reading the latest or an early edition of most daily newspapers? The printed front-page description is of little help: "Final," "Late City," "Four Star," "Bulldog," call it anything you want, and the papers do. It is as misleading as the gradings of meat (in which "good," was the lowest) or the courts of New York State (where the "Supreme Court" is far from the highest court in the state).

The real key of which edition buyers are getting is concealed in a code on the front page in the number of periods after the volume number, asterisks hidden somewhere, or other secret symbols known only to the editors. Similarly, magazines regularly date their covers a week, ten days or a month ahead of the date they are available, so they will not look stale to newsstand buyers or subscribers. Minor matters but deceptions that would be exposed and eliminated if practiced by others. Television is only slightly better about itself, labeling "file footage" and "re-enactments." But how often are documentary or segment reruns labeled as such? And the evening news, announced or promoted as "with" Tom Brokaw, Peter Jennings or Dan Rather, turns up to have a different fill-in anchor for the vacationing or traveling anchor announced. (Theatrical movies give their date of issue in strings of roman numerals that it takes a Latin scholar to decipher.)

More seriously, when the news media settle a libel suit, they almost always insist as part of the agreement that the terms never be disclosed. The demand they make of others for open agreements, open courts and full disclosure is one that most refuse to apply to their own cases.[4]

---

3. The paper, while full of good-humored staffers, notoriously lacked any sense of humor about itself. When a prominent New York businessman was asked to answer the charge of nepotism in his company, he replied with a laugh: "Well, I saw how well it worked at the *Times* so I thought I'd try it in our company." Neither the question nor the answer made the *Times* story, although it could have qualified as the quote of the day.

4. A rare and worthy exception was the *Wall Street Journal's* public settlement of a $5 million claim for $800,000, the largest such settlement without trial ever reported. The *Journal* had been sued by two federal prosecutors charged by the paper with having improperly harassed witnesses to get them to cooperate with the Federal Organized Strike Force. The *Journal* said it was making an exception to its policy of not settling libel suits because "in this case, where two important parts of the article turned out to be unproved, we thought it would be unwise for us and our people to undergo the financial and human costs of a long trial."

If the news media are so skittish as to be mostly silent in reporting on themselves, they are even worse in covering how they affect the other news they report.

Frequently journalists are the engine that generates important news, not just the spectators reporting it. That is a fact of their existence, not necessarily a criticism. Their searchlight is as valuable as it can be blinding. In a national U.S. or Philippine election, a congressional investigation or Supreme Court confirmation, an exposé of chicanery in government, a terrorist kidnapping, an Iranian hostage scam or countless other stories, the media are major players. They do more than focus world attention. They are very often the stimulus for, and the most important influence on, the news they are reporting.

On other subjects, they are impressively determined. Politicians personal lives are minutely examined. The rise and fall of the price of oil is tracked by the press from well to gas pump. Protected witnesses and anonymous sources are pursued in back alleys to get leads and stories. Information, interviews and access are traded and bargained for as wildly as soy beans, corn and gold futures. Planned events like political conventions, summit meetings or street demonstrations and such unplanned uproars as urban riots or national disasters create media spectaculars in which the press sometimes outnumbers the principals. Sports, entertainment, government and business are raked for every leaf. Yet the role the news media themselves play in making or unmaking such news is mostly considered unworthy of coverage or analysis, unless it cannot be overlooked.

Perhaps it is too much to ask of newspapers and broadcasters that they report fully and candidly on themselves, except when it is unavoidable, after a public scandal on their own premises—a Janet Cooke at the Washington *Post,* a *Wall Street Journal* stock profiteer, or a Philadelphia *Inquirer* reporter who lived with and was showered with gifts by a local politician she was assigned to report on. Very few people or organizations are capable of ongoing public confessionals or disclosures about themselves. When I covered the press for *Time,* my editors wanted intensive reporting and criticism of others. But it was taken for granted that when I had to write about some development at Time Inc. itself, I would shift into the spare prose of a corporate press release.

It is possible to overcome such self-conscious restraint, even when a news organization reports on itself. It takes no great leap of imagination in such instances to assign special reporters and editors, giving them the free hand they have when covering others. But if self-coverage is a lot to ask, there can be no excuse for the news media's not regularly covering and criticizing one another.

This major fault is so indefensible that it is being remedied—but much too slowly. Fewer than a dozen of the biggest papers now have media reporters, most notably Eleanor Randolph of the Washington *Post* (who in 1987 began one of the very few syndicated columns on the press, although rarely in the *Post* itself) and Alex Jones of the New York *Times*. Other notable full-time press reporter-critics are *Newsday's* Thomas Collins and the Los Angeles *Times's* David Shaw. The latter's unique assignment is to write long series reporting and criticizing press practices, including, without interference, those of his own paper and other dailies owned by the Times Mirror Company.

Television is both reported on and criticized in almost every American daily. In the past it was mostly covered as an entertainment medium, or a business or with a focus on celebrity newscasters.

Most papers assign generalist critics, rather than critics of journalism, to comment on television's news and magazine fare—treating even the documentaries the way they do Broadway openings. There is no better example than the Washington *Post's* Tom Shales who writes and reports with more bite, wit and enterprise than any television critic, for which he won the Pulitzer Prize in 1988. "News broadcasts," he says, "deserve more benefits of doubts than entertainment programs do." But he rarely gives them the benefit of his doubts. Very often he punishes them in his skillful prose for what he considers their theatrical gaffes.

To be reviewed as if they were theater outrages television journalists. Lately, bigger news organizations have actually started assigning different kinds of critics as well as intensively reporting on the workings and affairs of television. Some—a small few—even have media reporters who cover the whole news spectrum. The New York *Times,* which was slow to accept television as journalism, now gives it increasing coverage, including the full-time commentary of John Corry. Most others who report on television news are as obsessed with ratings comparisons as the broadcasters they write about.

For its part, television self-consciously tries to ignore itself as a subject. It also almost never comments on news in print except to use it or to follow up stories it gets from newspapers and wire services. Giving credit to a competing news organization in both print and television is done almost as grudgingly as sharing stories with the competition. Most newspapers are even worse than television in this self-serving concealment, although some are getting better. Television does run an infrequent special program or critical commentary on the media by commentators like ABC's

Jeff Greenfield. But television is even more erratic than daily print journalism in covering itself and reporting or commenting on others in the news media.

For both print and television, imagine the not farfetched notion of reviewing and analyzing news coverage and news organizations the way the stock market, politics, sports, restaurants, business, books, movies and other subjects are critically scrutinized. Imagine devoting some of the attention to journalists that leading business figures, politicians, other celebrities or sports figures routinely get. Imagine regularly covering the coverage of major news events where the media play a central role. A bore? Trade news? Unnecessary? Not at all. Rather a much-needed focus on some of the most important, interesting activities and some of the most influential people and institutions in America.

The New York *Times* rejected an interesting report by one of its reporters on how White House correspondents court sources by taking them to expense-account dinners. Nothing wrong with the practice. But the reporter was told that the *Times* prefers not to run such stories about the press (the *New Republic* published the piece).

Yet the need to cover the press became so obvious to the *Times* that it began selectively covering both print and television journalism more (still not as much as the Washington *Post*). It even started a weekly "Press" column, with short items about the news media, but dropped it after several weeks. ("We call it 'Press,'" said an editor at the time because 'media' is not in the Constitution, 'press' is.") Under the more open regime of Max Frankel, when the paper advertised "New columns, new ideas . . . clothes, health, sports, food. The law, rearing children, better ways to do things," there was no mention of new columns or coverage of the news media, which it began to expand later in the business section.

Weekly magazines have carried press and media sections for years. Journalism reviews on both local and national media practices have spread across the country. Trade journals and newsletters cover the media but only for those on the inside. Daily coverage of the media by the media is so simple to accomplish, its benefits so great, that it is gradually happening. Why not now at a faster pace—everywhere, as routinely as other news is covered and other subjects criticized? "We must stop acting," writes press critic David Shaw, "as if what we do every day is an arcane secret, too complex for the reader to understand, or a state secret that's none of the reader's business."

Until daily news coverage and commentary on the news media for the general public is regularly available and as rigorous as it is on other subjects, the press will continue to abuse its special status.

The effect is not hypothetical. The outstanding example of such coverage is in the September 1986 reporting on CBS's troubles by 28-year-old Jonathan Alter in *Newsweek*. He assiduously tracked the internal problems at CBS and in its news division. On the eve of a crucial CBS board meeting, *Newsweek* ran a cover titled "Civil War at CBS. The Struggle for the Soul of a Legendary Network." Fairly and with detailed reporting, the story laid out the problems and tracked down the crosscurrents of conflicting values and personalities at the country's most prestigious broadcasting company. It was neither gossip nor trade news but an intensive examination of one of the most influential corporations in the United States.

As a result, there was no way for the management and the board to ignore the reporting, not just in *Newsweek* but, taking the magazine's lead, in the rest of the press as well, including an excellent, balanced analysis by Peter Jennings on ABC's evening network news. "In the end," said the New York *Times*, "it was a news article [in *Newsweek*] that reportedly was the catalyst" for a major corporate shakeup. The *Wall Street Journal* added: "The sudden jump in media interest persuaded CBS directors that the turmoil couldn't be tolerated any longer." With that example behind them, the press then tracked dollar-by-dollar, person-by-person changes in the news operations of all three networks. The press allowed the real stockholders of CBS—the public—to become a key factor in decisions affecting that public's interests, just as the press refuses to allow other big institutions or public figures to shield themselves from public opinion.

It should not take a libel suit, like Westmoreland and Sharon, corporate takeovers, stakeout exposés, celebrity newscasters breaking ranks with their management or a confrontational interview of George Bush by Dan Rather for the media to report critically on one another. The *TV Guide* article that stimulated the Westmoreland suit was a good example of the press critically scrutinizing the press. And the uproar in print following Renata Adler's condemnation of both *Time* and CBS, for all the faults in her analysis, was equally healthy.[5] Such free-for-alls of opinion and criti-

5. Although it led to its own collection of absurdities, as heated arguments often do. None was stuffier and more restrictive in its definition of "serious" journalism than a review of Adler's book in the Washington *Post* by the former New York *Times* editorial writer and sometime columnist William V. Shannon, who became Carter's ambassador to Ireland and taught journalism at Boston University. Shannon wrote: "I regret that Adler had to erect her brilliant book on the dubious premise that *Time* and CBS Reports are serious journalistic enterprises. Although millions of readers and viewers may regard their output as journalism, [they] are both part of the entertainment industry. Notwithstanding their own pretensions and swollen self-esteem, it is unfair to judge them by the rigorous standards of daily print journalism evolved in this century by the Associated Press and good national newspapers such as the Washington *Post*, the New York

cism are standard fare in all areas of American life. They should be encouraged in the media, not surrounded by a wall of habitual trade association discretion. Just as public officials should not expect to be protected from press scrutiny, neither should the press itself nor the journalists who have access to its pages and airwaves.

The news media also need a second major reform to temper the effect of their power. They must respond to a constant public frustration to which they give such reluctant attention: once people or groups feels they have been wronged by the press, they most often find it impossible to answer back.

For public figures the news media have too pat a reply. They say that people in the public eye, if they are important enough, have means to express their points of view or disagreements with what has been said about them. They can hold press conferences, give interviews, make speeches, defend themselves in other public forums.

Presidents can and do answer back. Nixon lost against the news media, the Congress and the public not because he was not heard or seen but because when he was, he looked even worse. Ford and Carter, respectively characterized in the media as bumbling and lacking in presidential stature despite their accomplishments, were rejected at the polls because both oversimplified characterizations were personally harsh but substantially true.

Reagan is the first president since the full growth of television to prove during his first six years that the media can be made into a bigger presidential asset than a liability. His nomination and then election were initially greeted by the press with surprise and disdain. But in office, his optimism, charm and visible skill in advocating his policies were more convincing to the public than the early media reports of his ignorance, shallowness and misstatements. Over Iran and Central America, the stock market meltdown, and confusion over Supreme Court nominations, indictments and ethical accusations against his appointees, the reality of his disengaged management, not the press, unraveled even Reagan's consummate theatrical presidency (see page 227), despite his earlier accomplishments.

Although presidents have a chance to be an equal match for the power of the modern media, no one else does. Even high public officials find that the accusations, characterizations and arguments against them get a

Times and *Wall Street Journal.''* That may be Shannon's definition but it is not shared by a single senior editor I know in any of the news organizations he mentions.

quicker, louder voice than their defenses, explanations or corrections—if they have them. Lesser public figures, in and out of office, are completely outgunned. Westmoreland could have held endless press conferences, made speeches all over the country, written letters and collected petitions in his favor. They never could have had the national impact of the one network television program he wanted to answer. In Sharon's case, not much would have changed his basic reputation after the official Israeli condemnation. But a different response from *Time* would have helped rather than hurt the magazine's reputation.

Of course, government and non-government figures alike use the press on the offense, damn it on the defense. Entertainment celebrities selling themselves, politicians or business leaders hustling their products and policies seek the exposure on the way up, resent the lack of privacy when they arrive, and complain about the shrillness of the coverage when they trip or start down. The more experienced know they use the media as much as they feel abused by it. The occasional, often inadvertent wanderers into print or broadcast news (grieving families, shy heroes, rape victims, the falsely accused) have it worse than any. They have little effective means to protect themselves or answer back if they want to.

The most galling frustration is the inability of them all to make their case directly to the jury of the public without being overruled by media judges.

For the most part, newspapers and magazines in the past kissed off or responded to that complaint by letters columns, and more recently, brief paragraphs of daily corrections. Right after its embarrassment in the Sharon case, *Time* searched for a feature that would give louder voice to its readers. It too quickly abandoned the quest and simply resorted to sprinkling its letters column, at first almost too easily, with the phrase *"Time* regrets the error" or *"Time* erred."[6] Other weeklies and dailies increasingly are more receptive to different forms of corrections or apologies, printing longer letters and soliciting detailed replies. Even television, more often than it did in the past, corrects itself on the air when the mistake is bad or misleading enough (for example showing footage of what was supposed to be the smoking Chernobyl nuclear reactor but was actually a Yugoslav cement factory).

Only about thirty dailies in the entire country have independent om-

---

6. A year and a half after the Sharon trial, *Time* bent a little more. At the end of its letters column it printed a longer letter than it usually runs under the heading "A Dissent from Edwin Meese." In a precede to the complaint about one of its essays from the U.S. attorney general, the magazine announced: "Occasionally, *Time* will use this space to let readers respond in detail to a story involving complex issues." In the years following, no such responses were printed.

budsmen or their equivalents, who mostly answer complaints from readers about practices in their own paper. They are hardly a nibble at the problem. They tend to ease editors' consciences rather than satisfy the readers' appetites. Most newspapers and magazines also allow those who can afford it to take out ads that are uncensored—except for libel and taste—expressing their views. A far from satisfactory solution. But television networks, as a matter of policy, do not allow even that on the grounds that it would make the airwaves available only to those who could afford to buy time or clutter up their air with inflammatory diatribes. (Local television stations do allow replies to editorials—a hangover from the days when the FCC rigorously required them.) The need to create new formats for corrections and replies is compelling enough in print; it is essential in television, which now has no way to "talk back to the box."

There are better ways to open up avenues of access to the public for both television and print. The one-way freeway the media now control is not enough. The public wants at least one lane of its own to buck the media traffic. It should get it. How?

Begin with television, where the problem of access is the worst and the progress the least.

The government and the law are no help. The best proof of the theorem that the more government is involved in the news media the less the public gains is in the history of broadcast regulation. In 1949, when radio was in its middle age and television newborn, the FCC adopted the "Fairness Doctrine," which grew into a safety net of laws and regulation including rules on "personal attack," "editorial reply" and "reasonable access." Congress stepped in ten years later and created the "equal-time" rule, requiring broadcasters to allot the same amount of free reply time to *all* political candidates in an election. When cable television vastly increased the number of available television outlets, the FCC required every cable operator to create "public access" channels.

By definition, the problem of fairness and public access in broadcasting was solved—on paper. In practice, the reverse proved to be true. The rules created more air pollution than the fresh air of public debate. The equal time provision almost prevented debates among the major candidates in elections by qualifying more than a dozen presidential candidates. Personal attack and editorial reply requirements got mired down in such complexities and abuse that they defeated the very purposes for which they were intended. Some public access channels on cable are more noted for their public pornography than their public service.

Over the years rules governing broadcast speech have been embroiled in the courts, buried under millions of pages of FCC complaints and petitions. (Only *one* small station has ever had its license lifted in the whole history of the Fairness Doctrine.) In one landmark case, the Supreme Court ruled that "it is the right of viewers and listeners, not the right of broadcasters, which is paramount." To be sure—but how to exercise that right? Laws and government rules proved so ineffective that broadcasting has become less and less regulated. Today available air space is not much scarcer nor at times more expensive than print. There are seven times more radio (10,128) and television (1,611) stations than there are daily newspapers (1,657). Broadcasting is the biggest, most powerful part of the news media, that "press" whose freedom the drafters of the Constitution and courts guarantee. Why not treat it that way and abolish regulations on its *content* altogether?

There are complex answers to that question and heated arguments over whether finally to eliminate the atrophying regulations and laws governing broadcast journalism. The trend is steadily in that direction. In 1986, the U.S. Court of Appeals for the District of Columbia Circuit, which hears most of the important communications cases, signaled the ending of federal regulation of broadcast content when it ruled that "the line drawn between the print media and the broadcast media, resting as it does on the scarcity of the latter, is a distinction without a difference." I pass over the tangled web of issues in this dispute because they have become largely academic. Given the experiences with past rules, few people any longer believe that the only or best solution to television's one-way power lies in more and tougher federal rules, although it remains a hotly debated issue in Congress.

As with the print press, the answer to providing the public a fairer chance in responding to the media lies not with government regulators but with the broadcasters themselves, hearing the voice of legitimate and convincing public pressure.

Not that the broadcasters very readily respond, as their election-day voting projections proved. The public and Congress were indignant at the networks for having "stolen the spirit of voting from the American people." Congress threatened legislation. Network executives paraded up Capitol Hill in lockstep to give their traditional arguments against any restrictions on their electronic wizardry. They said they could not withhold from the public important information they had. Such voluntary suppression was against their free press obligations.

As hoary as the media position was and as earnestly as they advanced it, the networks also began to realize it was publicly unacceptable. So even before the House passed a bill that would—if it ever became law—create a uniform poll closing time across the United States, the networks finally listened to the wail from the public and said they would do the right thing rather than pursue their legal right to do whatever they wanted. They voluntarily agreed to withhold polling predictions in any state until its polls were closed.

Because compelling television by law to give the public access to its airwaves does not work, what would?

The occasional reading of letters from viewers is certainly not the answer. When that is done, it is most often a selective entertainment rather than a form of reply, pitting a few words without pictures against full-scale television production. Public access channels on cable are no better. Even if they were devoted largely to replies to the media, they have minuscule audiences compared with local television or networks.

Network television has made a few erratic forays into examining itself. NBC devoted one full hour in prime time to "Warts and All: A Portrait of American Journalism." ABC's "Viewpoint" was created to allow the public infrequently to question journalists' performance. Until it was cancelled for lack of a sponsor, Hodding Carter's "Inside Story" examined press coverage on the Public Broadcasting Network for two years.

CBS, which had already broadcast a "60 Minutes on 60 Minutes," collaborated with Fred Friendly's Columbia University's Graduate School of Journalism Media and Society Seminars.[7] Together they put on the network hour-long discussions on the press and privacy and the media and business. Other major media organizations joined in, co-sponsoring "Media and Society" PBS network programs on libel, terrorism, fair trial versus free press, the media and the military and other press problems, followed by newsroom workshops with their own staffs. PBS's "Frontline" covered the press covering election campaigns. ABC's "20/20" ran a segment criticizing reporting of the "Subway Vigilante" story, but used some eyebrow-raising reenactments.

Most surprising, CBS's entertainment division ran a two-hour drama in prime time called "News at 11," attacking the worst excesses of local television news chasing higher ratings. The cheerful newsroom ambiance of Mary Tyler Moore, from an earlier era, this time was replaced by the tawdry excuses of a local news director manipulating a Barbie-doll anchor to exploit sexually abused school children. NBC started running thirty-second promotional spots called "Tuned In To America," in which critics like Ralph Nader and others were allowed to say what they thought about television. The reason for these short messages, said an NBC vice president, was to demonstrate that "we hear you." ABC sent its anchor out to

7. I am the non-salaried chairman of the board of the now renamed Columbia University Seminars on Media and Society.

local stations to moderate ninety-minute specials called "Ask the Media," in which journalists from the station's staff and from newspapers responded to questions from the public.

It was all a small start but not yet a trend. The real remedy for the public must be found in access to network and local television, where the programs to be answered originated.

Periodically, especially when broadcasters are under attack, they discuss formats for the public to answer back. But a meeting on the subject is different from following through with a specific plan for a talk-back program. After the Westmoreland trial, CBS—as did *Time* after Sharon—reconsidered such proposals but reached no conclusion. As the Westmoreland debacle faded into memory, the idea was again allowed to wither away. Yet it can, must and will be done.

Don Hewitt at CBS, President Lawrence Grossman at NBC News, and others elsewhere have proposed such programs. ABC has a starting point with Ted Koppel's "Viewpoint," on the air no more than five times a year. Grossman's proposal had the working title "Talk Back to NBC," on which, in prime time, network executives would take calls and questions from viewers in the audience, responding to disagreements and answering questions about the network's programs. Hewitt's ideas are more expansive and promising.

He suggests his network create the video equivalent of the newspapers' op-ed page. A network editorial board, possibly with some outside members, would be in charge. It would determine who should be allowed to use an independent fully funded production unit that would produce viewers' replies to the network's news and public affairs programs. The production unit would operate in the interests of the viewers selected, using network television standards to supply visually the same impact as the program or point of view it was answering. Viewers, in effect, would be given the chance to be editorial supervisors of their own segments. (If he had been offered that, Westmoreland says he never would have sued.)

There are dozens of other proposals. One is to rotate such a program regularly among the three networks, thereby assuring that no single network could tip the balance in its own favor on its own airtime. Another alternative—if the commercial networks will not produce such prime-time programs—is for all three to provide the endowed financial backing for a weekly program produced and broadcast not by the networks but by the Public Broadcasting Service.

No innovations come easily. Valuable new television formats are not created, nor do they take hold, overnight.

The most frequent excuses—and they are just that—for not doing talk-back programs is that it would be difficult to make the selection of which grievances or points of view to put on. There are also the questions of how much latitude the viewers on the program should be allowed, whether they should be challenged, and when and where to broadcast the programs. Nor is it possible to ignore, although there is reason to deplore, another obstacle: television's traditional shortsighted reluctance to put low-rated public affairs programs in commercially valuable time slots, regardless of how important such programs may be.

Deciding which complaints to air would have to be arbitrary, measured by standards of fairness and importance. But so are all judgments made in editing public affairs programs. It could be helpful to have outside partici-pants in the selection process, even if they were a minority on a selection board. Replying to the replier would also be a matter of judgment. It need not be a case of having the final word. It could create a moment to admit error, present another point of view or explain why the journalists did what they did. There would still be complaints about the programs them-selves. But the heat already generated by not producing them is greater and more justified than whatever criticism might grow out of their execu-tion.

As to where, when and how often to broadcast such regular programs, that too should be an exploration. Three imperatives, apart from a fair selection process: One, the programs must be well financed and staffed so that the quality of reply is equal to the claimed offense. Two, such reply programs should *not* be put on when the fewest people can be expected to be watching. Three, local network outlets and independent stations should not only run their network's program but create their own community equivalent, just as they do in news.

The admittedly open questions are no harder to solve than any other programming dilemmas in broadcasting. The reason television has failed to provide access programming is not a lack of funds or program imagina-tion. It has been a lack of will and an unwillingness to give up commercially valuable network time—people stuck in their past prejudices and practices.

For the print press, giving readers new opportunities to reply requires no invention. It takes only an expansion of the space allocated for that purpose and a more responsive attitude on the part of the press itself.

Newspapers and many magazines already have op-ed pages and letters columns. They print corrections. They run their own and syndicated columnists expressing a wide variety of views. A few have ombudsmen or readers' forums. Some, as a periodic check on their reporters' perform-ance, initiate accuracy surveys, mailing stories to the people they are about and asking how acccurate the subjects found them. But none of these small opportunities for counterpunching can match the heavyweight effect of press knockout blows.

When the press accuses, the accusation is bigger news than the reply. Charges, indictments and convictions are given more space and bigger type than acquittals, vindications or retractions. People who turn up in the press in a bad light often fade away in dim light if they turn out to be innocent rather than guilty of the accusations originally made against them.

The press is fickle. It can swing wildly from blasé inattention to ferocious overconcentration, more as an expression of press ego than public need. By exposure, the news media set standards of law and public morality. Yet journalists are self-indulgently hypocritical about the press's own *ad hoc* laws and erratic morals. They need to be challenged and exposed as much as anybody else in positions of trust. Taking them to court in libel suits is an unsatisfactory, expensive last resort. When the press itself is accused, its coverage faulted or labeled as just plain wrong, its critics need the satisfaction of a much broader outlet for their complaints. They get almost none from television. They still get too little in print.

The credibility of newspapers and magazines is damaged by their defensive attitude toward complaints and the grudging space they devote to them.

Quick demands for redress or correction often come in by telephone. Unless those who complain are known or have some high-visibility community standing, they most often get the kind of bureaucratic runaround they expect when they make a similar call to a government office. It is hard to know to whom they should speak or write, given the jurisdictional and hierarchic division of labor of large news organizations. If those with a grievance reach the reporters responsible for the story, they will most often be greeted first with defenses or excuses: "That's the way I saw it," "I don't write the headlines," "That's not how I reported it before it was edited," "There was no time to call back," "I don't decide whether or where stories should be printed." All these responses may be true; none is satisfactory to the callers. If the complainers persist, they are likely to be confronted with disdain or hostility. If instead of calling the reporter, they can get the editors or publisher and if they have a point that on its face sounds reasonable, the best they can hope for is a promise to "look into it," or the suggestion that they write a letter.

When the complaint is clearly trivial or factual, not questioning the publication's judgment or fairness—a wrong title or address, misspelled name or incorrect picture caption—there is a good chance for remedy. A footnote-size correction is likely in the daily column most papers now print to straighten out small mistakes (e.g. a *very* small one from the New York *Times:* "Because of a mechanical error, an apple pie recipe in The Living Section yesterday omitted an ingredient. A corrected version appears today on page C11."[8] Yet it is remarkable that not until as late as 1967 did the first daily, the Louisville *Courier-Journal* and its sister paper, the *Times,* make a regular feature of corrections.[9]

Corrections columns are now printed in most dailies all over the country. The New York *Times,* once the most impregnable of all, not only runs daily corrections. Long before he retired as executive editor to become a columnist, A.M. Rosenthal initiated the occasional but important "Editors' Note," which "amplifies or rectifies what the editors consider significant lapses of fairness, balance or perspective."

An even more recent sign of changing attitudes was an unprovoked correction that appeared in the New York *Times* in the middle of the Iran-contra hearings. Without having received any complaints, the *Times* ran a headline atop page 1: "A Correction: Times was in Error On North's Secret-Fund Testimony." Under the new executive editorship of Max Frankel, a *Times* subeditor explained: "We don't often get put to a test this extreme—thank heavens—but in this case, the error occurred in the lead story of the paper and in two of the three lines of the headline." The correction of a relatively fine point ran 1,300 words, the most prominent and longest the *Times* has ever run.

The Washington *Post* went beyond expanding its letters column and printing the views of an ombudsman. Once a week it runs a full page called "Free For All," printing criticisms of the paper and articles that had appeared in it. It also runs articles on its op-ed page titled "Taking Exception," and has printed spirited exchanges with its own columnists who criticized the editorials in the paper. In the summer of 1984, the San Antonio *Light* created a rotating, three-member community advisory

8. Or on a weightier subject: "An article in Science Times on July 14 about the Indian mathematician Srinivasa Ramanujan contained several errors. He was born in Erode, a town near Kumbakonam, not in Kumbakonam itself, where he grew up. His stay at Cambridge University lasted just under five years; the article said nearly six. And the mathematician Godfrey Hardy's middle initial was H."

9. In June of 1967, the New York *Times'* "Abe" Raskin wrote a piece for the paper's Sunday *Magazine* titled "What's Wrong with American Newspapers," calling for newspapers to establish departments of internal criticism to check the fairness and accuracy of the paper's coverage and commentary. After reading the Raskin article, publisher Barry Bingham, Sr. and executive editor Norman E. Isaacs appointed the first U.S. dailies' ombudsmen.

board to meet regularly with the paper's editors. The Hartford *Courant* opened up a seat on its editorial board, rotating in for a two- or three-month period someone picked from its community and allowing the person full participation, including writing editorials. The Nashville *Banner* took the most radical step of all, more a sign of the times than a sensible policy. It tried opening its daily news meeting to the public.

Many of the relatively new corrections columns are as misleading as they are welcome. They create the impression that the publication is readily open to righting its wrongs. In fact, they only rectify in small type the least important errors—giving editors too easy a feeling of comfort in their own openness. If there is a real difference of opinion not just about facts but about interpretation, emphasis, fairness, omissions and placement, then the option that may be offered is access to the letters column.

Letters columns in newspapers and magazines are more like op-ed pages. They are more a window of opinion on issues than a place to disagree with the publication's coverage. Only a small percentage of the published letters involve criticism of the paper or magazine. When a letter does directly argue with coverage, even the best papers often do not respond, explain or retract in print. They believe they have done their duty just by letting people have their say. If the letter does get into print, it will most often appear in edited, shortened form, often long after the offending story or article that provoked it. Space allotted the complaint is never as much as that given the original story, nor is it given equal prominence— no matter how justifiable or serious the complaint may be.

The inequity is so blatant that there are now a few, if only occasional exceptions. In one month during 1986 the Denver *Post,* Philadelphia *Inquirer* and New York *Times* all gave front-page news coverage to the replies of people and organizations that had been criticized in news stories the days and weeks before. In some newsrooms, such rare stories are called "skinbacks," and in effect, without actually saying so, give a point of view other than the one published before in the same paper.

There is a vast difference between caving in when you believe you are right and being unwilling to concede that you are or may be wrong.

When the press is widely accused of arrogance, what most people have in mind is just that stubbornness in considering its own performance as fallible, and providing adequate redress. The fallout from the *Time*-Sharon battle is the leading print example of that resentment. It is ironic that under the serious threat of libel suits or as a result of their settlement, complainers most often do force the satisfaction they seek. Ironic because journalists unanimously agree that libel suits are the worst way to resolve differences with the public. Yet the press's own haughty way of dealing with complaints from its readers, encourages, indeed, sometimes forces into court pleaders who could be satisfied in other ways.

In the important University of Iowa study of 700 libel cases (see page 99), four-fifths of those suing and agreeing to answer questions about it said their objective was not money but restoring their reputation or punishing the press. The researchers found that an overwhelming number of those who sued the media said they would not have gone to their lawyers or to court had the initial response by the press to their complaints been different. Those who felt unfairly or inaccurately treated reported that they had been ingnored, passed from one person to another, treated rudely and in general, given no satisfaction or alternative to dragging their complaint into court in a libel suit.

"The plaintiffs told us," said the professors, "that their post-publication experiences with the press influenced their decision to sue. The way people were treated when they contacted the media was a factor in their anger and the decision to sue. More editors need to recognize that how they deal with complaints has an important bearing on whether they ultimately are sued for libel. The same attention now given to prepublication safeguards to prevent libel should extend to postpublication practices." Adds James Squires, editor of the Chicago *Tribune:* "I think, in other words, the best defense against libel is the newspaper's response after it's done something wrong."

Newspapers and magazines need prominently to inform their readers whom to call or write, the way the Detroit *Free Press,* under David Lawrence, Jr., and other papers have started to do. They need to say what their policies are for correcting mistakes and providing access to their own pages. They also must give more space to criticism and go beyond just printing it. They should agree, when they do, and apologize; or disagree, then try to explain the collision of views, if it is not obvious. It is very much in order, too, when their readers have been especially stirred up by something printed, for them to indicate how much protest they received on a single issue.

The one-way power exercised by print and television journalists needs to be hospitable rather than hostile to criticism. To justify their unique right to say what they want, they have to be prepared publicly to defend their choices. They can quarrel with that criticism but they should not suppress it any more than they would tolerate being suppressed themselves.

The news media need to create a mirror image of the people's theoretical right to know: the people's actual right to reply. "A realistic view of the First Amendment," says a *Harvard Law Review* article, "requires recognition that a right of expression is somewhat thin if it can be exercised only at the sufferance of managers of mass communications. The difficulty of access to the media has made the right of expression somewhat mythical.''

Vigorous coverage and criticism *by* the news media *of* the news media, plus increased access to their airwaves and pages, are not in the Bill of Rights.

By law, judges are not able to order journalists to open their pages or airwaves to either improvement. The Supreme Court struck down in 1974 a Florida law compelling newspapers to grant the right to reply because ''press responsibility is not mandated by the Constitution and like many other virtues it cannot be legislated.'' Only the unwritten rules of fairness and decency demand more coverage of the press by the press and greater public access to the media.

The first change—increased coverage—takes news operations out of the shadows and into the open, where the press correctly insists other public business should be done. Whatever faults, shortcomings or assaults against decency the media then display, they will have to answer for. Not as a result of vague opinion polls, punishing lawsuits or legal definitions of malice. They will be judged by a more informed public, just the way other powerful people and institutions in America are, often thanks to the efforts of good journalists.

The second improvement—increased access-responds to an enshrined American value: the right to answer one's accusers. People have a democratic right to talk back. That valued tradition is known as free speech. The institution in which the right of free expression is most controlled is in the most uncontrolled free speaker of all, the news media. Unless they voluntarily change that anomaly, journalists will continue to undermine the privilege on which they depend for their own essential freedom. Of such one-side privilege tyrants are born—and are overthrown.

By being more open about themselves and more accessible to the public, the news media will immeasurably improve their performance and their relations with the public. The worst disservices of the media will tend to be driven out by the embarrassment from scrutiny and reply. Their best services will flourish by acclaim.

In infantry basic training, I once had a mess sergeant who ruled his greasy domain with the dictum; ''When you talk to me you shut up!'' His food was as bad as his grunted command. The news media, with a world command, cannot afford such imperiousness. From a loftier perch, Judge Learned Hand pronounced a better rule for their domain: ''The spirit of liberty is the spirit which is not too sure it is right.''

Afterthoughts

The public will not accept shoddy journalism for long. We have no guarantee the First Amendment will be with us forever. We in journalism hold it sacred, but a huge segment of the public is not even aware of what it is. The press does not have a divine right to exist. We must deserve our place in society and carry it out responsibly. Only then will the public feel that the press is indeed a credible, honorable institution worthy of full support.

—Robert P. Clarke, outgoing
President of the American Society
of Newspaper Editors, 1986

Ending the tension between the press on one hand and the public and the government on the other is not only impossible but undesirable. The hypertension of the 80's, however, was dangerous to democratic health. It was brought on more by media abuse and growth than by actual government or public infringement on press freedom.

The American constitutional system, called by some our "civic religion," is based on tension, not on enforced accord. Its intent is to produce orderly change, not disruptive confrontation. The system is purposefully untidy, not oppressively efficient. All three branches of our government are supposed to oppose and check each other. Congress, the president and the courts will always be in disagreement. So will the news media, which are not a fourth branch of government but a fourth power center, intentionally placed outside the laws that govern the other three but not outside the force of public opinion. The four, pulsating in intended dissonance, are the heartbeat of the American governing system.

By the mid-80's, the news media, omnipresent and technologically transformed, were being challenged and confronted on all sides. They were finding it harder simply to hunker down unresponsively in their legally protected fortresses or to fire back aggressively after a direct hit. Behind their own walls, their sensitivity level was rising even without the help of staff psychiatrists or evangelists of ethics and morality.

No single administration in American history has ever been satisfied with the press, nor the press content with the government. They will always battle each other. American democracy was created that way. The press is supposed to curb the power, even the pretense and secrecy, of the government. The government was given no such powers over the press. Only the public, by its ballot, has indirect power over both.

Much as the government and the press complain about the other, neither succeeds in overwhelming the other. Nixon, the media's most powerfully active enemy in modern times, failed. In open and legal ways, the Reagan government, has tried to restrict the flow of information available to the press. It has threatened criminal prosecution for violation of security laws. It blamed the press for its worst troubles. But it barks more than it bites. Even Warren Burger, the conservative chief justice of the United States for seventeen years, who expressed a deep distaste for the news media in his speeches, maintained a record of protecting press freedoms under law in his decisions.

I do not believe that the American news media will come under tighter government control or even seriously damaging judicial restraint as a result of government or public pressure or changes in the Supreme Court. In the spring of 1986, the Court ruled in a decision written by conservative Justice Sandra Day O'Connor, that on matters of public concern "there will always be instances when the fact-finding process will be unable to resolve conclusively whether the speech is true of false. Where the scales are in such an uncertain balance, we believe that the Constitution requires us to tip them in favor of protecting true speech."

In early 1987, almost as if to underscore that point, the full U.S. Court of Appeals in Washington, D.C., overturned the panel decision of its own judges in the case of Mobil's former president, Tavoulareas v. the Washington *Post* (see page 103). In its decision, the court found the *Post* story—although not faultless—"substantially true." More important, the 7-1 majority opinion said: "An adversarial stance is fully consistent with professional investigative reporting." Tavoulareas' lawyers had argued that in office memos, notes and conversations, the *Post* was clearly out to get the Mobil boss. But the court thought that irrelevant: "Nothing in law or common sense supports saddling a libel defendant with civil liability for a defamatory implication nowhere to be found in that published article itself."

Then in February of 1988 came the most resounding affirmation of all. In hearing the appeal on the *Hustler*-Falwell case for "emotional damages" inflicted on the preacher by a parody in the sleazy magazine (see page 100), the court—now considered conservative—*unanimously* overruled the award. Speaking for the entire court, Chief Justice William H. Rehnquist strongly reaffirmed the Sullivan press protections in "vehement, caustic and sometimes unpleasantly sharp attacks" even when that "speech is patently offensive and is intended to inflict emotional injury." Rehnquist, who had been considered "soft" on press protections, said for the court that the decision "reflects our considered judgment that such a standard is necessary to give adequate 'breathing space' to the freedoms protected by the First Amendment."

No matter what hostility the press had experienced from the public, judges and the government in the climate of the mid-80's, the tradition of American press freedom ran deep. The opposition to formal restrictions or even legal accountability remained strong. The courts were resolute in protecting the press.

The press and its advocates have proved equal to the task of combating government efforts to rein it in. The courts and the judges have ultimately always seen to that. If the courts have been valiant, the Oliver Wendell Holmes dictum must also be remembered: "In shaping and reshaping rules of law judges are moved less by logic than by experience, by such things as the 'felt necessities of the time' and 'intuitions of public policy.' " The real brake on attempts to curb the press cannot be left entirely to history and the courts. The news media require support from the public, which has too much reason to be fed up with real examples of media arrogance, excesses and abuses.

Public support can be counted on only if journalists themselves and their bosses recognize that as much as their role has changed, so must many of their practices. They cannot proclaim policies and values in the public interest that are at odds with their own behavior and performance. They need to understand that beyond malice in its constitutional meaning are patterns of media behavior that are unacceptable. They cannot produce an information product as if it were any other profit-oriented commodity. If others are to be prevented from restraining them, they must temper their new and growing modern power with more awareness, self-restraint and initiative in the interests of the public.

After setting aside more complex philosophical nuances, I have long thought that the two most important goals for people who have acquired privileged positions are to try to be both strong and kind at the same time. (A sense of humor helps too.)

As a standard, the two are inseparable. To be strong without kindness is to bully. To be kind without strength is to be ineffective, possibly wimpish. (To be without humor—including about yourself—is less damaging, leaving you only stuffy and grim.) Perfection in achieving both goals is unattainable. Trying to reach them—in work and in life—is not. As good a compass as I believe that is for individual behavior, it is not a bad one either for journalists at work.

For the news media, there need to be some subdivisions under "strong," like enterprising, unintimidated and accurate; and under "kind," like fair, reasonable, careful and compassionate. And these can only be objectives, not the means of achieving them. There is another crucial difference between personal and media value. The media, especially with their overwhelming television clout, are muscular just by their very presence, more powerful than any single person or group. Even without flexing their muscles, they can have a controlling effect on lives, events and institutions, large and small.

Very often the news media implant the earliest and even the most lasting impressions. Reporting an arrest, arraignment or indictment can be an early public conviction of a presumed crime no matter that the person is theoretically innocent until proved guilty. The news media have become the judges not of last but of first resort. As judges, the reason they are so often resented is that they are not accepted as good or as fair enough to justify the power they have. Unlike judges in court, their standards of judgment are *ad hoc* and unknown. They are, unelected, unregulated, bound only by the intentionally permissive laws of libel. They are, in a familiar phrase, accountable only to themselves.

It is a big responsibility. Neither they nor their public are satisfied with how they exercise it. Those who have always had power or privilege can become so accustomed to it that they fail to recognize it. They often casually accept it, to the point of denying they have special standing among the millions who do not. As hard as this is to imagine today, the rising, thoughtful and now presiding or retiring journalists of my generation did not sense we had the power that others—from press agents to presidents—obviously thought we did. With all our self-assurance, we felt less important than others considered us to be.

Fifteen or twenty years ago, I heard some of the key gatekeepers of the U.S. press honestly say, "What is all this talk about our power? We don't feel it." Perhaps it was better that in either ignorance or arrogance we felt that way. The cover of *Life* magazine could make or break a career, but that was not in the minds of those who picked it. President Kennedy thought the lead editorializing story in *Time* could have a critical effect on "swing opinion" in the United States. Those who wrote and edited it never assigned it any such grand importance. The managing editor of the

New York *Times* once objected to a group of his peers that although he
certainly understood the importance and high velocity of news, "We just
put it in the paper where it belongs. The only power I can exercise is over
wedding announcements and obituaries." It was an incredible shortsight-
edness but it was authentic.

The world and the news media have radically changed since those days.
Now the power is unmistakably present. There are no junior or senior
journalists in print or television who can be unaware of what effect their
work has on the lives and governance of others. Not that they sit around
bragging about it or glorying in the power and seeking even more. But with
the new media environment that has developed in the past twenty years,
today journalists cannot avoid awareness of their enhanced power.

There is an analogy in another field of created power: the apocalyptic
force of nuclear energy. *Everyone* agrees on at least one aspect of that
complex subject. There is only one way to handle the power of nuclear
energy and bombs—very, very carefully. The change from the old-fashioned, preelectronic press to the modern news media has no such ultimate
bang. But their effect on day-to-day living is even greater. And like nuclear
power, the only way for the press to handle its new power is more carefully
than it does now. Much more carefully.

Acknowledgments

Among those to whom I owe a large debt of gratitude are:

The Twentieth Century Fund, which as part of its long interest in the press and public policy, sponsored this book from the start. Stimulated by a piece I wrote for the New York *Times* on the press aftermath of the Grenada invasion, the Fund invited me to undertake a book on the subject. The Fund's director, M. J. Rossant, has been an understanding presence from the beginning, aided most directly by the able and unfailingly congenial assistant director, Marcia Bystryn, as well as Beverly Goldberg, Laurie Ahlrich, Wendy Mercer and others at the Fund.

It is impossible to overstate the encouragement and advice I received from my friends the late Theodore H. White, Osborn Elliott, Ken Auletta, David Halberstam, William F. Buckley, Jr., Harold Evans, Irwin Ross, Christopher Buckley, James Hoge, Charles Eisendrath, Hedley Donovan, Thomas Guinzburg, Amanda Urban, Robert D. Sack, Samuel S. Vaughan, Fred W. Friendly, Simon Michael Bessie, Stuart Woods and others who read and made comments on a work in progress.

No journalist could want better research support than was provided by Hedva Glickenhaus and Naushad S. Mehta (the latter, who works for *Time,* was recused from the parts of the book that involve Time Inc.).

William Brink, Tammy Mitchell and Betty Seaver took on the task of editing the manuscript with meticulous, thoughtful and most helpful attention.

Harry Harding, from his well of talent and friendship, designed the jacket. Trina King provided the index.

Transaction Publisher's president Irving Louis Horowitz, Mary E. Curtis, Kimberly Jesuele, Alicja Garbie, Anita Stock and Joseph Bertucci demonstrated that authors and publishers can be collaborators rather than adversaries.

My invaluable assistant, Barbara Peterson, manages my complex office life with the invisible aplomb and visible good manners of a consummate professional.

Perhaps my greatest debt is to the innumerable journalists, sources and friends I have lived with, worked with and been around for most of my life, and most recently to those mentioned and unmentioned in the text who covered the Westmoreland and Sharon trials.

My wife Shirley, a sometime journalist herself, knows and appreciates at least as many of the aforementioned as I do. She not only puts up with my preoccupation with the subject but has for thirty-one years provided the atmosphere and surroundings in which I could enjoy their and her companionship.

And my three grown, dare I say, children, Michael, Carol Clurman Duning and Susan Emma Dockendorff, who have passed the point of being nourished by their father and now nourish him.

Finally, I am indebted for my home care and feeding at various times and places in the course of my writing to several attentive helpers, Betty Lee, Jules Kelly, Leslie Brinkworth and Regina Cardoza.

One last note: none of the above should be considered endorsers of my opinions or mistakes. Indeed, neither have I asked anyone to endorse (i.e., blurb) this book, which is as often an act of friendship as of judgment. As I observed earlier, *in print* I try to have no friends—or enemies.

Index